From Rock Bottom to Mountain Tops:
My Journey Through Faith, Hope and Love

FRANKIE M POWERS

Copyright © 2021 Frankie M Powers

All rights reserved.

ISBN: **978-1-7370679-0-0**

DEDICATION

To Nori and Jonathan:
Every single time I begin to wonder why it is that I am doing what I am doing, every single time I am tired, when I feel defeated, I look at you both and no words need to be spoken. Nori and Jonathan, my unconditional love for you, and your unconditional love for me, has made me desire and strive to be the best dad I can be, to be the best human being and example I can ever achieve. Nori, Jonathan, you two are the most "imperfectly perfect" children any parent could ever dream of. My love for you has no limits.

FRANKIE M POWERS

CONTENTS

	Acknowledgments	i
1	My Early Years	1
2	My High School Years	21
3	College and the US Marine Corps	37
4	Marriage and the Birth of Nori	53
5	Jonathan Completes Our Family	67
6	Divorce and the Downward Spiral	87
7	Hello Rock Bottom, My Name Is Frank	125
8	Visualizing the Mountaintops	137
9	Seeing the Mountains in the Distance	153
10	Standing at the Base of the Mountains	173
11	Climbing the Lower Slopes	183
12	The Summit is in Sight	195
13	The View from the Mountaintop	205

FRANKIE M POWERS

ACKNOWLEDGMENTS

First, I don't know where I would be without my faith. God has had His hand on me, looked over me, and carried me time and time again throughout my journey in life. The whispers of the Holy Spirit inside of me, the example set by Jesus Christ, my Savior. The one thing I am most grateful for, as far as me standing here, is I have never wavered in my faith and God's grace and mercy.

My kids, Nori and Jonathan, you have been my why. My desire to become the best version of myself. My desire to show you the example of the miracles God can do, and how blessed, fortunate and grateful I am for God to have gifted me the title of being your father. I would have never started this journey without both of you in my life. You were the driving force to make me the man I am today.

My parents, Mami and Papi. Thank you for loving me the best way you could. For giving me all the opportunities to succeed that you never had. For caring for me so deeply and instilling in me my faith, which I hold so dear to my heart. Thank you for giving me the best that you had inside of you. I am beyond blessed and fortunate to be your son.

 Lisa, thank you for all the years that you stood by my side. Your faith in me never wavered. I am eternally grateful for all the countless hours you sacrificed yourself and your family and showed me the true value of friendship.

Jessie, thank you, thank you, thank you. I don't know where I would be without your presence in my life and your presence in my children's life. You have been my bedrock over the last few years and are not my friend, but my other sister. I love you Jess.

Julie, my little sister. Thank you for the precious gift of introducing me to Yari. Without you, Nori and Jonathan would not be here. Thank you for the beautiful gift of my two wonderful nephews Gus and Chino, who I love so dearly. I love you, Jules.

My grandparents and aunt in heaven, especially you Abuelo Papo. Thank you for showing me what the love of a grandparent felt like. You were my hero. You showed me what it meant to live with integrity. I love you and miss you all so much.

Yari, thank you. Thank you for being so hard on me, for making me accountable for my actions. Thank you for the gift of our precious children, Nori and Jonathan. If it wasn't for your constant pressure, I would never have turned my life around.

Robert, thank you. Thank you for being such a loving and caring stepfather to my children. You are a blessing in their lives and in being so, a blessing in mine.

Norma, my mentor. Thank you for guiding me throughout my transformational journey. I do not know where I would be without your influence and direction along the way. I will forever value you.

Cynthia, Lauren, Charles, Barry and Jessie, thank you for your counsel, whether in the court room or therapy sessions, your listening ears, your soft, gentle and, when needed, tough love has helped awaken the giant within me.

Hanley Rehabilitation Center and the staff, counselors and members in it. Thank you for your presence, encouragement and wisdom. I told you all that no one that had ever walked into that building would ever outwork me (I say smiling)!

Noel, Ivan, Auri, and Edzo, thank you for your friendship throughout the years and letting me know that no matter what was going on in my life, I could always count on you.

Randy and Pep, thank you for Landmark. Thank you for your precious souls and in only by desiring what was best for me, did you push me to enroll in a program that kickstarted my transformation. I will be forever indebted to you.

Ralph, no matter how many years go by, you are the essence of a true friend. No matter the time or place, I wouldn't trade our friendship for much of anything.

Manny the Magician (Shabum), my brother from another mother. Man…you and Neri saw magic in me before I ever did, and you, sir, are a professional magician. You both saw something in me that I missed. Thank you for your love, we are forever family.

Richie, thank you for your dedication and help with the music and editing of my videos. You have one hell of a bright future, young man.

Theo, thank you for your kind-heartedness and the peace that you have given me. Thank you for your friendship and loving heart. I value you so much. You are such a beautiful soul.

Rob (Tamiami), thank you for giving me a second chance to coach my son Jonathan's basketball team even though I probably didn't deserve one. Your compassion is admirable.

Landmark, Dale Carnegie Program, Les Brown, Tony Robbins, ET, Don Miguel Ruiz and Sons, Kyle Cease and the countless others, thank you all for what you do on this earth. Because of people like you, I found a place where I belong. I found my purpose.

Mrs. Barbara Jordan, my St. Brendan High School teacher. Thank you for planting the seed of psychology in me almost thirty years ago. My lifelong love affair of people, emotions, the mind and human behavior was sprung to life in your classroom.

Mrs. Lourdes Abella, my first religion teacher in school. Thank you for teaching me about love, Jesus and faith. A special thank you for changing the Moms-to-Moms prayer group on Friday mornings to Moms-to-Moms and Frank.

Caesar Costero, thank you for your never wavering friendship. You are such a kind and generous man. I love you, my brother.

Alfred, Flaco, Tico, and the rest of our CU2 clan, thank you for the countless forgotten and unforgotten moments of some of the most fun and glorious years of my life.

Melissa Henriquez, Isa, Lisa T., Beth, Brenda and Mel (Rockstar group), thank you for your support and words of encouragement throughout the last few years. You have no idea how much your words have mattered to me.

Steph and Terri, thank you for giving me a helping hand, listening ear and gracious smile. I love you, my friends.

Armando (mi hermano), me salvaste la vida en los momentos llenos de desesperacion. you literally saved my life in my most desperate moments. There is not a day goes by I am not thankful and grateful for you. You may have worked for me, but I owe my life to you. I love you, my brother.

Caty and Andy and the rest of my family, thank you for being such a dear and loving part of my life. I love you deeply.

Gus, Chino, Kyle, Kazzandra, Gabi and Gianna, my godchildren, niece and nephews. I wish I had more time with you. I want you to always know that Padrino and Tio Frankie deeply love you.

Gaby, Danny, Sophia, Pipa, Jay and Max, thank you for your never-ending friendship with my children, Nori and Jonathan. Thank you for caring and loving them so deeply. I will be forever grateful for what you mean to them.

Lynn and Laurie, thank you so much for your support and listening ears through this emotional rollercoaster of a journey that this book has brought me. A piece of you is always with me and forever reside in this book.

Anthony Profeta, thank you for the value of your presence in my life and your friendship. You are an embodiment of peace and love. This world needs more people like you.

Len, Fidelina, Christine and my IPEC friends, thank you for all of your wisdom. I have learned so much from you on how to live life in abundance.

Mike, Alicia, Aide, and Ally thank you for your graciousness. Thank you for being such wonderful hosts and treating my children and myself like family. Mike, our friendship never missed a beat. You are not only an all-star coach, you are an all-star friend.

Olgita, gracias por tu amor, por tu carino. Por haber sido como una segunda madre para mi. Siempre te tendre, en mis pensamientos y oraciones. Te quiero mucho.

Lars, thank you brother! You saved me. You saved my life. My call for help didn't go unanswered from you. I will forever be indebted to you my friend.

Carol Di Giacomo, thank you. Thank you for your love, your concerns, your kindness and your thoughtfulness. I am so grateful to have you in my life.

Phil and Alex, my two childhood best friends. Thank you, guys. Thank you for your unwavering friendship. Thank you for all the laughs, smiles and for just being there. Time stands still in our friendship. You two are my brothers. I love you guys!

Melissa Duffy, Oh Melissa…Thank you. Thank you for your time, for your support, for your shoulder to cry on, your listening ear and your friendship. You are more dear to me than you will ever know.

Reyna, thank you for your listening ear and for your words of inspiration. I value your presence in my life immensely.

Dunia D…Oh Dunia. After nearly two decades of very seldom contact, you opened up the St. Brendan Reunion chat at just the moment in time in which I needed it. God sent you back into my life at the perfect moment. Our friendship will forever be tattooed inside of me.

To all the members of the front lines, be it the Police Department, Firefighters and military personnel, who put their lives in harm's way so I, and millions of others, have our freedom. Thank you, and Godspeed, my brothers and sisters.

To all the pastors, priests and members of all churches throughout the world that serve and give glory to God, thank you. Your time and your service will be rewarded one day in heaven and watch out, some day you may have to make a little room for me beside you on the pulpit.

If I missed anyone, please forgive me. For anyone who has ever blessed me with their smile, their presence, with a handshake or an embrace, thank you. Thank you for allowing me to be part of your life.

As I wrote this book, massive amounts of awareness arose in me. Moments that were buried subconsciously have come to light. "The light has strengthened me and cleared my path."

I ask, if I knowingly or unknowingly have offended any of you or hurt you in some way with my actions or my words, I humbly ask for your forgiveness. I am no longer living in the darkness of my old ways. My heart is filled with light and it is my desire to serve all men and women in my path, to spread the love that so graciously fills my heart and has become my calling. Thank you.

FRANKIE M POWERS

FOREWARD

Wow! Wow! Wow! Talk about incredible transformation. Frankie M Powers, you didn't simply transform your emotional, physical and mental make-up; you seem to have changed your human DNA. Your story and message is going to impact a lot of lives. Inspiring, Jaw-Dropping, Dedication and Resiliency. Unwavering sheer will and desire to change the world and help many overcome the obstacles that keep us from achieving our greatest potential! What you have accomplished and done is nothing short of a miracle and you prove that anybody can come back and win big in life. The Comeback at its best. What Unadulterated Love and Devotion to humanity and to those whom you Love and care about.

Readers will respect not only what drove you to get back on track, but that you can always continue to operate from your heart. People talk about accountability and taking responsibility; you have taken those words to a whole new level and show us how to as well. Raw. You share your story in a very Real and Vulnerable way, giving those with the desire to overcome the greatest challenges and true insight of the beauty and ugliness of transformation. The men and women who come across you and your story have such a divine opportunity to expand and grow into their greatness and change not only their own lives but the lives of those around them. God Bless you and all those people who are blessed to be a part of your journey. Best-selling author, Motivational Speaker and Seven Figure Empowerment Coach in the making is coming at you. You will be lighting up the stage and people's hearts like a fury of Fireworks on the Fourth of July. Buckle up, it's grow time!

All the Best,

SassBoss CEO
Best-selling Author of "Not Born this Way"

Sara Weiss

FRANKIE M POWERS

INTRODUCTION

On the morning of August 24, 2018, I called my children on their way to school. Nori, 13 at the time, and Jonathan 9. I told them how much their father loved them and that their dad was going to get help and come back better than ever. I had no idea what that meant, I just knew that my life's trajectory was about to turn full circle. Some call it instinct, some intuition. I call it faith.

After three weeks of having relapsed, I entered Hanley Rehabilitation Center in West Palm Beach. A rehabilitation center for alcoholics and drug addicts. I had no idea what I had in store for me but having been in Marine Corp boot camp over twenty years prior, I prepared mentally for the journey before me. My experiences throughout my life had been rooted in heartache, disappointments and anger. I resented many people around me. I continued playing over and over in my mind my regrets, past failures and feelings of not being enough to those I loved.

Upon exiting Hanley, I surrendered. I fully surrendered to life, to control, and to the only One who dictated the obstacles and blessings that would come my way, I surrendered to God.

I took a two-year hiatus traveling throughout the country, discovering endless possibilities and a far different way of living. I learned to fully love myself, which, without that, I would have stayed paralyzed and stuck in regret, frozen in fear for the rest of my life.

I learned about the power of our thoughts, the importance of being present and the need to find fulfillment in life. I became an expert in communication skills and relationships and became aware that most of us don't even see a glimpse of what is possible and attainable in them.

I learned that where you focus your attention, your energy and emotions in your life attach to that. What I also discovered, along the way, was my purpose for living, my passion, the one thing that sets my soul on fire.

I became aware of my lifelong love affair with people, with watching people glow and helping people grow. I learned that every single individual is born with certain inherent gifts given to them by their Creator, that they are graced with, that are uniquely theirs. It is their mission in life to discover what that is and gift it to the world. I learned the value of serving my fellow man and being a giver rather than a taker in every opportunity presented.

Every experience I share with you in this book, my memoir, has made me the man I am today. There is nothing that has occurred or happened to me that was an accident or a mistake.

In my journey, it was through the virtues of faith, hope and love that I overcame and conquered any and all obstacles and hardships that I had ever endured. I now spend my life giving unto others as an empowerment coach, life guide and strategist; to explore with anyone who I have been blessed with their presence, with the opportunity to jointly find what it is holding them back from having the breakthroughs in life they are destined to discover.

I have developed my logo being the, "Tree of Hope," the seven branches signifying the seven paths to keep you lifted up in even your deepest moments of despair. They are gratitude, forgiveness, growth, love, joy, faith and serenity. The symbolism of the roots being the core to find a life filled with abundance by seeking surrender, being present and finding fulfillment. These tools have utterly transformed my life. I have completely reshaped my physical body, as well as my emotional, spiritual, and mental makeup. I have overcome obesity, alcoholism, divorce, heartache, depression, anxiety, as well as, suicidal thoughts and desires. I may not know the hardships that some of you are going through, but I understand what it feels like to feel hopeless, alone and afraid.

The transformation process was a long journey, but the end result has given me a whole new perspective in life. In doing so, I have become a better man, friend, father and human being.

This book and its sole purpose is to let the reader know that regardless of your situation and what you are going through, you have the strength inside of you to get out of it. Every single one of you has a bright, shining lamp inside of your being just waiting to shine on through. Remember, your past does not dictate your future. My test has become my testimony.

Everything you desire in your life is there for the taking if you can get out of your own way. Seek and thee shall find, knock and the door shall be opened. If I can be of any assistance, please seek me out from the information down below. This is not my job; this is my vocation. Empowering others to live a life filled with passion, love and fulfillment. Helen Keller once penned, "Alone we can do so little, together we can do so much". Blessings to all of you and I hope you enjoy my journey. God bless you
.

PROLOGUE

Beep…beep…beep…resting heart rate 160. "Mr. Lopez, everything is going to be okay. We're going to give you some medicine; it is going to lower your heart rate." Beep…beep…beep…five minutes later. Okay, it's not working. As I look around, I quickly notice another three to four nurses scurrying around, coming to tend to whatever is happening to me in this moment.

A sudden sense of dread comes over me and tears start flowing down the side of my cheeks. I feel a warm, gentle hand hold mine. It's one of the nurses. She compassionately tells me, "Mr. Lopez, it is going to be okay. The medicine has not lowered your heart rate yet, but we are going to administer a little more medicine (medicine injected into IV)." Five minutes later, my heart rate is 162.

Anxiety and panic set in as I glance back to the right corner, behind me, and notice the reading on the machine. Oh gosh, confusion and terror set in as I notice that the medicine is not working. The lovely nurse, who so kindly and gently held my hand, yells out for more personnel! Within seconds, and like a movie in slow motion in the Emergency Room at Jackson South Hospital I was surrounded by so many nurses I couldn't even count them all.

Could this really be happening? No, it can't! I've got so much more to do. Rapidly, the situation gets worse. My resting heart rate is now 165 and climbing. In this moment of panic, I realize that a Doctor or some kind of medical professional is walking near me with a machine that is marked with an X on it, that is unmistakable to anyone. It is a machine I had never seen before outside of a movie.

In confusion, I turned to the soft-spoken nurse standing beside me and grab her hand, pleading. I can barely get the words out, "Please, I have two children, a ten-year old-daughter and six-year-old son. I cannot leave my children without a father; please help me. I cannot leave my children without a father," my voice cracks as the fear is consuming me.

Minutes later, a cardiologist came to see me to say that my heart was out of rhythm. They needed to do a standard procedure to jump start my heart and put it back in rhythm. Oh, my, God, I thought! Please, God, help me, I prayed.

Ten-minutes later, which seemed like hours, I open my eyes to see standing above me cardiologist, Dr. Ivan Mendoza. He tells me, "Mr. Lopez, everything is going to be okay. We were able to get your heart back into normal rhythm. You are one extremely lucky man. You need to take charge of your life and lose weight. You were going into cardiac arrest. If you had not come in today for a routine checkup, within 24 hours you would probably not be with us." That moment defined everything for me.

1
MY EARLY YEARS

"Life is a journey. A journey of coming full circle in unlearning much of which we inherently learned." -Frankie M Powers-

It was fall 1977. How I remember that I am not sure because in Florida we do not have the change of seasons, but the memory is so vivid and impactful. I'm just two years old. I look down and remember being barefoot. I feel so frightened, helpless and alone. As I stand in the living room of my parent's home in Westchester, a suburb of Miami Dade County, Florida. Just being two years old and finding myself alone, I felt abandoned and started crying The scene is forever engraved in my mind. The living room space was not a large one; it was about 12 by 12 I remember the feel of the rug as if I was standing there right now in this very moment, almost 43 years later. It was brown and light blue, colors woven together. It was soft, almost like the feel of a blanket. At that time, I was an only child, the first-born son of Frank and Amanda Lopez.

My little bare feet intertwined with the rug, the rug being the only comforting feeling I had at that moment. I was wearing a sleeved Superman shirt and red pants (not quite sure if it was an outfit or a set of pajamas). I remember hearing my mom, at a distance, telling me that she was leaving. I remember crying and crying uncontrollably as I looked around wondering what was happening. Where did they go? Why did they leave me? I was frozen. It was almost as if my body was immersed in concrete. I could not move. I recall feeling desperate, desolate and alone. I was…alone. This was the first of many memories where I felt alone, abandoned and unseen.

Then, I remember my mom coming towards me almost a half hour later and consoling me. I was shaking and my breath was shortened. Immediately, my fear turned to relief. I wrapped my arms around her and made sure never to let her go, and for the first half of my life, I did just that. She was my everything; when she was with me the world was right. I never wanted her to let me go. I needed her comfort, her security, her love and acknowledgement. That day stayed with me forever. It haunted me for the following 41 years.

Remember that number. I am 45 years old now, as I write my story.

In my early years of life, Christmas is what I remember the most. It was simple times. I remember how the whole family gathered on the back patio. The patio was large, and we would construct a table out of wooden panels and place cylinder blocks for chairs. Pretty creative, right? I love that memory. My grandfather (Abuelo Tata, as I would call him) would cook a whole roasted pig on Christmas Eve (Cuban families normally celebrate the holidays roasting their own pig) . I recall these memories with fondness. In those years, I remember him most, Abuelo Tata gave me my first taste of alcohol. It was spiked cider, I believe. It was probably funny seeing the look on my face as I had my very first taste of what would later become my best friend and companion. Still today, I recall the memory of how he would show his affection, his arms cradled me and softly with the tips of his fingers he would run his hands up and down my arm and gently and lovingly stroke my belly. I felt so protected and loved, it was so easy to fall asleep, knowing Abuelo Tata was there holding me and protecting me. Til this day I'm a sucker for the gentle touch of a soft hand running down my arm and belly.

Christmas WOW! For me, they were always spectacular. I was spoiled rotten, every desire and then some was granted. There was nothing that would stop my parents from making me feel like a king that day. That holiday was especially made and tailored for me. Come to think of it Christmas for me has become a most important holiday where I express massive amounts of love and it is my joy to give and light others up. Regardless of our financial situation back then, I was clueless because my parents made me feel like the most special and loved little boy on the planet, I now realize this is why I love to give so much to others. No one leaves me without letting them know and feel how special they are. This becomes a common theme in my life. By all means and cost, I will love you to the deepest parts of my soul. I later learned to channel this a different way when self-love was born. More on that later. My father, Frank, who was an avid carpenter, would stay up all night building my swing set and any other toys or presents that Saint Nick decided to leave me. As I sit back and recall, I see my dad smile as he would watch my eyes open in amazement at all the gifts left for me to discover. I realize I was and have always looked for that smile, that acknowledgement of, "That's my boy." The need for approval and being loved is a strong constant in my heart, I would continue and continue to chase it from my dad. As I write my story, I recognize that regardless of my age, my feelings have always been worn on my sleeve. I am extremely expressive; every emotion has always been felt and clearly shown.

It was 1979; I am four years old and now I am going to be a big brother. I remember feeling so excited; I was going to have a little sister. I recall one specific moment when my parents were going through their list of names. My mom, Amanda, asked, "Frankie, Any ideas for names for your baby sister?" I replied, "Yes, mommy, I have the perfect one…Frog." I found it hilarious for about three seconds until I got a slap across the right-side of my face, I can still feel the sting of her hand. Mom did not find it very amusing. I guess I should have realized then (make mental note) that there are certain jokes that one does not make to a pregnant woman. So, on October 30th, 1979, my baby sister Julie was born, and this completed our family nucleus.

*****

My father was born Jesus Francisco Lopez on June 7th, 1948, in Havana, Cuba, the second of two children. Later, upon his arrival in the U.S., he changed his name to Frank Lopez. His father, my grandfather, Dr. Francisco Lopez, was a judge and ran for political office, for congress, at one point in his life. He was also a newspaper writer. My grandmother, Yolanda Lopez, was an athletic woman and piano player, with extraordinary craftmanship. My grandparents were very rigid, they steered a tight ship, hence that rubbed off on their offspring. It is now 1960, tensions were rising between the United States and Cuba. My grandparents sent their children, Yoly and my father, to the United States. My father was 13; my aunt was 18. At the time, the plan was to immigrate with them to Miami, Florida. Then, the unthinkable happened. Flights to the United States ceased. Families were separated. It was the closest moment in the history of the world to Armageddon and my family was somehow stuck in the middle of it. It would be five long years before my father would reunite with his parents. This took place in the most critical years of a person's life, years 13 through 18.

My father does not speak much, but I know, whether he would ever realize it or not, that those lost years have forever impacted his life and the man he has become, my father was lost even before I was a thought in his life. Upon arrival in the United States, there were eleven family members living in a three-bedroom apartment. Originally, thought to have been welcomed to live with an aunt and uncle, they rescinded their offer upon my father's arrival. This created a series of broken promises from the people he trusted most that created feelings of distrust toward others. As he and my aunt began to search for places to rent, he remembers seeing signs that would read, "No Jews, no blacks, no Cubans." He was a 13-year-old boy forced to become a man almost overnight, facing the harsh cruelties of abandonment, whether by choice or by chance, by his parents and relatives. In addition, he was feeling discriminated against in his new home, his new land.

Feeling no sense of home and no one to rely or depend on and not speaking the language, he soon realized it was up to him to figure out how to survive, how to eat and how to live.

He would wake up every morning at 4:00 am, get on his bicycle and begin to pass out newspapers. He would get home, quickly shower and go to school at Miami High. Once school ended, he would ride his bicycle to Winn-Dixie, where he had a part-time job bagging groceries. Life was hard; nothing was handed to you. You had to go out and make it happen. During those years, he lived off so much coleslaw and rice and beans, that, let's just say, he is not a big fan of rice these days. I would venture to say, somehow, he associates those difficult times with the foods he ate. He was forced to be hard, to be strong and to be tough.

*****

My mom was born Amanda Perez on January 6, 1950, daughter of Gregario Armando Perez and Julia Perez in Matanzas, Cuba. She was their only daughter and was born a beautiful, small, blonde, firecracker of energy with a jubilus spirit. My grandfather, known to me as Abuelo Tata, was a kind, generous, loving man, as well as an extremely brilliant one. He had invented a machine in Cuba that would speed-up the process of cutting sugar cane. He had also patented an invention of the disposable razor that upon his untimely death, the patent had expired, and Gillette jumped on it. My grandmother, Abuela Tata, on the other hand, was a lively, charismatic woman of humble upbringing and limited education. Her studies concluded at the end of her third-grade school year.

My grandfather immigrated to the United States with my mom and grandmother a few years before the Cuban Missile Crisis, and lived in Dallas, Texas, for one year, before returning back to their home on the island of Cuba.

On his second and final voyage to the United States, he was forced to come alone. He then called for my grandmother and my mom to join him in Miami, Florida. However, there were certain documents my grandfather had forgotten to sign. Upon calling my grandmother over the telephone and trying to explain to her to look at the documents he had signed (wink, wink), then to have her turn over those documents to the appropriate Cuban government offices, my grandmother began arguing with my grandfather, known by his middle name Armando. "Armando! Armando! The documents you are telling me about are not signed," she explained. He then asked to put my mother on the phone, who he referred to as Armandita. With my then seven-year-old mother on the phone, she listened to her father's instructions of where the documents were. He then told her, "Do you see the documents, Armandita?" She said, "Yes, Papi." "Don't you see my signature on them?" My mom instinctively understood what he was saying. My then seven-year-old mother signed over the documents, forging my grandfather's signature: and they were able to join my grandfather in the United States.

As I write this, I cannot help but notice the intuitiveness my mother had then, and how closely it resembles my own daughter, Nori's, instincts. Before leaving the island for good this time, none other than second in command, and future Cuban President Raul Castro, came to visit my grandfather and told him, "Armando, I need you to go to the plantation to fix a sugar cane machine because it is not functioning properly". Little did Mr. Castro know that my grandfather purposefully disassembled it and never did return back to put it in functioning order.

After settling in their new country, the United States of America, my grandparents, much like all new immigrants, went through various hardships in their journey to achieve the American dream. My mother often reminds me of one particular Christmas that has stayed with her throughout her 71 years of life. My mom was ten to twelve years old and she knew the financial burdens her parents were going through. She had absolutely zero expectations for that Christmas year. However, that Christmas morning, upon awakening, she saw she had received a ball and a beautiful girl doll. Those two simple gifts became the most treasured gifts my mother has ever received.

My grandfather was a go-getter, an entrepreneur. He ended up opening an import/export textile company and was continuously traveling throughout Latin America. My mother was a sweet, strong, independent woman. She stood a whopping four foot, ten inches, but what she lacked in height, she made up for in fight, in wit and in smarts. My mother, throughout her years of life, felt betrayed by many members of her family who she loved deeply. This led her to have difficulty in forgiving others, and to hold on to pains and hurts she felt others gave her. As a mother, she loved with all she had inside. She loved me more than any mother could ever love a son. For the first thirty-years of my life, she was my rock. I can never forget all the love she gave me. I reminisce with fondness of those younger years.

*****

It was 1970, five years before I was born. My grandfather, Abuelo Papo, was turning blue, almost purple. He was rushed to the hospital. He could not breathe. He was ill, doctors believed it was terminal. They told him it was cancer. He was a heavy smoker at the time and the doctors gave him six months to live. My father was furious. "How dare they tell my father how much time he has left on this earth? Only God has that power." He slammed the door in the hospital room, and he pulled a chair next to his dad. He grabbed his own pack of cigarettes (my father was a smoker too), looked at my grandfather and said "Papa, no more. I quit today, and you quit today," and so they did.

It was now 1981; I am six years old and big brother to my sister Julie. We have since moved to a beautiful two-story home in west Miami. It was a quiet neighborhood with a cul-de-sac at the end of the street. Family life was a little different.

I didn't see my Abuelo Tata as much, however, my dad's parents, Abuelo Papo, as I would call him, and Abuela Yolanda, were a constant presence in my life. Every Saturday morning, they would come over to my home and we would spend the day together. They slept over and stayed with us until Sunday afternoon. It was during these years, my bond with Abuelo Papo grew immensely. He still hovers over me, I still feel his presence, I still can hear his voice. It has been thirty-five years since I lost him, yet I can still feel him inside of me. My grandfather, Abuelo Papo, was born with club feet. He was a survivor of lung cancer. I did not realize it then, but his health was not so great.

I remember playing catch in the backyard of my new home with my grandpa, my mentor, whom only through God's grace, did I ever get a chance to meet. I have fond memories of those times. Abuelo Tata was not around as much. He was busy working and his work required a lot of overseas travel. So, Abuela Yolanda took over his role as far as the bedtime caressing me to sleep. I felt deeply loved then, I felt deeply loved by everyone, everyone, except my Dad.

The year was 1982. I was seven years old, living in our new home in west Miami. I attended Green Glades Elementary School, a public school just a few miles from my home. My first-grade teacher was Mrs. Davila. She was a heavy-figured African American woman. School was fun, or so I thought. I remember one day having a food fight in the classroom, which seemed like a good idea at the time, but quickly shifted when I was sent to the principal's office to receive my reward. "Hands off your butt cheeks Frank," wooden paddle smacked right on my butt cheeks, a well-deserved whooping if you ask me. Throwing that chocolate pudding was not the cleverest of my decisions. School was fun, home…was different.

My dad worked hard. He was an aircraft mechanic at Eastern Airlines. His work ethic was second to none. I do not believe he ever went in late or ever called in sick. I remember every morning mom would pack his big, black, rectangular lunch box to take to work. Mom would take care of the house, cook supper and work from home as a property manager. She would also serve as a guardian-ad litem and help out at Saint Kevin's Catholic School as a catechism teacher. She was a school lunch mom and on top of all of that…she was pure "love". As I write this, my eyes swell up, just remembering feeling my mother's love every moment of every single day. I wish that every child born could feel, even if for just one moment, the love by their mother that I felt from mine.

Every day I would get home from school, do my homework and run outside to play. I would run in, just before dark and we would sit as a family to have dinner. Dinner was always a treat, mom was quite the cook, whether it was a plate of rice and beans, or carne con papas (beef stew), mom knew what she was doing. No matter what she was cooking, the secret ingredient was a big pinch of love in every recipe.

Dad was different. He was serious. He would come home and say hello, but he always looked angry. I was afraid of him. He did not really hit me, at least nothing that I did not deserve or that was too painful, but it was what he would say or perhaps what he would not say. I always kept searching for his love, for his praise, wanting to feel he was proud of me. Still, I keep searching and desiring that from him. Perhaps, I always will. I always felt that no matter what I did, I could never gain his love, his approval, his acceptance. He always seemed angry at me, I always felt that I was a disappointment to my father.

He would purchase model cars for me and as I would attempt to build them, they would break. He would scold me. I felt dumb, I felt inept, I felt…useless. His disappointment in me fueled my anger. I was angry. I was insecure. I felt that I could never gain my father's approval. No matter what I did, it was never enough to gain his love. It was during these years that I first began to see a psychologist to test me for behavioral issues.

It was now 1983 and I embarked on my first season of organized sports. It is January and I am playing little league baseball at Tamiami Park in West Miami. This would kick off a lifelong love affair with sports, as well as bonds and relationships that have progressed to this very day. Baseball was fun, it gave me something to do after school and on Saturday mornings. My parents took a liking to sports, especially my father. He was always present.

He worked at Eastern Airlines Monday thru Friday from 6am to 3pm. This would give him enough time to coach me in my baseball practices. Although my dad was always present, he was tough. He was a pretty well-rounded athlete, while I, on the other hand, was all effort and not much talent.

In October 1983, our family's whole world changed. My grandfather, Abuelo Tata, was involved in a serious car accident. A young man was speeding in excess of 80mph on a residential street. He slammed into my grandfather's 1983 silver Oldsmobile. My grandfather was not wearing a seatbelt and he flew out the front windshield. He was seriously injured. He was rushed to the hospital and spent 33 days there, until his body could go on no longer and he died. Our lives changed.

My grandfather was a successful businessman, but he did not leave a will. My grandmother was sick and on many medications. She was unable to handle not only his loss, but also his personal matters. To make matters worse, since there was money and my grandfather's brothers knew about it, it was a fight of every man for himself. His widow and only daughter be damned. My family turned against my mom. My mother, 33 years old, mother of two young children, had to fend for herself. She hired a nanny, hired attorneys, fired nannies, and fired attorneys. She finally found a nanny that suited her, who was able to help around the house, take care of my sick grandmother, cook, and take care of the children.

Mom then went to work. Although she had helped my grandfather on some business ventures, there were others that she knew nothing about. She was forced to travel to South America and Mexico. She enrolled at the University of Miami to become a paralegal. Those were a tumultuous few years. She did all this while looking after her sick mother. To this day, I do not quite know how she did it. What I do know is that she was a fighter. She was determined; she always had tremendous faith in God and our Lord, Jesus Christ. She planted in me, from a very young age, the mustard seed of God and the importance of loving him above all and anyone else.

I remember my mother not wanting me to go to my grandfather's funeral. She felt it was not something she wanted her 8-year-old son to experience, so she bargained with me. She told me she would give me ten packs of baseball cards not to attend the wake. I was a huge, avid sports card collector and I accepted. It was a decision that I would come later to regret.

A lot happened in my life in 1983. I started baseball, I started seeing a psychologist and I lost my grandfather. I had also started in a new school, albeit, for only a year, Francisco Baldor.

It was now August 1984. I am ready to start my new school, Saint Kevin's Catholic School in Miami. My children would attend this very same school, 30 years later. I recall the very first day of class, being a new student, the teacher, Mrs. Chau, asked me if there was any name or nickname that I wanted to be called. I was nervous. I panicked. I froze. I answered no, a decision that I would regret for the next 35 years (you see, all my life, my nickname was Frankie. I loved Frankie). Til this day, every time I hear the name Frankie, it does something to me that is hard to explain. It soothes my heart. In that moment, in that classroom, when I answered no, I changed my identity. It changed who I was. I was no longer Frankie; I became Frank.

Anyhow, I made friends easily. School was okay, however, my relationship with my father proceeded to get worse and worse. We were always arguing, always fighting. I began to throw objects. I would yell. I would scream. I would cry. I felt so unheard and so unappreciated by my dad. I often wondered if I would be better off dead. I continued to see different psychologists. What I remember most is them showing me different pictures and asking me what do you see? What I recall seeing most often is a butterfly or a spider. I could not comprehend why I had to continue to see these people (don't they understand? I am fine. I just want my dad to love me, I told myself inside). Why can't he hug me, why can't he be proud of me? Why can't he smile when he sees me? Why is he always so angry with me?

So, I acted up. His anger, my feeling of being unseen, spurred aggressiveness in me. I would fight; I would fight anyone. There was no one too big or too old, bring them on, win or lose, it did not seem to matter. I could express all that deep-seated anger and resentment that I felt inside. However, one thing, to this day, I have never been able to hit anyone with all my strength. There was always something, somewhere, this voice that would whisper to me, "Don't hit them too hard." I never truly wanted to hurt anyone, at least not too much. Yet, fighting became routine. Not a week would go by without a fight; it became part of who I was. It was so much so, one year a friend of mine's dad, after a baseball state championship ended, one in which I punched a kid in the middle of the game where he was vomiting blood, gave me the nickname "Tyson."

It was now January 1986. It is Sunday; my mom and dad call me and my sister over to their room. I remember the look on their faces. I instinctively knew something was wrong. They said, "Frankie and Julie, Abuelo Papo has lung cancer." Now I was only ten-years old, but I knew that he was dying. I immediately ran into my room, jumped on my bed and began crying, and crying, and crying some more.

Me with Abuelo Papo

Memories of my favorite grandparent, my closest grandparent, came racing through my mind. The memories of playing catch outside my parent's home. His body so broken, yet he was happy as a clam playing catch with me. I remembered all the baseball games that I would dictate play by play over the phone from beginning to end because he did not have cable television in his home. Never once did he voice an objection. On the contrary, he was just filled with joy to be talking to his grandson. He was my world, and I was his. I remember a lesson he told me that I have carried with me since that very day over 35 years ago. He told me "A man is only as good as his word. The day a man breaks his word, he loses his value as a man." Living with integrity is a testament I hold dear. I hold that testament as a badge of honor for my grandfather.

A few weeks later, some time in February 1986, my parents came to talk to me and told me "Frankie, Abuelo Papo is not eating. He adores you; he listens to you. See if you can help get him to eat." I said, "Sure, I know just the trick". You see, my grandfather and I used to love those Ritz club crackers with cheese. The ones that come prepackaged with a red rectangular stick to spread the cheese. I said, "I've got this. Now one thing, mom and dad, I need to stop at the grocery store first," and so, we did. I went straight to the aisle, grabbed the crackers, paid for them and we were off to see my grandfather.

As I write this, for the first time in 35 years, I see him. I see his face, as I saw him that day. I see him lying in bed with his royal blue checkered pajamas. He is frail and weak, yet with a huge smile bursting out on his face that showed that he was so happy to see me. I sat next to him. I was frightened. I was scared. I looked at him and offered him the crackers. He looked at me, grabbed my hand and said, "Macho, I'm not hungry now. I promise I will eat them later. Give it to your grandmother and I will eat it later." I left on that day, not realizing that would be the last time I would ever hear his voice. I was hopeful, but not overly optimistic.

A few weeks later, on March 10, 1986, I got home from school, with my sister Julie, to hear the news that I feared the most. Somehow, I knew it. I felt it. "Frankie, your grandfather, Abuelo Papo has gone to heaven." I immediately ran upstairs to my room and jumped into my bed, however, there were no tears inside of me. I remember feeling guilty. How could I not cry? How could I lose my grandfather and not cry? I was ashamed of myself. The very next day was the wake. My mom came to me and said, "Frankie, tomorrow is the wake. I do not think you should go. I will give you ten packs of baseball cards if you do not go." I told her, "No, Mom, I am going." She upped the offer to twenty packs of baseball cards. I looked up at her and said, Mommy, I don't care if you give me all the baseball cards in the world, I am going," And so, I went. When I saw him dressed in his grey suit, I hugged him in his coffin and gave him a gentle kiss on his forehead and cheek. I wiped the tears streaming down my face and told him goodbye.

About a week later, I went to my grandmother's house, the one that she shared with my grandfather. As I walked to the kitchen and opened the refrigerator, I could not believe what I saw…what I saw became the mantra that has run my life ever since. It was the pack of crackers with cheese; he never opened it. At that moment, I told myself, "If I would have only tried harder, if I had only pushed harder, he would have eaten them." If he would have eaten the crackers, he would have lived. My mantra was that I should have tried harder, there must be a way, there is always a way. You must push, pull, climb or barrel through but you must!

After a few months, in the summer of 1986, my parents put me in martial arts. I started taking Taekwondo at Chi/Tai Kwon Do school in Tamiami Park. As I stated earlier, I was an emotional young boy. If I was happy, you knew it; if I was frustrated, you knew it. Chances are, if I was angry, you felt it. After the loss of my grandfather, I became angrier. It was my first deep loss and I felt partly responsible. I did not realize it then, but I believe my parents put me in martial arts hoping to have them teach me how to channel my anger and how to gain self-discipline.

*****

Sixth grade shortly came around and I loved it. I was teacher's pet. My homeroom teacher was Mrs. Bassing. Most of my classmates were not fond of Mrs. Bassing, however, for some reason or another she took a real liking to me. I became her favorite student. I remember how she loved to pinch my cheeks and nicknamed me "Frankie baby." Perhaps it was the feeling of nostalgia I felt when she said my nickname, "Frankie." I never gave it much thought until this very moment. I loved it and I ran with it.

My days were jam packed. August through December I had Taekwondo on Tuesdays and Thursdays, basketball practice at Tamiami on Mondays and Wednesdays and basketball games on Saturdays. I was never the kid that enjoyed video games. On my days off from school and sports, I would spend my days running around the block with my friends. Boy, did I love the outdoors. There was something about being outside, I felt light, I felt free.

From January through April was baseball season. My days were immersed with sports. Taekwondo one day and baseball the next. I was extremely competitive. Every time I stepped on the field or inside the dojo, I gave everything I had. I took every ounce of fire, of passion, of talent and left it all on the table. Although I was never the most talented, I always took great pride in being a leader and in giving full effort. I strived to be the best that I could be. As I sit back and wonder, I contemplate if I was doing it to prove it to myself, or if I was trying to prove to my dad that I was worthy.

It was the summer of sixth grade, going into seventh, and changes were brewing inside of me. My voice was changing, muscles developing, deodorant goes from being a decoration on the bathroom shelf, to a necessity. My body is changing, testosterone is moving into high gear. As the summer of 1987 came to a close, I remember getting ready for school. As soon as the first day begins, I develop my first crush. Her name was Carol DeCardenas. I remember her living a few blocks from my parent's home. I would get home from school, put on my coolest attire (or so I believed), splash on some Old Spice (my Abuelo Papo's favorite cologne) and head on over to see her. Carol became my girlfriend for a whopping three days. She was also the first girl to break my heart. Seventh grade was the beginning of nighttime parties. I recall being overwhelmed with excitement. It was also around the time I forged my greatest friendships of my junior high years.

My two best friends were Caesar Costero and Michael Balado. Together, we were known as the Three Musketeers; we were inseparable. It was hard to spot one without spotting the others. We each brought uniquely different traits to our friendship. Caesar was the smart and mysterious one. He also had these incredible blue eyes that made many of the girls melt. Mike was the tall, blonde, funny one. He was always cracking jokes and was one heck of a dancer. I admit now that I spent plenty of hours behind the scenes having him teach me a thing or two, so I was ready to move when I hit the dance floor. As for me, I was the fighter. I was the defender. I was the outspoken one. Together we made a great team. It was a beautiful friendship, one that I miss and cherish to this day.

Sports continued to be an integral part of my life. Every three months, I had a Taekwondo examination that I had to pass to move up in rank. Baseball became more intense, so much so, that my dad bought a batting cage for our home for me to practice after school. I became quite the baseball player by sheer dedication and commitment to my craft. The discipline that was the main reason for placing me in Taekwondo never came to fruition, but I was getting fit and getting strong.

It was April 1988. Baseball season was coming to an end. We won first place in our division and we are in the state playoffs. Game after game we grind and win. I was the team catcher and number three hitter. I was on fire this season. I hit .538 in the regular season. Now we make it to the state championship and the team to win the best two out of three becomes State of Florida champions. I remember the first game. It was the top of the 7th inning and we were up by five runs. Our team, the New York Yankees, are on the field. We have one out and the bases are loaded; the batter from the other team hits a shot to right field. Gilbert makes the catch, the runner tags on third base and comes running home. I square my body, bracing for impact. Gilbert threw a perfect strike, right to me, as the Tampa kid came charging through and as we collided, I dropped the ball.

What happened next was unfathomable. Upset at myself, I took it out on the young teen. I picked him up, slammed him on the ground and began pummeling him with my fists. We were separated and I was thrown out of the game. The ambulance came because the young man was throwing up blood. Thankfully, he was okay. I remember the field was packed with spectators that Friday evening. We had home field advantage. The game was played on our turf, in Tamiami Park in Miami. I recall everyone was cheering me on for my aggressiveness and my feistiness. That was the day that a friend's dad gave me the nickname "Tyson" (for Mike Tyson). We went on to win the championship, however, not in the manner that one would have wanted. The very next day, after we had won that first game, the Coach of the other team objected to me being allowed to play.

He believed I should have been ejected for the remainder of the tournament. The officials and umpires disagreed, so the boys from Tampa forfeited the game and drove back home.

It took me 33 years to recognize that that Coach, that father, the boys from Tampa made the right decision. The officials, my hometown, and those that cheered on the nickname Tyson, were wrong. I had no business playing; I should have been thrown out of that tournament! I was a punk, a young preteen punk. Those Tampa boys deserved better. My anger that day got the best of me. This time it happened on the baseball diamond. Where would it happen next?

*****

On Friday, May 13, 1988, something happened as I fell asleep. It was a mystery unbeknownst until this very day. On Saturday morning of May 14, 1988, as I got out of bed, I looked over at my brown trophy case which sat right on top of my mattress. As I looked up, there was a newspaper article and a royal blue rosary laying on top of it, right next to one of my baseball trophies. I was bewildered. I remember walking to it, picking it up and reading the article. I recall holding the rosary.

As I read the article, it was about the Lady of Fatima. It was an article about the Virgin Mary who appeared to three children in Fatima, Portugal, on May 13, 1917. She appeared to them on the 13th of the month for several months. Something beckoned inside of me, a feeling that for many years I have been unable to describe until this very moment. It was a feeling of a sense of peace, of protection, of, "You have a special and divine purpose."

As I write this, goosebumps and chills are running up and down my spine. I had completely forgotten that sensation. I immediately ran downstairs and looked at the Miami Herald, our community newspaper. As I stared at the front page and looked at the center, in bold black letters it read, "Saturday,

May 14, 1988." I immediately asked my mom about the newspaper and the rosary.

"Mom, what is this for?" She responded, "Where did you get that?" I looked at her puzzled, "Mom, you put that on my shelf with the rosary…didn't you?" She replied, "No," so the mystery continued. Mom asked my father, knowing the answer well before she ever had to ask the question. "Honey, by chance, did you leave these items here for Frankie?" He replied "No, you know I would not have done that." My mom looked confused. She could not understand where this newspaper and rosary came from. She picked up the phone and called the handful of people who would have been in our home and could have possibly left those items. She made three phone calls, all of them provided the same answer. No one knew anything about the rosary or the newspaper.

The Rosary

The very next Friday, May 20, 1988, at the school morning mass, I sat in the second to last pew at Saint Kevin's Church and began what would be my daily and weekly prayer. It was something that I prayed and asked God for years on end. It was "God, the day that you bring a woman in my life, let her be the one I marry."

As I look back, I recognize how bizarre that was, complete and utter insanity. In hindsight, I was in love with love. From the tender age of twelve, all that I ever could imagine wanting, was to be a husband and a father. It became my ambition. I always believed that God had something and someone special planned for me. I just needed to do my part.

Faith became core to who I was. It was part of my identity. To this day, I do not know how many people outside my home really understood or knew what my relationship has always been with God. As I sit back and ponder, I remember that during this time, I began my artistic expressiveness. Less than a month after I received this beautiful gift of the newspaper and holy rosary, I performed my very first song for friends and family. On June 4, 1988, in celebration of my dad's 40th birthday, I playfully sang the song "Faith" by George Michael.

*****

It was now the summer of 1988 and my eighth-grade year was coming up. As eighth graders, we would officially be known as BMOC. (Big Men on Campus) at St. Kevin's Catholic School. I was excited for my upcoming year. Wow! What a year. Over 30 years later, I must admit, that was one of the two to three most fun years of my youth. The year was filled with great friendships, fun times, many laughs, lots of gatherings and parties. Lots of great memories came from that '88 to '89 school year. I finally had my first kiss. Her name was Vanessa. It was October 30, 1988, my sister's birthday. We were outside by a friend's house on the golf course, and I went for it. Wow! I must be honest, it was incredible. I remember saying to myself "Wow, Frankie, what have you been missing?"

Being that it was the day before Halloween, we were all eating candy and yes…candy had a role in that incredible kiss. Her mouth tasted like peppermint. So, after 13 long years, yeah, that is right, I am the man. It is funny, all these years, and for every single one of us, we never ever forget that very first kiss. I am so glad to say that I definitely was not disappointed. Throughout the year, I engaged in various sports at school including cross country, basketball, and, of course, my sport, the one in which I dominated, or so I thought, baseball. At the end of the year, the athletic awards ceremony would be held in our cafeteria.

I remember that I was aiming toward and gunning for the "Athlete of the Year" award. The athletic award came down to two of us, myself and my dear friend, Tico Munecas. In baseball, I was certain, as a matter of fact, assured of getting an award. In fact, in May,1988, Coach Diaz gave the MVP in baseball to another young teen; his name was David Lorenzo. He told me, "Don't worry about it, Frank; you will, for sure, win it the following year."
It was a lock except…the following year, future New York Yankee draftee and future starting second baseman for the University of Miami Hurricanes, transferred to our school. His name was Rudy Gomez. Rudy and I became really good friends. We got along great. We had so much in common. We did some crazy, funny dances together. We both loved baseball and we both fell hard…really hard, for the same girl. Her name was Vivianne Sanchez.

Often times, when we compete in life or in sports, it tends to force us to take our game up to another level. Well, this was not one of those times. Rudy and I were the best players on the team. I pitch, he catches, I bat third, he bats fourth. There was a lot of talent amongst the baseball players and teams that we played against at that time. Rudy's superiority on the baseball field did not translate into bringing my game up, I felt the pressure. I put the pressure on myself to outperform and to out hit him. Ultimately, I could not compete. It was not so much that he was athletically more talented than I was, however, he was without a shadow of a doubt more driven. He was hungry.

Baseball was not a past time but a passion, it was not a game, but a job. I have not seen my childhood friend in over 25 years. I do not know what he is doing in his life, but what I do know is, if he is half as dedicated to his family and his career as he was to the baseball diamond, then my dear friends, he has definitely had a hall of fame life.

The season ended and the athletic awards came. The announcement, as expected, "Athlete of the Year Award" went to Robert (Tico) Munecas, St. Kevin's baseball Most Valuable Player Award goes to, Rudy Gomez. I did not get the much anticipated and desired MVP in baseball. I did not get the long hoped for "Athlete of the Year Award". Truth be told, I did not deserve either one of them.

A few weeks later, as I sat in class joking around with Rudy as we were signing each other's year books. I looked at him and told him, "You may have gotten the MVP, but I got the girl." Vivianne Sanchez, had become my girlfriend. When I think of my junior high and high school years, she was my first childhood love. She truly was an incredible human being.

Well, not everything about my eighth-grade year went so smoothly. Every year, each student was responsible for selling their share of raffle tickets. The top three classes would receive a special honorary award. My class was 8B and we won third place. The other eighth-grade class, 8A, won first place. One particular day in May 1989, our class prize was pizza and a popcorn movie day in school. That was great…except 8A's first place prize was a day at the beach. Now, my girlfriend, Vivianne, was in 8A, along with many of our friends, including Rudy Gomez. I wonder now if insecurities had arisen in me at the time. Honestly, I am not quite sure. However, I came up with a grand idea.

I gathered with my other two buddies, fellow musketeers Mike and Caesar, and orchestrated a plan. We would not go to school the day of the movie and I would have my mom take us to the beach to hang out with our friends. Brilliant, I thought, except umm…I know that we are not supposed to be at the beach. So, we all talked to our parents and came up with an alternative. We would not go to school that day. Mike and Caesar would be dropped off in the morning at my parent's house and we would hang out all day in my pool. When the day was over, we would reunite with our friends. Fantastic, except when 8:15 am hits and our homeroom teacher, Mr. Gonzalez, takes attendance, he reads Michael Balado, Caesar Costero and Frank Lopez, absent. Oh, no, "Something is going on," he says out loud. By 8:30 am, each of our parents were called and were threatened to take us to school or there would be dire consequences…so they did.

After much pushing and prodding by Mrs. Martinez, the eighth-grade religion teacher, we admitted we never had any intention of going to school that day and that our parents were aware of us having a secret pool day. You see, in explaining the reasons why we did not go to school, I supposedly had an orthodontist appointment, Caesar had complained of a migraine headache, and Mike was supposed to be accompanying his grandmother to the doctor's office in Hialeah.

Once we admitted this to Mrs. Martinez and after assuring us that everything would be okay, we proceeded to go back to our classrooms while she went to the principal's office. The next day, Mike and I were called to Mrs. Novas' (the Principal) office. I still am not quite sure why Caesar got out of this ridiculous over reaction. Mrs. Novas made us aware that she was going to speak to the school priest, Father Morras, and expulsion was being considered.

I remember feeling scared, frightened. As I sit back, I wonder what the hell was wrong with these people? What major rule or school law did we break? Two days later, the students were called for a special talk. They gathered all the classrooms together on the patio and told the students how some classmates had lied and described to them how our actions were reprehensible. As I write this, my blood is boiling. They humiliated and embarrassed us. These are the things that for some young adults can create psychological and/or emotional trauma that can last a lifetime. How dare these people call themselves followers of Christ and Catholics. These are not Christ-like teachings.

Nevertheless, that Friday, my mother was called to a meeting with Father Morras. Father Morras told my mother that I was going to be expelled. My mother pleaded with him, "My son is only a few weeks away from graduating. Please, what can I do?" she asked. He replied that he would reconsider under one condition. She said, "Anything." He told her, "Get on your hands and knees and beg me for forgiveness." She humbly obliged.

To this day, I have no idea how my mother did that for me. My mother was, and still is, an extremely strong woman. On this day, she kneeled and sought forgiveness. I cannot understand or comprehend what was going on during those days at my school and alma matter St. Kevin's Catholic School, a school my daughter went to and my son currently attends. I question if upon enrolling my children in this school, did I dishonor my mother and dishonor myself? Members of that administration are no longer there, and I have forged great relationships with many of the current faculty members.

However, it saddens me how some people dress up as wolves in sheep's clothing and bear the name of Jesus Christ and preach forgiveness yet fail to turn the other cheek.

Somehow, I did it; we did it. We finished the year. I made it…barely. It never would have happened if not for the love of a mother for her rebellious son.

2
MY HIGH SCHOOL YEARS

"In life our desire for our identity is often placed in the eyes of others, when to find ourselves what we need to do is blindly look within." - Frankie M Powers-

Summer 1989 came to an end and high school is just around the corner. I was accepted to Christopher Columbus High School, a prestigious Catholic High School in Miami, Florida. It was an all-boys school that was geared to athletic and academic excellence. It was, and still is, one of the finer high schools in south Florida. Yet, I was not happy there. I wanted none of it. I wanted to go to St. Brendan. I was 14-years old and testosterone levels were in overdrive, yet there was nothing I could do. I voiced my opinion to my parents, and we made a deal. If I was to make the baseball team and was successful athletically, I would stay; if not, I would transfer to St. Brendan.
High school started off as a challenge. I was no longer ruling the social scene. I was just trying to find my way. Caesar and Mike joined me, but high school was a different animal, a different breed. My anger continued, fights soon followed. The discipline that Taekwondo was expected to give me never came to fruition. I packed on the freshman 15. For the first time in six years, my school had a hot lunch cafeteria and soon, food became my comfort.

In December 1989, I received my black belt from Chi Taekwondo School. During my examination, the culminating part for me was fighting three other black belts while I was under attack. When the fight was stopped, I had one black belt on the ground, and I was holding on to one leg of each of the others.

January 1990 came. On the day of the Tamiami baseball parade, I had some choice words with my father before we left the house. I could no longer control my anger, and I said enough is enough. I took a swing at my dad, we tussled and wrestled on the living room floor. That was the only day that I ever raised my hand to my father, yet one day, is one day too many. It is a moment for which I will forever feel ashamed.

Something would often happen in me when I would get angry. I would lose complete control. I would smash walls, throw plates, throw punches. It was as if I was possessed by demons. I believe, in a way, that I was. It was a battle within, that I kept losing time and time again.

Every day when school ended, I would walk by the front of the school on the sidewalk, where my mom would come to pick me up. This became a daily ritual. One day, there was another teen, his name was Jesus. He was a big guy, a sophomore. He outweighed me by about 40 pounds, and he started bullying me. For the first time in my life, I felt insecure. I was afraid and I was scared to fight back. He would make fun of me. He would crack jokes and then, he began pushing me. On one particular day, a Friday after school, we began wrestling each other. In the heat of the moment, I pulled on his shirt and I heard it tear. We immediately stopped. His face turned candy apple red, and it looked like smoke was coming out of his ears. He looked at me dead center in the eye and said, "Frank, you better sew my shirt by Monday, or I am going to kick you're a**." My mom picked me up that day and I frantically told her what had happened to me. She assured me not to worry; she would get it sown by Monday.

When we got home, an argument ensued. My father scolded her, "Do not sew that shirt. Our son has to stand up for himself. If not, that boy will never leave him alone."

I have to say, my father was right. However, my mother went against my father's wishes and sewed the shirt. Sewing the shirt ended up becoming a big mistake. I gave Jesus the shirt that Monday afternoon, a move I thought would gain me some favor. It was a move that worked completely the opposite of what I had envisioned. The emotional and mental bullying became worse. I soon began to feel like Daniel Larusso from the Karate Kid. As I would exit school and search for another pick up spot, I would do anything to avoid confronting Jesus. I lived in fear for most of those days. I patiently counted the days till summer came, so that I could run away and avoid the fear of my fellow student.

I continued to play baseball at Tamiami Park. The fire and passion that I lacked in standing up for myself I brought out on the diamond. I remember one particular incident that is permanently tattooed in my memory bank.
It was Thursday night, and we played a game in which we lost 7 to 6. I busted my tail off in that game. I went 2-3 with 2 doubles, 4 RBI's and a walk. I threw out three runners, trying to steal, but we still came up empty. Our coach, my confirmation Godfather (Pepe), ripped our team to shreds. He told us that we lacked hustle, discipline and the will to win. As I walked to the parking lot, I saw the unthinkable. My father and Pepe got into a shouting

match. My father said, "My son busted his tail off and you showed him no recognition." I was floored, shocked, and for the first time in my life, I felt truly loved by my father. For the very first time in my life, I felt my father was proud of me.

*****

The first year of high school was really tough. I felt alone, confused. I had never in my life been afraid of anyone, yet all of a sudden, I felt intimidated by this schoolmate Jesus. Furthermore, my ex-girlfriend, that I'm still crazy about, Vivianne, has absolutely no interest in me and has a boyfriend. My friendships with Caesar and Mike had also changed. My feelings for my father were being challenged. I felt overwhelmed and conflicted. After lunch, in Columbus, as I finished eating, I would go to the chapel and pray. There was a small prayer room in Columbus. I would grab the bible and pray for ten minutes or so. It was my sanctuary, my refuge, my safe place.

I stopped going out as much during this time. My childhood neighboring friends, Alex and Phil, would become my escape from the real world. My weekends had now consisted of renting movies and watching them with friends, instead of going to parties and get togethers. I went from non-stop physical activity to lounging around and getting filled up with tacos and pizza. I was depressed, I was lost. I felt defeated. During the summer, I began to question my self-worth. I had also been injured playing baseball. That was the one thing in which I had taken great pride in myself. Now it had also been taken away.

I got into a fight with my best friend Mike, and our three-musketeer friendship was forever fractured. I also wronged my friend Mike. I love that guy. I apologized but I never really said I am sorry. I owe him that, I owe myself that. Before I publish this book, I will go out to do just that.

Halfway through my sophomore year, I pleaded with my parents to let me change schools. I did not make the Columbus baseball team. My damaged arm never fully healed. I hoped that a change of scenery would be welcome and that I would be able to find myself once again.

It was January 1991 and Christopher Columbus became my school of the past. I transferred to St. Brendan High School that was located right next door. I hoped to start a new beginning and forge myself a new path. Now there was definitely an adjustment period. I had made the junior varsity baseball team, although my athletic skills had eroded significantly. I lacked the fire, the drive, the passion that I once had. I still seemed lost, lacking direction. I continued to live like a hermit on the weekends. I was literally a shell of my former self. I continued to cope by eating, by fueling my satisfaction with food. I stopped fully living. I decided to get a job and start working and find some sense of self-satisfaction and fulfillment.

I was a dishwasher at Sizzler Restaurant in Miami. I was excited. Starting pay was $3.90 an hour, enough to continue my hobby that lay dormant for a few years…baseball card collecting. The job was short-lived, just a few months, until the dog days of summer. Truth is, I really had no financial need to work. It was money to splurge, to have for fun.

People often say that change takes years, but I believe differently. I have proof of that. Change happens, in an instant. Something clicked in me during my sophomore year summer.

I said, "Hell, no. I am not going to continue to live this way." A fire began burning inside of me that sought to find my fun, feisty and athletic eighth-grade self once again.

So, I set out on an improbable exercise routine. I would run 4 miles, do 250 pushups, 1000 sit-ups, box and swim for an hour every day. I exercised for approximately four hours a day. I would eat a small breakfast, light snack for lunch and a nice sized dinner. I was shredded. I went from 195 pounds to 150 pounds of pure, lean muscle. My braces came off about a week before school started. I also cut my hair and got a new hairstyle. I was a new man; I was determined to become engaged and popular once again, and I did, I sure did.

On my 4th attempt, I finally passed my roadside test and received my driver's license after not hitting an orange cone, car, or mailbox this time around. Often, we hear the phrase, third time is a charm…well, for me, it was the 4th time.

It was now September 13, 1991. A friend of mine, a high school senior named Mari, is having an open house party. It is Friday the 13th and they are going to be having two kegs. I wanted to go…but with who? An old friend, my former baseball teammate Eddy, was going to be going and he would be going with the DJ for the party named Nomar, so I decided to tag along. Little did I know then, but that night would become the beginning of my love affair with my greatest vice and kryptonite, alcohol.

Two beers, that's all it took. My first taste of alcohol was two beers from a Budweiser keg. It was also the first time I ever smoked, two cigarettes. The party was on. I recall somehow ending up in the pool in my underwear. Wow, what a night! I remember the feeling of pure joy and happiness. I was able to be myself without judgement, without thinking, without fear. Alcohol became my companion; it became my best friend.

That night I met one of my lifelong best friends, his name is Aurelio Infante, Auri, we called him. Auri, Eddy and I became quite the trio. We were the smaller of a larger group of 12 friends. We called ourselves CU2 (Care Unit 2). Till this day, I have no idea what the heck that name stood for. We were weekend drinkers. It was all good-natured fun. Whether it be Colt 45, Mickey's beer or Cisco's, we were sure to be having a good time. Drinking became my oasis, my escape from anger, from home, from feelings associated with not being enough. As a result of my newfound friendships and my constant partying, my school grades suffered quite a bit. I was too concerned with harnessing my newfound friendships.

I had joined the drama team at my high school. We were a duo; my partners name was Betty. We were pretty damned solid, if you ask me. Betty was a beautiful, blond, young woman with big, bold green eyes. We were just friends, but I remember one day, I abandoned her. On one particular Saturday morning before a drama competition, I stood her up. Cisco got the best of me the night before. I do not believe I ever gave her an explanation or ever told her I was sorry. I quit the drama team and never looked back, hence began a particular pattern of behavior. Alcohol became number one in my life. Everything and everyone else be damned.

During this time, Mark Wahlberg, also known as "Marky Mark," became a one-hit sensation. The song "Good Vibrations" shot up the radio charts. All of a sudden, the entertainer in me came back out. That song hit me like a bolt of lightning. I love to entertain. I heard Marky Mark singing Good Vibrations, one day on the Arsenio Hall show and I remembered saying to myself "Heck, I can do this. I can be a white rapper." So, I started practicing, rehearsing for the upcoming talent show at St. Brendan. I remember auditioning and us all being selected. It was me and Patti who did the woman vocals and we had two backup dancers who were phenomenal. One of them was Cindy and the other, my former drama partner, Betty.

I still cannot believe that after I betrayed her, after I stood her up, she still chose to dance for me. That shows the character that that young woman had. We performed and we crushed it. Wow, that was fun, I thought. I could do this; I believed. I started thinking of a catchy name, "Frankie Fresh. Frankie Powers." I was drawn to theatre, to performing, to entertaining others, to make them smile. As I go back throughout my life, I have always had a burning desire to inspire others to believe in themselves. To let them know that they matter. I suppose that I felt that way because for many years of my life, I felt like I did not matter. That I was unworthy of love. I always desired to someday have a platform to let anyone who would listen know, that their lives are worthy, that they matter.

Throughout my wishful thinking and hardcore drinking, somehow, I still managed to stay true to my faith. I would still find time, after lunch, to visit the chapel to say my prayers to the one whom I owed everything to and who I knew would never abandon me, my Lord and Savior, Jesus Christ.

On March 10, 1992, I awakened to take myself and my sister to school. I remember the sun was extremely bright that morning. As I made a sharp right turn, I was completely blinded. As I tried to switch lanes to ultimately come to a stop, I never had a chance to even tap the brakes. I slammed into an 18-wheel construction truck. I remember being dazed for what seemed like a few minutes. As my eyes slowly came into focus, I turned to my sister and asked her if she was okay. Thankfully, she was. However, one look at the car and no one could have imagined that anyone survived.

The paramedics came over as a precaution and took us to the hospital to get scanned for any brain injuries. My sister and I were cleared. However, as I laid down in the hospital bed, I remember grabbing my dad's arm, looking in his eyes and saying "Dad, do you know what day it is today?" He replied, "No." I looked at him straight in the eyes and said "Today is March 10th. Today is Abuelo Papo's six-year anniversary of his death." His eyes opened wide. I told him, "Abuelo saved us today." My father did not speak; he did not have to. His facial expressions said it all.

Lord of the Flies was a mandated book we were forced to read in our junior year. Piggy was one of the main characters. Somehow, lo and behold, from Frankie Fresh and Frankie Powers, the name that took hold amongst my friends and peers was "Piggy." Now let me explain.

It was a hot day after school and some of us guys decided to go swimming in a nearby canal. Boys being boys, we decided to swing from a rope into the water. In one instance, as I was swinging, my friend Alfred Melchor threw a rock. The rock hit me in the head as I fell into the water. For those of you who know the story of the book, "We just killed Piggy," he joked.

The name stuck; Piggy it was. I embraced it, it was fun and funny. I was without a nickname for quite some time and I didn't realize it then but I longed for one and now Piggy gave me an identity.

I finally found a sense of belonging my junior year of high school. Alcohol, cigarettes and marijuana became things I did to fit in, to find my crew, my boys. I did not want to lose that. My grades suffered; my grades suffered a lot. I remember in May of 1992, having a talk with my parents telling them I wanted to get my GED and go to Miami-Dade Community College. See, most of my closest friends were graduating that year and I wanted to follow them. My parents replied "Over my dead body. We have paid for private school for the last ten years. You will finish high school." They were absolutely right, and I did. However, I recall feeling a sense of loss. Most of my friends were seniors and in having them graduate, I felt, or thought, that I would lose myself once again.

Last week of school junior year, I was determined to end it with a bang. As my final contribution to my dear friends of the class of 1992, I decided to throw an open house party at my parents' house, with flyers printed that read, "Piggy's Open House, Saturday, June 6, 1992. Four kegs."

Every weekend my parents would go to their secondary home, a condo at the beach. Their condominium was located on 71st Street and Collins Avenue in Miami Beach. It was a large one-bedroom condo with a picturesque oceanfront view. It was waking up to the salty taste of the ocean and crashing waves every morning. Every Friday afternoon, my parents would head out to the Burleigh House condo and would not come home until Sunday evening. This weekend, I knew the odds of my parents coming home on a Saturday night were slim to none. On top of that, the following day, June 7th, was my dad's birthday. We were planning a beach picnic to celebrate with family and friends. Throwing an open house party on June 6th was foolproof.

I printed flyers and contacted Nomar to be the DJ. We had a five-dollar cover charge at the door. My friends (CU2) and I, were to split the proceeds. Nomar's dad helped us purchase the kegs. CU2 would work the security at the party to make sure no one got out of line. It was a done deal.

On Saturday afternoon, the party almost got disrupted, when my dad called and told me that he needed to come home to get some papers. I panicked and told him, "No! You can't! I have some girls that are coming over Dad. I don't want you to embarrass me." My dad sensed I was up to something, but he convinced himself not to worry. Phew…that was a close one, I thought. The checklist began. Kegs on ice, check; tables, check; money box, check; music, check; cups, security, etc., check, check.

As the day starts winding down and the night takes hold, cars begin to arrive. It was car after car after car. Before I knew it, my neighbors began coming outside asking questions and wondering what the heck was going on. I was friendly with all the neighbors...well, all of them, except one. Luckily that one neighbor was out of town at the time. My charming personality and people skills were fairly evident, as none of my neighbors notified my parents or called the police. There were cars parked five/six blocks away. As the alcohol began to hit the blood stream, libations were getting loose, and emotions began running hot.

Then, fights began to break out everywhere. People were fighting literally everywhere. Auri got cut on his head and began to bleed. Fists kept flying and the party began to become complete pandemonium. I got frantic and called the cops. Yes...yes...and yes, I called the cops to my own party.

Within 15 minutes the police showed up and broke up our event. We hurriedly grabbed the kegs and hid them inside the garage of the house. Someone accidentally left the back-sliding glass door open, which enabled the police to come inside the home. After asking to speak to the owner of the house, I approached the police officer. After asking several questions, they found the kegs of beer and asked to speak to my parents. I told them they were out of town, well...they were, kind of.

After some trepidation, I reluctantly gave them my father's phone number. After getting ahold of my father, they told my parents of the so called "girls" that I had over to our home. They proceeded to tell them of all the people, music and my bloody friend Auri, who they found in the bathroom. They also told my father I was drunk, which I vehemently denied. Truthfully, this was the one time that I really was not drunk. The only reason I was not was because the weekend before I drank so much that I had popped blood vessels in my eyes and was told by the doctor that I needed to refrain from drinking for two weeks. Keep in mind, I was only 16 at the time. I had nothing to drink that evening. That was about the only thing I did right that night.

After roughly 45 minutes, my dad showed up. I was petrified. After talking to the police, my father came up to me and we got into a heated argument. I immediately got into my car, a black 1989 Jeep Cherokee Laredo, and turned on the ignition. I sat in the driver's seat, idle, as my dad let me have it. He then looked at me straight into my eyes and said, "Thank you, Frankie, for my wonderful birthday surprise." That crushed me and I lost it. Damn it, Frankie. Damn it, Frank. You did it again, I told myself. With no walls in front of me to smash and nowhere to release my anger, I hit the only thing I could see. I punched the front windshield and smashed it. "Oh, no, now the windshield!" I exclaimed.

The next morning, my dad's birthday celebration was cancelled. I had to walk the six blocks or so picking up cans, bottles and cups. "What recklessness, what a disappointment!" I told myself. I just…I just, want to end it! I do not want to live anymore, I thought. "God, help me! Please, help me," I pleaded.

Summer of 1992, what a blast! Parties, get togethers, clubs, alcohol, girls, food. At the end of every evening, hunger seemed to kick in. Wag's Diner was our go-to spot. "I'll have the Sunshine Special." That became my go-to meal. $3.85, if I recall. It was two eggs, sunny side up, of course, bacon, sausage, hash browns and some good 'ole buttered white toast. I would wash it all down with a few cups of coffee. Let's just say, those calories started adding up after a while. In the span of a year, I gained about 40 pounds and there were no signs of downsizing from there.

Senior year had finally arrived. It was time to take a bit of an inventory of my life, my past, my present and my future. What did I want to do? Where was I going? As seniors, one of the traditions done yearly at our school was called, "Senior Skits." It was a way to poke fun at ourselves, our teachers and our time at St. Brendan High School. I was chosen to be the star of the show. I remember an epic moment in the play where Carlos Bustamante played the role of God. I remember at a particular moment in the play after loud music was playing in the background, it suddenly stopped. There was complete silence.

The lights were turned off and a huge spotlight was cast on me. Carlos (God), said, "Frank. This is God, Frank." I dropped to my knees and said, "Yes, Father.". "Frank, you need to start behaving, Frank. Frank, you need to do better in school, Frank. Frank, you need to slow down and find yourself, Frank. Frank, you need to lose weight immediately." It was a funny and humorous display of where I was in my personal life at that time. Then He said, "Frank, the most important thing you need to do, Frank…Frank…you need to stop using Sun-in, Frank." I said, "Yes, father," as I bashfully nodded my head. A huge outburst of laughter came from the audience.

You see my junior year, summer, I decided I wanted to lighten my hair a bit, so I purchased a bottle of Super Sun-in and poured the whole damn thing over my hair. My hair turned orange. I was called Sunshine and Strawberry Shortcake for quite some time. Lo and behold, a few months after the skit, I had dropped the weight, I became a studious scholar, and I began eating healthy and getting fit. I, literally, became a shadow of my former self. I had literally and figuratively obeyed God (Carlos).

During this time, I befriended someone who has become one of my best friends to this very day. His name is Manuel Soltero. He was known at the time as "Manny the Magician". Today, he is known to children all throughout the world as "Shabum." There was something about him that I was drawn to, that I wanted. He was an entertainer; he was electric. Truth is, he was someone that knew what he wanted, and he was driven. He was determined and passionate to succeed. We became the best of friends. During this time, we also got involved in promoting nightclubs on the beach. We were also driven to push each other. He kind of took me under his wing and taught me about lifting weights and eating healthy. In mentoring me, he helped me lose 35 pounds. I also pushed him and myself to excel in school. For the first time in my life, I was determined to make honor roll. Not only did I meet my expectations, we both surpassed them; both getting first honors in school. Not too different from what had occurred in my eighth-grade year with Rudy. Manny and I, both fell for the same girl; her name was Dunia. However, unlike in eighth grade, she did not want either one of us Although she did not reciprocate those feelings, we formed a tight bond together, that will never be broken. She became a dear friend to both of us, one in which, part of my heart smiles when I think of the value and impact she has had in my life. Manny and I developed quite the friendship; we became inseparable.

I always knew the value that Manny brought into my life; however, it was not until early March 2020, that I realized the value that I brought into his life. It is early evening, and I am sitting in a chair near his home in San Juan, Puerto Rico. It was just a few days before Covid-19 took hold and stopped the world in its tracks. I was going through some difficulties at the time, and he puts his left hand on my right shoulder looks at me and says, "Frank, let me tell you something. From the moment I met you, I was drawn to you. I really thought that you were going to make it. I saw Pitbull in you before there was a Pitbull. I saw this guy with charisma, with a certain spark, with unlimited talent.

Me and Pitbull

Then he proceeded to tell me, "You know the difference between you and me?" I looked at him and replied, "No." Meanwhile, I was taken aback and humbled by what he saw in me; by his belief in me. I wondered if I ever had that faith in myself. Then he proceeded, "The difference, my friend, is that I went out and did it. I did not accept defeat as an answer. I was relentless in my beliefs, in my goals, in pursuit of my dreams. You see, Frank, I had a goal, and I made a plan. When the plan failed, I changed the plan but never the goal." Wow, I thought. All these years and my dear friend Manny believed in me when I never believed in myself.

Backtrack back to senior year, Manny and I were always united. We would spend our weekend days at the beach then stop for a bite to eat at Chicken Kitchen, shower up and it was South Beach once again. I substituted the greasy diner meals of Wag's for the much healthier option of Chicken Kitchen and frozen yogurt. Chicken Kitchen was not yet a franchise at the time. It was a healthy treat for us high school youths in those days. I remember our orders as if it were just the other day. It was the only location back then, right by Sunset Place, known as "Bakery Center," at the time. It was located next to Ace Hardware off of 57th Avenue and SW 72nd Street. We would often order a boneless breast pocket with yellow rice, baked beans and lettuce and tomatoes. The man behind the counter, a middle-aged Haitian, would say "Chop, chop?" We would reply "Chop, chop," and there we would have it. Little did we know then, or do many know now, that Chop-Chop was born. Two young high school kids, just trying to get some chopped chicken, yellow rice and veggies alongside a humorous Haitian guy behind the counter trying to comprehend what we desired and hence "Chop-Chop" began.

Winter break was upon us, I was excited to be going with some friends on a much-anticipated road trip. There were 15 families, and we were headed to Grandfather Mountain, North Carolina, for a week filled with fun, shenanigans and heavy drinking. At the end of our trip, it was now January 4, 1993. After a long drive back to Miami, my parents, Julie and I arrived home close to 9pm. I was dying to go out to see my friends. My parents advised me against that, but I did not listen. Perhaps, I should have taken them up on their suggestion. I called my friends Hector and Alex and asked them if they wanted to join me to go to the Abyss, a nightclub in South Beach.

The Abyss was located on 5th Street near Alton Road. It was in the exact location where the greatest of all time, none other than "Muhammed Ali", used to train when it was a boxing gym.

Anyhow, Hector and Alex decided to join me. I went upstairs, took a shower, got dressed and got into my car. I put on my Alpine pull out cassette tape and pumped up the base with my Rockford Fosgate speakers, onto the tunes of "Let Me Ride That Donkey". We made a quick stop to pick up a 12-pack of Bud Light and a few key-lime flavored wine coolers. My friends Carlos, Victor and Alfred were promoting the nightclub that evening, so we entered for free.

After a few hours of dancing and drinking, we got into the car to drive home. Alex and I were hammered. We were under no condition to drive; however, Hector did not have his license and after watching him drive a couple times, I was utterly convinced that an inebriated Frank, was a far superior driver than a completely sober Hector. Well, again, alcohol can convince one of many things, however true or untrue they may or may not be.

As I began driving home from South Beach, I took two red lights. Alex and Hector yelled at me, "Hey, Frankie, you took two red lights." I slurred, "No, man, those were yellow." After a few seconds, I noticed some flashing lights.

"Frankie, it is the cops. You need to pull over." With slurred speech, I told them, "No, guys, that is an ambulance." They then proceeded to tell me, "No, Frankie, it is the cops." I replied, "No, it is an ambulance." After about five seconds I hear, "Sir, you, in the black Cherokee, pull over. Pull over!" I immediately took a sharp right turn where my jeep's right-side tires were elevated and came to an immediate stop. After coming to a halt, I noticed that the street I entered was none other than the entrance to Star Island, home to celebrities such as Gloria Estefan, Will Smith and Jennifer Lopez.

The police officer came to the car and asked me for my driver's license, insurance and registration. After fumbling through the documents, the officer asked me, "Sir, how much did you have to drink?" I looked at him with blood shot eyes, disheveled, and my response was "Two beers." With a sly grin he tells me, "It looks to me more like two kegs." He then tells me, "Sir, please step out of the vehicle." As I open the door, I stumble my way out of the car. He then asked me if I would kindly do a roadside sobriety test; I agreed.

I recall the officer telling me to lift my leg up directly in front of me, with my foot pointing forward for 30 seconds. After about 3 seconds, I was certain that this was an impossible task and almost fell to the ground. He looked at me sympathetically and said, "Okay, look son, you are drunk. We are going to leave your car here where it will be safe, and I will call you a cab to take you home." One would have thought that this was a huge break; it should have been, but I was really lit that night. I replied, "No! Wherever my car goes, I go!" He looked at me, giggles, and proceeds to ask Alex and Hector, "Why the hell didn't you drive?" He looks at Hector and says, "You're sober." Hector just shrugged.

The officer once again looks at me and says, "Look, son, we are going to leave your car here. I have already called a cab to pick you up," (for all you young ones, there was no Uber or Lyft back in those days). So, just when it appeared that I had gotten my "get out of jail free card" the officer noticed the empty bottles of beer in the back seat of the car, which prompted him to ask me, "Hey, by the way, where did you get the beer?" I look at him with a sheepish, sly grin, and say, "Oh, that is easy. Look at this." I smile, proudly, and proceed to whip out my two-month-old fake ID. The officer could not believe it himself. He tells me, "Sorry, son, this is just too much. You are going with me."

I believe Alex's mom picked up Hector and Alex; I was sent to the police station. Being that I was a minor, only 17 years old, I was fortunate that I would not spend the night in a jail cell. My blood alcohol level was .19, almost twice the legal limit at the time, which was .10 (it is currently .08 in the state of Florida).

After a 16-hour drive from North Carolina and having only had a few hours of sleep, my parents received a phone call from the Miami Beach Police Department. Their son, Frank Lopez, received a DUI and needed to be picked up at the jail. My father wanted them to leave me there so I could learn my lesson. Fortunately, for me, that was not an option because I happened to be a minor.

The following morning, I remember my sister Julie waking me up and saying, "Frankie, you are in big, big trouble! Mom and Dad are super angry." I asked her where they were. She responded, "They went to go pick up your car." I was in trouble all right. I was grounded for a month of no parties, no get-togethers, and no phone privileges.

When I arrived at the court hearing, they really threw the book at me. They suspended my driver's license, gave me community service hours, ordered me to attend an advocate program and to attend a victim impact program, plus pay court fees and other legal costs. I remember thinking to myself, wow, this DUI stuff is serious. That same inner voice told me, "Well, hell yeah Frank, you could have killed someone." It was quite some time before I got behind the wheel again. Nevertheless, my reckless behavior did not cease.

During this time, my faith and spiritual beliefs never wavered. God was still ever-present in my life. I recall in my senior year at St. Brendan, one of my most memorable moments was called "Encounter." Encounter was a three-day spiritual journey that we as students would experience as a group. It was a reprieve, a time for reflection and to ponder who we are. It was an opportunity to connect with our Creator and recognize all those things to be forever grateful for. It was a spiritual awakening to say the least. I remember feeling a sense of euphoric love that permeated within all of us. It was definitely a beautiful treasure to always remember.

In my senior year, there was another defining moment in my life. One that had an everlasting impact in my adult hood. Manny and I took a class called, "Introduction to Psychology," taught by Mrs. Barbara Jordan. This class planted the seeds of understanding human behavior and emotional awareness that has so captivated my life and Manny's all these years later. Mrs. Jordan played a monumental role in cultivating my love affair with understanding people. What influences and affects who we become as human beings in society, and the way we view the world, our subconscious programing and the effect of ego, on how we act or react to the adverse effects of life?

As graduation neared, I remember senior prom, grad night, and all those final high school moments we shared together. While most of my classmates knew where they were headed, I did not have a clue. I was lost; I lacked direction. After graduation, we went to Cancun, Mexico, to celebrate for Memorial weekend. It was the first time in my life that I had ever left the country by myself (without my parents), and boy, did I live it up. During those days, I continued to promote clubs on South Beach and in Coconut Grove. I loved it. I mean, who wouldn't? I would be part of the event, I would get paid, have free drinks and we were "it." I felt like I was "Hollywood".

I managed to delay my completion date for community service hours for quite some time. I received my final extension, which was to have the hours completed by September 1, 1993. A friend of mine named Marcus, worked at Tamiami Park. He told me he would be willing to sign off on my community service hours without me having to do them. He had assured me back in June that it would not be a problem. "No problem, right?"

It was now August and there was no way to contact him. I decided to go to his house. On my way there, near 132nd Avenue and NW 7th Street in Miami, Florida, I saw him drive past me in the opposite direction. I immediately made a U-turn, trying to catch up with him. I began swerving into oncoming traffic and then swerving back into my lane. I continued to do this, passing car after car, as I attempted to get close enough to him to get his attention. Then…all of a sudden, when I went to pass the next car, I happened to run a Florida Highway Patrol officer off the road. Oh, s***. All of a sudden, the police officer turns on his lights and it was on.

I do not know what got into me, but I went Dukes of Hazzard on him. I was the "Bo" to his "Rosco P. Coltrane." I began driving thru the neighborhood as if it was a long desert highway with no one around. I knew the neighborhood well, since many of my friends lived in the area. I remember getting ready to make a turn. I put my left turn light signal on, began to steer left and then ventured a sharp right. I continued to do this several times. I told myself, "This cop must be seriously pissed off." Mind you, here I am trying to outrun a police officer in his FHP Ford Mustang, while I am driving a standard Jeep Cherokee Laredo. What the hell was I thinking?

After a while, I told myself I only have one opportunity to lose him. There was a red light on 132nd Avenue and SW 8th Street. It is almost 5pm and I made an instinctive decision, I am going for it. So, I gunned it. I do not know how, but by God's grace, no one hit me. At least three vehicles came within mere inches of slamming into me. I could have killed someone; I could have seriously hurt someone. I could have killed myself.

Once I got past the light, a few blocks later, I made a right into a cul-de-sac. As I pulled up into the driveway of a vacant home, a man doing construction work looked at me and my car wondering what was going on. Smoke was coming out of the engine. I got out of the vehicle and just sat on the street trying to figure out what I would do next. I continued to hear sirens of police vehicles in near proximity.

After approximately ten minutes, I see a police vehicle pull into the cul-de-sac, with his lights on. He yelled at me, "Put your hands up." I immediately obliged. He asked me, "Any weapons? Any drugs?" I told him no. He walked up to me, cuffed me and left me sitting in the driveway as he checked the car. After searching thoroughly, he looks at me stupefied and says, "What the hell is wrong with you?" I looked at him with a puzzled look, shrugged my shoulders and said, "I don't know." He then proceeded to tell me, "Here I am on my way home from work after a long shift and you almost hit me head on. Then you send me on a wild goose chase, and you almost killed someone!" My head was stooped down in shame.

I remember at that moment, that less than a week prior, I had turned 18. I am going to jail, I thought. The police officer then asked me for my parent's phone number to contact them. After asking me a few questions about my parents and what they do, I told him that they had a medical office near 87th Avenue and SW 40th Street near La Carreta.

He looked at me and said, "I think I know your parents." He called my parents, who were unmistakenly livid with me, and after speaking to them for several minutes, he proceeded to write me five tickets. Driving with a suspended license, reckless driving, fleeing an officer, et cetera, et cetera. While he was writing the tickets, a question arose in me, one which I cannot believe I had the audacity to ask him. "Excuse me, Officer." He looked at me and said, "Yes." "Hmmm…how did you find me?" He looked my way and said, "Young man, after driving several blocks and noticing that no vehicles had veered off the road, I realized you must have turned into one of the neighborhoods. It is not rocket science kid." I nodded. Approximately 20 minutes later, my parents 1992 black Lexus LS400 pulled into the driveway. My father gets out of the car, says hello to the police officer, who he knows, and looks at me with shame. I did it again. I am such a disappointment. "What the hell is wrong with me? "I thought.

3
COLLEGE AND THE US MARINE CORPS

"Courage is not about being unafraid. It is looking at fear as an observer, pushing it to the side and going through the fire anyway. -Frankie M Powers-

As the summer came to an end, I enrolled at Miami-Dade Community College. I will never forget my first day of ENC1101 (English class). I remember the teacher passing out a student's paper and having us read it. Once we read it, she asked, "I want you to raise your hands and tell me how many of you would give that assignment an A, B, C, D, or an F?" I remember reading the penmanship of the author and being extremely impressed by the student's work I truly believed that it was exemplary. She then replied, "That paper received an F." Whoa…uh-oh…I am in trouble, I thought. She then preceded to hand out another assignment paper, asking the same questions. I quickly realized that I was in way over my head, and I dropped the course. Never did I forget it. I made an attempt to take the same course two other times, believing it to be the professor that was the problem, not myself, the student. Well…time for a rude awakening. Truth is, I have no idea how I managed to pass through high school with my writing skills.

I was utterly unprepared for English Literature in college. I proceeded to see the guidance counselor and explained my current situation. She told me, "Son, there is a course called ENC 1130 that I recommend. It is a preparation course for ENC1101." I replied, "Perfect, I'll do it." After arriving in the classroom that very first day, I quickly realized I was not ready for that either. Fear, frustration and ineptitude started setting in. I remember going to see the counselor and telling her I needed something else, perhaps a remedial course. She forewarned me that these courses were not credited. I understood, however, I also understood that I needed to learn to walk before I could run, so I enrolled. Fortunately, that class laid the groundwork for the basic fundamentals that I was so desperately lacking. While my insecurities in English Literature were on high alert, on the social front, things could not have been any better. I would spend my Thursday thru Sunday evenings out with my friends. I reconnected with my older friends from CU2. My dear friend, Manny the Magician, had gone back to his homeland in San Juan,

Puerto Rico, to study and to live.

During this time, I was working with my parents who owned a medical clinic. My responsibilities were to check each patient's blood pressure, prepare payroll and do some basic accounting, not much else. My social life was where it was at and I was enjoying every minute of it. During this time, I was also hitting the gym, hard, and I continued to eat my Chop-Chops from Chicken Kitchen. I began to become extremely disinterested in school. School became a hindrance; it became a means to socialize, rather than a means to succeed in my future.

*****

It was now 1995 and my dad tells me "Son, let's go look at a car for you." I was hoping for a Mitsubishi Eclipse or an Eagle Talon. My father looked at me and said, "Hey, how 'bout going to the dealer and looking at some BMW convertibles?" What!? My head was spinning. I surely wish someone could have snapped a picture of me at that moment. I would have loved to look at my face...I was stunned, shocked... excited.

You see by this time; my parents had made it. They had gone from humble upbringings to an upper-class family. By the time I was 19 years old, they had arrived. They had achieved what we know as The American Dream and they wanted to share that with their son.

So, in July 1995, my father purchased for me, a candy apple red, BMW convertible with Fittipaldi rims. Man, I was killing it, I thought to myself. My days were spent working out at the gym, working at my parent's medical clinic, entertaining myself at school and promoting nightclubs at night. It was friends...girls...and alcohol everywhere. It was raining good times.

In the midst of all the fun, all of a sudden, something happened. I fell. I fell in love, or so I thought. Her name was Lia. Lia was a few years older than me and she would work out at the same gym as I did. It was called Spinellis. I remember her being cute as a button. She was well put together both physically and in the workplace. She worked hard and had direction. While I, on the other hand, was too busy having a good time and slacking off. I was immature and obsessive. I partied too much, demanded too much and drank too much.

When I met her, I remember thinking, is this the one I have been asking God for at church since I was 12 years old? Well...she wasn't. When she broke things off with me, I was heartbroken. All my life, I was used to getting my way. I was accustomed to…if I wanted it bad enough and I tried hard enough, it was attainable. Now, that may be a great model for business, it does not really work well with people. I did not know how to deal with it.

One night, I drank too much and slept over at my buddy Jorge's house. I recall waking up in the morning and Jorge telling me, "Whoa, Piggy, come with me to the Marine Corps recruiting office." I looked at him puzzled and said "What the hell do you want me to go with you there for? Hell no." He then promised to invite me after for lunch at Chili's, so, I obliged and accepted his invitation. Oh, boy, so off to the Marine Corp recruiting office we go. It was located near Tropical Park in Miami.

So, what goes on in a Marine Corp recruiting office? Well, they recruit kids like me. Never in my entire life had I even remotely considered joining the military. Well…until that very day. After taking some voluntary examinations, I heard what every single human being, and I especially, have longed to hear. "Hey, Frank, you did remarkable. You can have your choice of any job that you would like, if you decide to join the United States Marine Corps." As I write this, my chest opens. I remember feeling proud. I recall looking at a picture and seeing fellow Marines dressed up in their dress blues, formal attire, and saying, "Man, that outfit is bad" (aka in today's terms as "fire").

I remember that weekend we were having our happy hour on Friday and Saturday at Chris's house. This was our normal pitstop before a full night of drinking. I remember there being about 15 of us gathered together and there being a few extremely hot young women. After having a few drinks, we began talking about the possibility of joining the Marines. Those good-looking young women looked at each other, then looked at us and said, "Marines are hot!" I immediately turned to look at my buddy Jorge and no words needed to be spoken. Our eyes widened, our smiles shined, and I whispered to him "Well…maybe." The truth is, I was still struggling over the breakup with Lia.

I was sad and I could not find a way to stop thinking about her. On January 10, 1996, I signed up to become a United States Marine.

I signed up to be a reservist. That meant that I would go on to boot camp at Parris Island, South Carolina along with all the other young men who were soon to become Marines. After 11 ½ long weeks, I would come home to spend 10 days with my family and then, I would venture out to MCT (Military Combat Training) in Camp LeJeune, North Carolina. Shortly thereafter, I would go to my MOS school (Military Operations Specialty) and then come back home. My MOS was 0861, otherwise known as a forward observer. I was a spy. By all intents and purposes, that is what a forward observer is. I would be positioned with a small group, between two to four of us; our job was to spy in on enemy lines and call in naval gun fire, artillery and air support.

Needless to say, being precise with our coordinates could be the difference between living or dying. Our life expectancy, in the event that we engaged in battle, was a mere two seconds. Being undetected for us was beyond important. It was paramount.

My buddy Jorge signed up for active duty. He was going to be an aircraft mechanic which required five years of service. I was originally scheduled to depart in mid-March. However, an opening became available, and they pushed my date up to less than a month from having first signed-up to join the service.

On February 5, 1996, Parris Island would become my new home for the next three months. So, what was I to do? Well…it was time to do what I did best, party, party hard, Hollywood style.

The weekend before I left, on February 3, 1996, one of my dear friends, Freddie Melero, was hosting Saturday nights at a popular South Beach nightclub called "Amnesia" (properly named for not remembering a damn thing about evenings there). On this particular evening, Freddie closed off the upstairs VIP section and printed special flyers with the headline, "Frank Piggy Lopez" going away party. Wow, what a night! The VIP room was filled with friends, family and bottles of champagne were popping and overflowing everywhere. Talk about going out with a bang alright.

On February 5, 1996, I said good-bye to my parents, and I was dropped off at the check-in station of the US Marine Corp before we were transported to the airport. I remember feeling uneasy, my stomach was churning. I wondered what the hell I had signed up for. A few hours later, we landed at the South Carolina Airport and proceeded to a bus filled with young men from throughout America.

Our final stop was the Marine Corps recruiting depot, where young boys would become men. I will never forget the ride. It was pitch black outside. You could hear crickets. A few hours later, I was awakened. Next thing I knew, my fears turned to reality. "Get off the bus! Get off the bus! Get in line! Now! Now! Now!"

"Oh s***! What the hell have I gotten myself into?", I thought. How do I turn back now? I began following the masses going from station to station.

It was like an assembly line, except, instead of parts, it was people. We would get measured, get fitted and onto the next station. Over the next 48-72 hours, we were poked and prodded, as if we were cattle. We went to all sorts of different doctors, psychologists, dentists, et cetera. All sorts of questions were being asked of us. We received numerous injections. I remember wondering, What was all this for?" However, I was too tired, confused and frightened to ask. During these days, I remember only having two to three meals total and almost no water. I believe that was a mistake, as I do not think that was their intention. After about 72 hours, all hell was about to break loose.

I remember vividly, as if it were yesterday, on day three, a well-fit officer of the Marine Corps came to our barracks. We were platoon 3089. MIKE COMPANY, Third Battalion. The gentleman was a Brigadier General. He was the chief officer of Parris Island. He spoke to us for roughly ten minutes. I do not remember much about what he said, however, what I do remember, is at the tail end of his speech, him telling us, "I know that all of you have heard frightening stories about Marine Corps boot camp; but rest assured, it is not as bad as you think. I will not see any of you again until graduation day. I will now leave you with your drill instructors. Good luck."

As soon as the door closed behind him, all hell broke loose. "Get in line! Get in line! 54321, you're done, you're done! I said why are you moving, why are you moving?" I remember the drill instructors just yelling and screaming. It seemed they kept telling us different things to do, all at the same time. It was loud, confusing. I did not realize it at the time, however, in hindsight, they were trying to prepare us, as best one could, for what may soon come to us, the chaos and confusion that ensues during battle in war.

My head was spinning, I could not think, I was in full reaction mode. Come to think of it, in war there is no time to think, it is all about reacting to what comes your way. I will never forget drill instructor Sgt. Freeman. He was a fit, African American male, about 5' 10", 180 pounds, and he was loud and frightening. I remember him explaining to us the proper way to address the drill instructor in his quarters (office). We were to stand at attention (on the floor I remember there being painted footprints where we were to position our feet). We were then to raise our right hand and smack this yellow wooden hand sign that was screwed onto the wall. We were then to put our hands, cuffed, at attention, chest upright, and say "Sir, Recruit Lopez, requests permission to speak to Senior Drill Instructor, Staff Sgt. Graham, sir." It was a mouthful, especially when everything everywhere seemed to be flying all around us. Sgt. Freeman never repeated what he had expected us to say. He said it once.

After about another 20-30 minutes of complete and utter confusion, I lost it. I freakin lost it. I had enough and I was going to let them have it. I had absolutely zero recollection of what I was supposed to repeat or how I was supposed to address the senior drill instructor, Staff Sgt. Graham. However, I did know one thing…I was done, I was going home…or so I thought? Hoped? I remember trying to talk to the Marine in his perfectly ironed, well-groomed uniform. He looked at me and began yelling. The other drill instructors looked at me, got in my face, and loudly reprimanded me saying, "That is not the way you address the Senior Drill Instructor!" I snapped. The anger that had been my go-to emotion all my life, came out and I unleashed my fury. I said, "I don't give a damn what the hell I am supposed to say. I don't belong here; this was a mistake!"

I pointed out my upper-class privileges to all of them. "I have a condo at the beach, a BMW convertible and I promote nightclubs on South Beach. This is not for me!" Man…in hindsight, I am surprised they did not just laugh at me and all my entitled bull crap, I was spewing out. The only reason I think they didn't is that I believe they said to themselves, "This Hispanic boy must be pretty freakin nuts." So, I continued, "I am crazy," I exclaimed, "I am F'n crazy. If you don't send me home right now, when we get to the rifle range, I will blow your freakin head off." I don't exactly remember what happened next, however, what I do remember is that I was sent to talk to another fellow Marine. He was a middle-aged African American Sergeant. He was built like a tank and I remember him having glasses. I remember him speaking to me quite calmly and having a soothing presence. After speaking to me for a while, he managed to calm me down quite a bit.

After 20 minutes, another Marine walked in and snarled at me. I barked back and gave him a piece of my mind. Whoa, big mistake. The calm, soothing sergeant told me, "Hey, don't you dare talk to a commanding officer in that manner! That is your company commander. And his name is Captain Sinecro." This time I immediately shut the hell up. The sergeant had gained my respect and I assuredly listened. Soon after, I apologized and Captain Sinecro came to me and whispered these words, that I will never forget, "Listen here, boy, there are two ways off this island. One, you graduate, or two, you try to swim off of it. What I can tell you is that in all the years the Marine Corps has been here, no one has ever made it out by swimming." As you can guess, my options were limited, graduation it is. I was then transported back to my unit 3089. I remember every single day, keeping a mental note of the countdown to graduation. Absolutely nothing was going to deter me from that goal.

I began counting the days and weeks, looking at each weekly milestone as one less hurdle in my path. Every day, except Sundays there were three things to look forward to, meals, sleep and seeing if we received anything through the mail. On Sundays we had a little extra time. By extra, what I mean is, we were able to have four hours to ourselves. This was to our self; however, we were not to leave our barracks with the exception of attending church services. Sunday always included church for me. Now, for those of you who do not know, in boot camp there were no phones, no calls, no computers, no dining out, no television, nothing. We had a bed, our military gear, our homework and our rifle. We were being trained for war; no perks allowed.

As one looks and sees the physical intensity of the rigorous training it takes to be a Marine, what one does not see, is that the reality is that it is more about 90% of your mental attitude and only 10% of your physical endurance. A Marine must train their mind to go places that the body does not know it is capable of advancing.

So, I pushed…and I pushed…I pushed harder than I ever had before. In week three, we had physical benchmarks we had to hit in order to advance in training. We had to do a certain number of pushups, a certain number of sit-ups and we had to run three miles in a certain allotted time. For myself, everything was a countdown. It was, "Frank, check that off your list. Frank, you are one step closer to graduation." In hindsight, I guess the future motivational speaker in me was motivating myself. I surpassed the pushup challenge, I surpassed the sit-up challenge, and I was well on my way to easily surpassing the three-mile run challenge.

Then it happened…just about the time I had passed the one-mile marker, I felt a sharp pain in my left calf. "Damn it, damn it," I said to myself; I pulled my left calf. How in the hell am I going to continue? I thought to myself. "Frank, you cannot stop. You have to find a way. If you do not make the time, you will be sent back in training." I then told myself, I will be damned if I am one more day in this so-called Parris Island, it is more like Dragon's hell in this place. So, I limped, I limped hard. I practically ran on one leg, putting all my body weight on my right leg. I did that for the next two miles. As I crossed the finish line, I collapsed. I had nothing left. I made the allotted time by about 7-8 seconds. I was sent straight to medical and was on light duty for the next two days. Most importantly though, I passed on to the next stage of my training.

It was now week six and we are off to the rifle range. More importantly, I am halfway through boot camp. I must tell you; I do not know what I would have done without those letters. There was not a single day that would go by where my mom would not write me or send me a package. Even my father wrote me a letter. I still remember how he ended it, "Frankie, this is the first letter that I have written in 34 years."

Now, back to the rifle range. I had never shot a gun, much less a rifle. The instructors indicated to us that those of us that had never shot before would be at an advantage. That there were less bad habits to have been acquired. It made sense to me; however, it did not seem to work in my favor. All week, I struggled. It was now Thursday, and it was pre-qualification day. I did not stand a chance, I said to myself. I was frustrated and disheveled. I could not will myself, or my body, through this particular training.

On Thursday evening, I went to recruit Miller who had the bunk right next to mine. I asked him "Miller, do you think you can help me with my positioning? I don't know what I am doing wrong." You see, throughout the week I kept looking at Miller and telling myself, "Wow, this guy can shoot." Unable to practice with my unloaded M16A2 service rifle, I proceeded to grab a broomstick, position myself as if I had my rifle, and he then began to show me how to grab the handle and then the mantra that ensued, "Breathe in, breathe out, stop breathing, focus, squeeze, repeat, breathe in, breathe out, stop breathing, focus, squeeze." I continued to repeat the sound in my mind. It is now Friday, and it is rifle qualification day. Failure to qualify meant I would be held back in training. The mere thought of that sent chills up my spine. To qualify as a Marine rifle marksman, one needed to hit a total score of 190. 190-210 was needed to qualify as a rifle marksman. A score of 211-219 would qualify one as a sharpshooter, and with a score of 220 and beyond, you would qualify as a rifle expert.

A rifle would hold a magazine clip that would hold up to 30 rounds. To qualify, we would have to shoot from different positions including upright, seated, and lying down at a distance of up to 500 yards. There were no scopes on the rifle. To get an idea of the visual of what you can see as far as the bulls' eye was concerned, it was the size of the dot of a pencil at a target of 500 yards away. A bullseye was 5 points. If it hit anywhere else on the target, it was 3 points. My turn came up and I was quite nervous. All I kept thinking was I have to get to 190 or I am going to be held back in training.

I can still smell the gunpowder as I write this. I began shooting and remarkably the broomstick idea, and recruit Miller, seemed to have helped me quite a bit. As I continued shooting, the points kept adding up. Lo and behold, before I knew it, I had qualified. Now I had one final shot left, 500 yards away and my score at this time was 215… "Breathe in, breathe out…stop breathing, focus, squeeze." I nailed it, I freakin nailed it! I am a rifle expert! I cannot believe that I am a Marine Corps rifle expert. I had a grin from ear-to-ear. Drill instructor Sgt. Freeman looked at me and said, "Lopez. Rifle expert, huh? Good job. Now you have 5 seconds to wipe that smile off your face or I will send you to the pit to do leg lifts and pushups." (For those of you who are unfamiliar with what the "pit" is, let's just say, that is not where you want to be headed.) The pit is a sand pit where when we would not do what was expected or misbehaved on some level, we were sent for extensive and vigorous physical punishment). "54321, you're done, Lopez," and I was. I was feeling elated. Recruit Miller ended up having the highest score in the entire boot camp training. A score that somehow, I still remember till this day. His score was 246.

The days and weeks came passing by. Now we arrived at week nine, field week. This was the week that we would spend on the field, outdoors. This was the week that we would practice combat drills, go to the gas chamber and handle grenades. For any of you that heard the word tent and thought this would be fun, let me assure you, it was no picnic.

My greatest challenge in boot camp caught me completely by surprise and almost cost me my life. It was Friday of field week; it was also the day we were to handle and throw live grenades. Everyone was jacked up. I remember the Marine Corps instructor giving us our safety tips. He explained to us that the grenade had two pins. We were to pull on one pin and hold it like a baseball. We were to have our front arm extended outwardly and the other arm, the one holding the grenade, pulled back. We were then to throw the grenade, as far as we could and duck for cover.

I remember having a conversation with myself, "Okay, Frank, this is simple enough. Heck, you have played baseball all your life. This will be a piece of cake."

Shortly thereafter, my name was called. "Recruit Lopez, on deck." I grabbed my grenade, pulled the first pin, pulled my arm back and held it like a baseball. Before I knew it, all hell broke loose. All I heard was hollering and screaming, "Throw it! Get rid of the grenade! Throw it!" I felt panic and launched the grenade as far as I could. Within a few seconds, I remember being lifted off the ground by a fellow Marine and thrown into a bunker. As soon as our bodies landed in the bunker, you could feel the shrapnel of the grenade ricochet off the concrete walls.

"Lopez! What the f*** is wrong with you?! Do you know that you almost had another Marine killed?! You were about two seconds away from us having to call your mother and father to let them know that their son was dead." I remember thinking, what the heck happened? I later realized that the instructor must have misspoken. He told us to hold the grenade like a baseball. While most people would probably imagine that meant to hold onto the baseball/grenade tight, it is quite the opposite. A baseball is to be held gently, like an egg. I then realized what had occurred. Once I pulled the first pin and pulled my arm back, I loosened up my grip on the grenade, the second pin must have gone off, unbeknownst to me. In that moment, the grenade became live and almost ripped my body into pieces.

I spent a good portion of the next week in the pit. Let's just say, I probably developed at least a 4-pack of abs that week, over that almost deadly miscommunication.

My biggest fear going into boot camp was the gas chamber. I remember seeing the videos and seeing the people's faces in horror. I remember agonizing, in watching the young men choking and gasping for air. However, not unlike most of our general fears, it was nowhere near as bad as I anticipated. Actually, it was not bad at all. The worst of the week was, without a shadow of a doubt, the no-see-ums. No-see-ums are these very small mosquito-like insects. They are called no-see-ums because...you cannot see them. These little insects packed quite the punch. Now that was the least of our concerns. The problem was we were not allowed to move or scratch. Doing so would be seen as a lack of discipline. Imagine being out on the battlefield and the enemy is lurking nearby, one small movement or sound and it could be the difference between life and death.

I remember getting eaten up, but proud of resisting my desire to scratch. It did not go unnoticed. When drill instructor Sgt. Tillman said, "Lopez, what the hell is wrong with your face?" "No-see-ums, Sir," I replied. "Great job, Lopez, in showing discipline." I felt really proud of myself that day.

That week, we were also introduced to MRE's (Meals Ready to Eat). Let's just say, they give new meaning to the term, "food for fuel." As week eleven came around, I could finally see the end was near. I remember the drill instructors smirking...looking at each other and then turning to us and saying, "Hey, guys, by the way, you may have noticed that some of your body parts were not functioning as they used to, don't worry, that will soon pass. We gave you an injection to make certain that no funny business would be going on during your stay here." We all smirked and smiled as we felt relief as we thought something had happened to our masculinity.

April 26, 1996 had arrived. I finally graduated as a United States Marine from Parris Island, South Carolina. My parents and sister came to see me graduate. On the way back home, upon arrival at Miami International Airport, as I exited the plane and looked up, there were about 20 of my friends there waiting to congratulate and celebrate with me, with an ice-cold Corona in tow. They were stunned to see the new me. I was lean, serious, and stoic. I remember them trying to get me to relax. I could not...I was still in combat mode.

Private Lopez

US Marine Corps

After a few days of partying with my friends, I was off again to military combat training at Camp LeJeune, North Carolina, for a 30-day stay. Once the training was over, I came back home for a small reprieve before I was set to leave again for my M.O.S. training in Ft. Sill, Oklahoma. Now, what is a young, fit, 20-year-old Marine to do but party like a rock star? And party I did. Heck, the nickname for Marines is "Jarheads," so drinking fit me like a glove.

For two months, alcohol rained on my body like a warm shower. It was friends, girls, booze, and music.

It was now late July 1996. I was set to sleep at a friend's house before he would drive me to West Palm Beach Airport to head out for my M.O.S. training. I stopped at a local food spot to grab my usual 32-ounce cup of Diet Coke. As was commonplace, I left my car on with the keys in the ignition. I had all my military fatigues, as well as my civilian attire, packed in my suitcase in the car. After I paid for my soda, I walked outside. I noticed my car was gone. I froze, it felt like a dream…well, better yet, a nightmare. I was stunned. I raced back in and told the cashier to dial 911. I immediately picked up my cell phone and called my friends who were at a nearby party, to see if they were pulling a funny prank on me. They replied no. Within a few minutes, my friends came to the food spot and waited with me until the police arrived to take a report of the theft of my BMW. I was with my best friend at the time, Tico. After they finished the report, Tico drove me to Denny's. We grabbed a bite to eat, had a whole lot of coffee and pulled an all-nighter.

After the meal, Tico drove me to West Palm Beach 4th Anglico Marine Corps. Reserve Base. "Private Lopez, are you ready to leave?" "Well, I don't know. Can I?", I asked. I proceeded to explain and show the sergeant the police report of what had happened just a few short hours ago. They had told me not to worry about it and that training would be rescheduled. So, Tico and I drove back home.

After finally getting a few hours of sleep, my good friend Ralph received a phone call from Iliana, a girl who I had been dating at the time. She informed him that she had seen my car the night before and that she had found it strange because she thought I would have been sleeping since I had an early flight. She even mentioned that she was considering leaving a good-bye note on the windshield visor. I immediately called her and asked where she had seen my car, because at the time she had seen my car, it had already been stolen. After giving us the address, my friends and I drove to the location…to no avail. Nothing. For several days we drove by the area where my car was spotted…nothing.

About five to six days later, while riding shotgun in my friend Ozzie's car, I told him, "Hey, Ozzie, can you pass by that address again?" He replied, "Sure." As soon as we turned the corner, I could not believe my eyes, there was my red, BMW convertible parked in a driveway. I said, "Ozzie, call 911 right now. Someone is going to get their a** kicked." As I got out of the car and walked to the open garage, there was a middle-aged man sitting down doing some carpentry. I yelled at him, "What the hell is my car doing here!? Who are you!?" He looked at me puzzled and said, "Wait one second. I will be right back." Less than a minute later, a young man comes out the front door wearing one of my US Marine Corps tee shirts. I almost floored him. He instinctively jumped back and said "Hey, it was not me. It was my friends inside." Being young and naïve, I believed him. He then went through the house, exited out the back, jumped the fence and took off. The cops arrived shortly thereafter and after some hesitancy as to the validity of the story, they found my keys, a report was written, and they started searching for the suspect.

A few weeks later, he was finally caught wearing my prescription glasses and some other clothing of mine. I swear it was almost too surreal to believe. In all these years, I have never forgotten him. A few years later, a friend of mine that had become a Miami-Dade police officer told me, Frank, that guy calls the station every so often and says, "Hey pigs, got another one (car), catch me if you can." Incredible…

My 21st birthday came and went and now I was drinking...legally. It was now October 1996. I got a job at Commerce Bank in Coral Gables, Florida, as a bank teller. I loved that job. The same day that I was hired, so was a young woman, as a customer service representative. Her name was Danay. I was absolutely smitten with her. We dated for a short while and I fell for her; I fell hard. I mean, that is my MO (Modus Operandi) ...see girl, like girl, fall for girl, get heartbroken, repeat. It was a short-lived romance; however, I could not stand the thought of having to see her every day in my workplace so, in early February 1997, I asked for a transfer to a bank at another location. My transfer was granted, and I was now a teller in Hialeah, Florida, also known as Little Cuba.

It was now April 1997. I am sitting in class at Miami-Dade Community College. As I look over, sitting next to me is my close friend Sylvia. I see Sylvia talking with another young woman, who immediately catches my eye and I quickly become enamored. After class I tell Sylvia, "I have to meet her. What is her name?" Sylvia replies "Ari, Ari Vasquez." As I told Sylvia of my interest, she advised me against it. She said, "Listen, buddy, she has been in an on-again, off-again relationship with someone for four years. Forget about it, let it be." However, I couldn't, or better yet...I wouldn't. I was a man on a mission. I was focused. I was determined. I became the hunter and she became the hunted. I looked for every opportunity to see her, to find out where she was at and make my presence felt.

After a few weeks of pursuit, I finally got my catch, or so I thought. We dated on and off...and on and off. Truth is, she was still in love with her ex-boyfriend, yet, somehow, I believed if I tried hard enough, I would convince her to fall in love with me. I did not realize at the time that love is a feeling, it cannot be forced, it is to be felt. I fell hard. I fell...real hard. After dating on and off for a while, I came up with the delusional idea, I believed, if I would propose to her, that she would somehow fall in love with me. So, in May 1998, I took her to Sandals Negril, Jamaica, and did just that. I asked her to marry me. She said, "Yes" ... and we lived happily ever after, right? Nope, not a chance.

During that same time, my sister was on the verge of getting married. My baby sister, Julie, was 18 years old. She was going to marry her high school sweetheart, Gus, on October 30, 1998, which happened to be her 19th birthday. However, the back and forth of my on again, off again, relationship with Ari was starting to become quite a concern for my sister, as Ari was chosen to be a member of her bridal party. Ari and I made it to the event together. My sister Julie and Gus married, and he became a much welcome addition to our family. Gus became like the brother that I never had and the one I always wanted.

*****

It was late afternoon on a Saturday in the summer. I was at 4th Anglico in West Palm Beach, a day training with my fellow Marines. We were all drinking from a keg, outside. A Master Gunnery Sergeant was retiring, and we were celebrating. I remember receiving a phone call from a friend letting me know that my girlfriend Ari was confused about her ex-boyfriend and myself. I panicked. I told everyone. I said my good-byes, and impulsively made the decision that I was leaving the Marine Corps for good and there was no turning back. My Marine Corps friends thought I was crazy, that perhaps I had too much to drink. Nevertheless, I left. I stopped at a gas station, filled my tank with gas, bought a six-pack of Icehouse and dropped the top of my BMW and I was out.

I took the ramp to I95 South, for the hour and a half trip to Miami. I showed up at my friend Tico's house, knocked on the door, and lights out. The next thing I remember is my buddy Alfredo telling me, "Yo, Frank, its 4:30 in the morning and you need to go back to your Marine Corps base." I looked up at him and told him I was done, that I had been searching for love all my life and, although it is only one weekend away a month, that I was not letting this girl go, so I quit. I quit the Marine Corps. I still struggle with that decision to this day. And so, I drank, and drank some more. I drank when I was happy, I drank when I was sad. When in doubt, drink was my motto.

Ari and I continued our on and off, back-and-forth relationship until February 18, 2001. It was the same day that Dale Earnhardt Senior had died. I remember sitting down with my close friend Auri, at Doral Ale House, eating zingers and drinking bottles of Miller Lite when I received the dreaded phone call from Ari saying that our relationship was over and there was no going back. It was another relationship, another failure. I was desperate for love, desperate for the love that seemed to forever evade me. So, I drank, and drank some more.

*****

September 11, 2001, a day in infamy for all Americans. It was a day that changed my life for almost a decade.

I turned the ignition on the car and drove to a nearby newsstand I used to frequent. As I listened to the radio, I heard about a plane crashing into the World Trade Center. I then heard that another plane hit the second tower. I remember telling myself this must be a joke, a ploy similar to years ago, a radio hoax portrayed as an invasion called War of the Worlds, except this was no hoax, this was the real thing. I remember going to Miami-Dade Community College that day; classes had been canceled. I stopped at a nearby Subway to get a turkey sub, and I remember looking at the Middle Eastern young man behind the counter. I looked at him with disdain, with hate. "What is going on?", I thought. I blamed it on the Palestinians. I knew it was terrorism, but I could not understand why.

On this day, I began to see the world differently. I became somewhat obsessed. I tried to comprehend what had just happened, but my logical mind could not. In hindsight, how could I? I did not understand the mindset of people willing and able to kill innocent others. I could understand someone feeling irrevocably broken enough to take one's own life, but countless others? I could not understand leaving families devastated, children orphaned. I just could not…until, I did. I immersed myself in world history studies. I read two different Korans. I read the Hadith. I began researching and reading about anything and everything that had to do with US history and Islam. I then remembered the Marine Corps hymn (from the Halls of Montezuma to the Shores of Tripoli). Tripoli, I remembered, the Barbary pirates, Muslims. I remembered the Marines.

I drove to the Marine Corps recruitment office where I had not been since the day I signed up, almost six years prior. My original recruiter, Sergeant Santiago, now Gunnery Sergeant Santiago, was somehow still there. He looked at me, smiled, and said "Yo, what's up my boy? What the hell are you doing here?" I told him I wanted to go back. I wanted to re-enlist. He looked at me and said, "Okay, let me see what I can do." I left him my number and I vaguely recall him calling me about a week or so later. He said, "Frankie, sorry man. The only way you would be able to rejoin the Marines would be if there was a draft. Before a draft, they would seek those with prior military experience and at that time, we would take you back." I assume with the war being as long as it became, that the rules must have changed. However, I never bothered to follow back up. I left it at that. I continued researching and searching for anything and everything I could find on the middle east. I became almost as obsessed as those men must have been when they hijacked the planes. I studied all that I could on Osama bin Laden, Khalid Sheik Mohammad and the Prophet, Muhammad.

4
MARRIAGE AND THE BIRTH OF NORI

"To have regrets, is to not treasure experiences. Experiences, when looked at objectively, give us jewels of wisdom that can never be taught." -Frankie M Powers-

It was now November, 2003, and my nephew was turning three years old. It is a week before his birthday. I ask my sister, "Hey, Julie, you have been telling me for a while about a girl you want me to meet. Do you remember? Why don't you invite her over to Gus' (my nephew's) birthday party?" She replied okay, I will. She did and she came. Her name was Yaribey Lopez and she soon, thereafter, became my wife. I remember my sister introducing me. I smiled and said…H-E-L-L-O. I remember her having a wonderful smile and telling myself, maybe…just maybe… A day or so later, I asked my sister for her number and we soon began talking. We hit it off. We both had over the top personalities and we were fun to be around. After a few dates, we made love. The very first time we were intimate, she got pregnant. I remember during the act of intercourse with Yari, looking at her and saying…whoops! I remember her looking at me with slight concern.

When we awoke the next morning, we talked about what had happened and we agreed to have her take the day after pill. I did not really know then what the day after pill was. I somehow believed it would have the same effect as a condom. The day after pill, fortunately, did not do the job it was intended to do. Often times, I hear people say, "The baby was a mistake." The truth is, God does not make mistakes. I have never been so glad to receive the completely opposite outcome that I had desired. God had a plan, an incredibly precious one at that, in store for me. Often times, God makes better choices for us than we could ever have imagined having made for ourselves.

Once I found out I was to be a father, I was excited, frightened, anxious and overwhelmed all at once. There was never a question of what I would do, it was just a matter of when. Yari, as I would go on to call her, told me, "You don't have to marry me, however, I would like you to be a part of our lives."

I looked at her dead center in the eyes and said, "Without question, of course, I am going to marry you and you will be my wife. I will not have our child grow up without their father being present in their everyday life."

My emotions were all over the place. The day after I found out that I was going to be a father, for the very first time in my life, I began to bleed profusely out of my nose. I was panicking. I remember calling my Primary Care Physician, Dr. Torre. He got on the phone and told me I was having an extreme emotional reaction and prescribed me some strong medication that he thoroughly warned me about. He was so adamant about the strength of the medication that it scared the heck out of me. So much so…I never took it. I was still living with my parents at the time. I remember in just a moment's notice, I went from living with my folks to becoming a father, husband and out living on my own. My parents, being wealthy, loaned us a beautiful two-story home, just two houses away from them, for us to live. I was happy; I was elated. The day that I had been praying for all those years since I was 12 years old, in the second to last pew of St. Kevin's Church, had finally arrived.

However, there was just one thing, well…it was kind of a big thing…I was not in love. I somehow convinced myself that that would be okay. I mean…I love to love. I am in love with the notion of being in love, so, hey, it will come in time. However, it never did. My mom was ecstatic, as were both of our families. We set the date of April 3, 2004. It would be the beginning of my lifelong dream of having my very own family coming to fruition.

I never finished school. I was unmotivated and undisciplined. Truth is, I was afraid. My fears of not being enough, of continuously failing my father since childhood bore fruit throughout my life. I was afraid to take a chance, to learn. I was intimidated by technology, so I ran away from it. During the whole tech explosion, I watched from afar and drank and drank and learned about the book of Revelation and the battle between Christianity and Islam. I was quite fortunate for my parent's wealth. For that was the only thing that kept me afloat. I ran a 100-unit apartment housing complex in Opa Locka, Florida, named Michelle Village Condominiums. I have always been a sociable, charming and charismatic man, but I lacked focus, I lacked drive. Truth is, I was not hungry; I was lazy. I was unmotivated.

My life looked like it was all set. I soon got a phone call from my soon to be wife. On the other end of the phone line I hear, "It's a girl. It's a girl." I was excited! I was angry! Excited! Angry! I was excited that I knew the sex of my child, but I was livid that I was not part of that moment, a moment that I can never have back again. Now, I understand that perhaps for most men, it may not matter much. Again, I also understand most men do not tend to visualize their wedding day as a cause for celebration. For most men, it is a day filled with fear of a lifelong commitment. Well…I guess I have never been the typical man. All my life, I deeply connected emotionally with women. I have always understood their feelings. I have always understood the emotional component of one's life more so than our rational minds. All my youth/teen years and adult life, I have had many women best friends. Yeah, this big, tough Marine on the outside was a real teddy bear on the inside. I guess, perhaps, it was the love that I had been yearning for and missing throughout my life that allowed me to deeply connect with members of the opposite sex. I remember one day watching Father of the Bride and recalling in the movie, when the couple found out they were going to be having a child. I saw myself in that moment. I envisioned that moment. It was a moment that I felt got stolen from me. I built resentment towards Yari over that. I really loved Father of the Bride, so much so, that that movie became the inspiration for my wedding day. We were married in my parents' beautiful home. My wife, Yari, never really cared for having a wedding. This was her second marriage. The truth is that the wedding was all my idea.

Before I knew it, April 3, 2004 had arrived. I woke up early and proceeded to go from cemetery to cemetery. I visited my two grandfathers, my grandmother, and my soon to be wife Yari's mom.

My high school best friend, Manny the Magician, was arriving, from San Juan, Puerto Rico, for my wedding day. I picked him up at the airport. We stopped to have lunch at none other than our old hangout Chicken Kitchen, and then I dropped him off at his hotel. The wedding was a blast. It was just what I had always envisioned it to be…my friends, my family, my wife. Everything that I had always wanted my whole life was before me, except…the feeling that I expected never arrived.

There was one other thing I always envisioned as far as my wedding day, as well. The day that I got married, I asked my father to be the best man in my wedding. I wanted to give him that honor. I had never been to a wedding where a son had chosen his father to be his best man. I wanted to do it. I recognize now, that unbeknownst to me at the time, it was also an attempt to once again seek my dad's approval, his affection. I was still desperately craving my dad's love.

The very next morning we headed to Miami International Airport to get on our flight to St. Lucia, for our honeymoon. I spent nearly every night of our honeymoon outside the room looking at the ocean, smoking cigarettes and drinking rum and coke. My wife would have to call me in to bed to make love. I was not feeling it. I kept playing the record of my whole life over and over again in my mind, trying to figure out what was missing.

Before I knew it, it was August, and our daughter would soon be born. As we were going over a list of names, I remember looking at my wife and telling her I wanted to name our daughter Vivianne. Yes…Vivianne, the name of my childhood girlfriend who I cared for deeply. Vivianne was a beautiful woman, a beautiful person, and a beautiful soul who left this earth, way too early. My wife, understandably, was not too keen on my idea. We decided to name her Nori Amanda Lopez. Yari's moms' name was Noraida. She went by the nickname Nori. My mother's name was Amanda, so we combined both grandmothers' names together. On September 9, 2004, Nori Amanda Lopez was born, and my life would never again be the same.

Tears rolled down the side of my cheeks. I am a father, I exclaimed…I am a father! Damn it, pinch me, I must be dreaming. I am a father!. It was real. She was real. There is not an artist or a picture that can-do justice to the beauty that entered the world that given day. She was perfect, she was jubilant and huh?? she was awake?!?! Those beautiful big bold eyes looked in wonder at all her surroundings. The nurses and doctors were in awe as to just how alert this newborn baby was. They laughed, they stared at one another in amazement at just how awake my precious daughter came into this life. I was jubilant! It was surreal as to how all her senses seemed to be heightened. A noise was made, and her eyes would immediately follow it.

I recall the day after her birth, September 10, 2004, the nurse came into our room to have Nori examined for her hearing. She looked at us, giggled and said, there are definitely no hearing issues with your baby girl. I was overzealous. On Sunday, September 12, the hospital released her to go home. I remember pulling up to the front of the maternity section outside of Baptist Hospital in Miami in my 2003 black Ford F150 and putting Nori in the car seat in the back of the car.

I remember gazing at my wife, taking a deep breath and pausing, before I left the driveway. I started recalling about how just a few short days ago I stepped into this medical facility, with my sole responsibility being for my very own life and now I have the responsibility to do all that I could for my precious baby girl. I slowly drove home, slowly…really, really slowly. A 15-minute drive somehow took over half an hour. I will never forget how nervous I was on that short commute home. I believe I was more nervous on that day, than on the very first day that I put myself behind the wheel of a car. Once we arrived at our home, my wife and I looked at each other in disbelief. Here we are, I remember thinking, now what? I unpacked the balloons, gifts, and flowers from the car and Yari and Nori went to rest.

Now, as for me, it was opening day of the NFL season and the Miami Dolphins were playing the Tennessee Titans. I was a father and I love football, so hence, I should be celebrating, I told myself. I went straight to the refrigerator and opened myself up an ice-cold Miller Lite and began to celebrate my accomplishment. One beer led to another. Every now and again I would check in on my wife and newborn. After a few hours, Yari and Nori woke up. I remember sitting on the sofa gazing into her precious eyes. Little did I know then about the long night we had in store.

My daughter was a night owl. She kind of still is. It was not until 3am that she finally drifted off to sleep. It was not until Yari and I held her in our arms and danced a sweet lullaby together that we lulled her to sleep. She was an angel. Less than a week from being home from the hospital and Nori did a complete turn on her back. Once we told the doctor, Dr. Castaneda, he looked at us with apprehension. Truth is, if my wife had not been present, I would not have believed my very own eyes. Nori was a wonderful baby. For the first three months she would give us about five straight hours of sleep throughout the night. I say "us" but truthfully, it was Yari that would care for Nori.

Typically, my wife would go to bed around 10pm. I would stay up having some Captain Morgan with a splash of diet coke. I believe the splash was for mere color or just to say it was a mixed drink. Because those drinks were pure alcohol. Around 1:00am, I would take my turn feeding the baby, not recognizing then that I was intoxicated; so much so, that I should have never been carrying my daughter in my condition. Luckily, by the grace of God, never once did I stumble or drop her. That, in and of itself, was a miracle. Somehow, I managed to fool my wife into believing that I was coherent. Truth is, I believed she would have packed my bags and changed the locks on the door, had she suspected that I had put our daughter's life in jeopardy. I was in love; I was in love with my daughter. I still am. She looked…well, she looks so much like me. However, she is a much cuter, prettier version, or as some friends like to joke around, "Frankie, she is you, in a dress."

I had gained roughly 30 pounds during my wife's pregnancy. You would think I was the one getting the cravings; actually, I was. My wife only had me run to the store with a craving one time. I believe it was for a frozen popsicle. I enthusiastically obliged. It was I who was going to the supermarket to go for the cookies and ice cream. You would think my life would be complete, yet, it was not. I had a great relationship with my brother-in-law, Gus, who had married my sister. My sister had two boys, my godson, Gus, and my nephew Chino, who was born only a month and a half before my daughter. I lived two houses away from my parents. I worked in the family business of managing properties. Yet, I was miserable. I was depressed. I was not living; I was merely existing.

Every night I would come home from work, say hi to my wife, play with the baby for a bit, and make myself a drink. Within an hour, I would go to my retreat…my mancave. My retreat was outside on the back patio. I would take out the black plastic cover that I had on my childhood 1987, 27" Sony television (they sure don't make TV's like they used to). I would then grab the remote and tune in to watch political newscasts and sports. I would light up my Marlboro Light cigarette, sip on my Captain Morgan's drink, and let the hours go by until midnight would hit. Every now and again, I would check on the baby and grab a snack to nibble on in my own personal, nightly, happy hour. Every day my wife would ask me to join her for dinner at the table, and every night I would conjure up an excuse. "I'm not hungry right now. Maybe later." Later never happened, at least never together.

After feeding Nori I would put her to bed, finish my drink and go to the kitchen where I would look for my plate of food that I claimed not to be hungry for at dinner time. I would discretely try to hide from my wife the fact that I was eating it now as I quietly turned on the microwave. After I finished eating, I would get rid of the evidence and drift off to sleep. Every night when I would go to bed, I would turn to my side of the bed, never caressing or being present with my wife, and snore myself into oblivion until the next morning. Upon awakening, I would go to the bathroom, smoke a few cigarettes with my Diet Coke for breakfast, kiss my daughter and wife and go off to work. I repeated the process day after day. This was ground hog day for me.

The properties I managed were in Opa Locka, Florida, one of the poorest cities in all of America. The demographics of the population in the city was a majority of African Americans and Hispanics. In managing the 100 units, I really did not have to do much. I dealt with some of the problems with the tenants and the occasional disruptions with the city. My time was primarily consumed in conversations with residents. My job was easy. I have always loved people; I love all people. I may not like all people, but I do love them. Nevertheless, I was unfulfilled. I was by all accounts just letting the days pass me by.

I kept trying to figure out why I was so unhappy. I seemed to have everything anyone would want. I now realize that I had a vision of what I wanted; however, it was always attached to things that were tangible, things I could see. For example, the picture of the family, of the home, of the vacation, of the job. Truth was, I was not in love with my wife. I immensely disliked managing those properties. I was unhappy with the relationship I had with my father and my sister. I was unfulfilled and unsatisfied with where I was and where I appeared to be heading in life. I was by all accounts, stuck.

My life consisted of reacting to the day's events or news cycle, instead of creating my own dreams, my own desires, my own destiny. I realized I was living like most people in America live, except I had nowhere to escape. Truth is, even the job that I had was mine only because it was given to me by my parents. I never had to earn it. I disliked the man, husband, and son that I was. I just did not know how to be any other way.

When the weekends would come around, I would always try to find a way to connect with my sister's family, and my sister-in-law's family. My sister-in-law, Yamilet, had a daughter Kazzandra and a son Kyle, who was born just two days after Chino. All three cousins, Nori, Chino and Kyle, were born within two months of each other. On top of that, my goddaughter Gianna, daughter of my best friends Lisa and Auri, was also born in July. My other best friend Ralph's son, Andre, was born within two weeks of Nori. In total, we had five babies amongst our dearest friends and family born between July and September. To say that there was some heat going on between the months of October thru December 2003 in South Florida would be an understatement.

I took it upon myself to be the planner. I was always searching, googling, or looking up possible adventures or outings that we could conjure up. For some reason, it always seemed my sister was too busy. Hence, my sister-in-law, Yamilet, and Kazzandra and Kyle spent a lot of time with us. The song, "Everybody's Working for the Weekend" comes to mind as I write this. The weekend was truly all that I lived for. I have come to realize that is what most people live for. Needless to say, even what I lived for, was somehow empty. I adored and loved my daughter. Unfortunately, through no fault of her own, I could not find a way to reciprocate those feelings to my wife. I cheated on her. I cheated on her every single night. I cheated on her with alcohol, with food, with politics, with sports. I neglected her as my partner, as my wife, and as a woman. We did have moments, although not nearly enough.

It was July 2005. Nori was nearly 10 months old. As I arrived home from work, Yari told me that Nori said her first word. I excitedly said, "Really? What was it?" She replied, "Papa." I was elated, overjoyed, it was me…it was me. Nori's first word was "Papa".

It was August 25, 2005, my birthday. More importantly, though, my nephew

Chino has an operation scheduled at Miami Children's Hospital related to his hearing. My parents and I, as well as my wife, were waiting at the hospital. Fortunately, everything came out okay. As we left the hospital, Yari, Nori, and I were on our way to have dinner at my parents' house. Mom had made my favorite, red beans and rice and lomito (pork loin). I remember that as soon as we sat down to eat, within seconds the lights went out. All of a sudden there was a strong gust of wind that knocked my parents' neighbors' old satellite antennae into their pool. We immediately searched for a radio. Soon the realization that Hurricane Katrina, which, as of just a few, short hours ago, was headed towards West Palm Beach and northward, took a sudden detour and ventured south. Being stuck in the middle of a Category One hurricane, we were forced to stay the night. The following morning, we awakened and assessed the damage. The effects were minimal; however, we were without power for roughly two days.

That following Sunday, August 28th, we went to a friend's baptism. After the ceremony, they had a small celebration at a banquet hall. On the television, they were reporting that Hurricane Katrina had become a category five and was barreling towards New Orleans. Immediately, I felt a sharp tug in my stomach. I remembered being there just a few, short weeks prior. I remember the tour guide telling Yari and myself that New Orleans was shaped like a bowl of soup. If a strong enough hurricane were to hit them directly, the devastation and death that would occur would be unfathomable. He also stated that he knew that it was just a matter of time before a storm such as this would inevitably hit the city. I then remembered that we were supposed to be there this particular weekend.

What would I have done? Would I had headed the warnings and left the Crescent City? Would I have rode the storm out? Or would I have been my stubborn self at the time and said nothing is going to happen. The answer to that question, I will never know.

I had always desired to go to New Orleans. For my 30th birthday, Yari surprised me and booked our trip. I immediately fell in love with the city. I loved the food, the drinks and the music; I loved all of it. Originally, we were supposed to arrive in New Orleans on August 25th, my birthday, but Yari had heard of a mini jazz event that was going on the weekend of August 3rd and asked me if I wanted to change the date. I wonder what would have happened if I had said no. Anyway, what I do know is the devastation that rocked New Orleans during Hurricane Katrina, stayed with me long after those levies broke on that fateful Sunday.

Throughout our first year as parents, we took several trips to Disney World.

I attributed the reasoning to be for our daughter, Nori. Although that was partly true, I was a huge Disney fan. In fact, I still am. It really is the most magical place on earth. I realize now that there was always something special to me about Fantasy Land in the Magic Kingdom theme park. Most adults look at Fantasy Land as being for children. While that may be true, it is also the land where the little kid in all human beings forever lives. I now know that in that place, in that land, little boy Frankie was able to still see his dreams, to still believe those dreams were possible. I guess I wanted to experience that. I wanted my daughter to know that. I am certain that without question, Walt Disney himself felt that.

I did not know then, but I recognize now, my wife would go along on these trips to placate my daughter and myself. Yari was simple. What she wanted was a family, a home, and a good job, which she had as an oncology nurse at Baptist Hospital. Yari also wanted to feel loved, desired and cared for by her husband, which she did not have.

*****

Nori's first year was completed before I knew it. Her first birthday party theme was ladybugs. Like everything else I did in life, it was over the top. We had popcorn machines, cotton candy, mechanical fair rides, and oh, how can we forget…ladybugs…loads and loads of ladybugs. We invited many friends and family. We had a food truck before food trucks even became a thing. We had the party at the same place we would do all family parties, at my parents' home. Their backyard consists of about half an acre with chimney-colored pavers, a pool, and a goldfish pond. This is the home where I grew up and where my children and nephews often gathered.

It was now October 2005, and as Halloween season nears, we started what became a yearly tradition for our family, a Halloween celebration at our friends Lisa and Auri's house. Auri was my childhood best friend. He was the one I spoke about a few chapters back who threw me in the pool back, on that first day I tasted my kryptonite, alcohol. I was the best man in his wedding. Through the years, our friendship changed, and his wife Lisa had become my closest confidant. I became godfather to their first-born daughter, Gianna.

Lisa and Auri would go all out for Halloween. Auri was extremely quiet; he was really reserved. Somehow, I believe there was something about Halloween that he always loved. The idea that he could get out of his shell and be someone else without anyone knowing. That idea greatly appealed to him. Every Halloween several of us would gather at their home, my sister and nephews included. Auri and Lisa were never big drinkers, so I always made certain I brought my companion…no, not my wife, but the Captain, Captain Morgan. I never could stray too far away from the Captain.

Shortly after Halloween, it was my turn for decorations. Ever since I was a little boy, Christmas fascinated me. I loved the lights, the music and the décor. I would often tell my wife, half-jokingly, "Hey, what if we keep a room decorated like Christmas year-round?" Let's just say, the idea did not resonate with her like I had hoped. As I decorated for Christmas, there was nothing with Jesus or Kris Kringle that would not catch my eye. I would google search, check on Ebay, look at garage sales, with one thing in mind, Christmas décor. Then it happened, I found something…(drumroll)…Disney Christmas décor. I had to have it. I was literally as addicted to Christmas, as a crack addict is to crack. See, the thing is, as many of you read this, you think I am kidding. I am, but at the same time, I am not. The same high, the shots of dopamine and oxycontin, would fill me up when I found something new or when a new package would arrive through the mail.

Thanksgiving and Christmas were by far the happiest and most joyful times of the year for me. As soon as Halloween was over, I would begin playing Christmas carols, turning on Christmas lights and begin searching for Christmas movies. I would go all out. Now as I write this, all these things were fulfilling and satisfying for me, however, never once did I even think about asking my wife how she felt. I just assumed everyone loved decorating for Christmas. The thing is, I was never too handy. Furthermore, most of the Christmas décor needed to be built, so, yes…you guessed it, my wife had to lead. Here she is, in charge of the house, working at Baptist Hospital, tending to Nori, and now being forced to put up all this Christmas décor that I wanted.

As far as Christmas gifts, I would be the one to purchase them and boy, would I outdo myself. Yari and I would have constant arguments about my purchasing too many gifts and not allowing her to partake in this experience. I did not realize then, but I was, number one, spoiling the heck out of our children, number two, not allowing her to partake in the experience of Christmas, and number three, after all this, having her be the one to package and wrap these gifts as well.

The holidays were also a great reason to drink and not be hounded about it. To be fair, my wife did not ride me too hard. In fact, only on occasion would she mention anything about my drinking. Rarely, if ever, would she talk about how much or what I was eating.

At this point, I was weighing roughly sixty pounds more than when we had met. Although she never spoke much about it, I knew inside of me that my drinking and eating were not normal. At the time, I felt relieved that Yari was not hassling me, although in her avoiding the conversation, it was just building up resentment inside of her. It had her feeling like lava brewing inside a dormant volcano before the eruption would inevitably take place.

In 2005, I began what became a short-lived tradition that I thoroughly enjoyed, a Christmas party celebration at the Lopez residence. It was an all-out extravaganza including lights, décor, food, drinks, and my famous New Orleans style, category five hurricane punch. A couple of those and your hips could not stop swaying.

This was also a time for me to show off my cooking chops. I loved cooking. I always enjoyed trying new recipes, but it was never really for me. What I truly enjoyed was looking at other people's faces when they would taste my food. My cooking was a way to show my deep love for others.

Mid-way through the party, an unexpected visitor would always arrive. It was, none other than, good 'ole St. Nick. I would run upstairs, put on my red suit and furry white beard and sit on a red wooden chair to await the beautiful children.

One by one, the children would sit and tell me their wishes. I would then hand them a red stocking full of goodies and they would excitedly run off to tell their parents. Everyone had a beautiful time, although I know for certain, that no one had as great a time as I did. I swear if being Santa Claus was a full-time job, I would be all in. Seeing the look on the children's faces, seeing their wishes and dreams through their eyes, there is no dollar amount that can ever give me the sense of joy and aliveness that those innocent and noble children had deep inside of them. As I looked at them, I saw what I see every time I enter Fantasy Land, as well. I see the childlike wonder of little Frankie in them. Many of the things that I am sharing with you now are realizations that I am discovering as I write. These are truths that were unavailable or unrecognizable to me during these years.

It was now March 2006, and my wife is about to turn 30. I decided to throw her a surprise birthday party and once again, just like everything I do, it had to be big. Let me clarify, when I say big, it is not about it being necessarily over the top, although more often than not, that was the case. It was about the attention to detail. It was in the big things as well as in the little things. As I have shared with you over and over again, the detached, neglectful husband that I was; but I was not that on this day. On this very day, it was probably the one time that I gave almost everything I had to my wife.

The party was a grand surprise, and the theme was Spain. Being that it was Spain, I had to have a paella, of course. I hired a catering company and cold and hot Spanish tapas were on full display. I hired a gypsy fortune teller to read people their future. There was a guitarist, along with a dancer, dancing Flamenco. We had a mechanical bull for the adults to attempt to ride. There was also a full-service bar with bartender, a large flamenco dancer cake and our wedding videographer to capture unforgettable memories. To top it all off…I had an adult piñata. The piñata consisted of adult trinkets, such as adult games, lotto tickets, cigarettes and small bottles of liquor. The night was a blur for most who attended. However, a blur for me was normal. I do not believe there were many nights over the last decade of my drinking career that I can say that I remember much of anything.

It was now, early summer 2006. I received an email from an old friend, Paul, encouraging me to purchase a book titled, "The Day of Islam." Never has a book had such an impact on my life like that book did. Thankfully, it was not a lifelong impact.

As I mentioned earlier, the events of September 11, 2001, had a profound effect on me. It had me trying to understand the deep-seated roots of evil. Here I was, almost five years later, and I was still searching for answers. I trusted Paul, so I ordered the book.

Three-quarters of the way through the book, I started feeling chest pains. To give you a small summary of what the book entailed, it was written by a CIA correspondent, who stated that Al Qaeda operatives had obtained suitcase nukes and were planning on detonating them in seven United States cities, Miami being one of the targets.

As I was reading the book, my co-worker and friend, Armando, happened to come into the office and saw my hands holding my chest. He asked what had happened and rushed to call 911. After the paramedics came and took my vitals, they assured me that everything was okay, that I was probably having an anxiety attack. They asked me what had happened. After explaining to them the contents of the book, they advised me to throw the book away. Of course, I rejected that idea.

I arrived home later that day to tell my wife what had happened. Yari, began to cry. She looked at me and must have thought that I was crazy, but she never said anything. I continued to buy more and more books, which confirmed the CIA operatives' beliefs. I was convinced that Al Qaeda was planning an attack on United States soil; I was going to find out when and alert others to take heed. I tried to do that. Around this same time, a documentary came out titled, "Obsession: Radical Islam's war with the West." Now, you want to talk about striking fear into the hearts of people, this documentary was it. I was petrified, but I was a Marine. I was willing, able, and ready to fight.

My poor wife, what she had to deal with during this time. I imagine she must have thought that Frank was insane. Truthfully, for a while, I unquestionably was. I talked and began to speak to almost anyone who would listen. Almost every single conversation I would have turned political. Every single one of them would turn to Islam and its war on America.

Nori's birthday came and went. Every invitee would get an earful of my new theory. Then, it finally came. I figured it out. I believed that I had figured out the date for the next attack. The date was October 2, 2006; I was certain. I told everyone who I knew to join me and escape Miami. The everyone that joined me was my wife, Nori, and myself. I decided to take a short reprieve to Sanibel Island. It was a three-day stay. Lo and behold, October 2, 2006, came and went and nothing occurred. Luckily, I was wrong.

As 2006 ended and 2007 arrived, I recorded a Glenn Beck special and shared it with my wife. After watching the program, she felt relieved. She began to believe me. She began to tell herself perhaps Frankie is not so crazy after all. Somehow, her believing in me made my anxiety dissipate. I still believed the threat to be real, however, I did not believe it to be imminent.

During this time, my relationships with those around me began to suffer. I continued to distance myself from others…or maybe not. Maybe they began to distance themselves from me. In hindsight, who could blame them? Frank has gone mad. I was a ray of negativity. Everything was gloom and doom. My drinking got worse, or at least my consumption did. I was drinking a little more than half of a jug of Captain Morgan a day. That was almost a liter, if not a liter, a day. My wife and I were barely intimate. Actually, after Nori was born, we seldom made love. When I say seldom, maybe five/six times a year. To celebrate Nori's third birthday, we went on a one-week Disney cruise. Not once during those seven days, were we intimate.

I studied a lot during these years. I became a student and scholar of United States history. I prided myself in what I learned. I recognize now that although I learned quite a bit, I also only read those ideologies that supported my beliefs. I refused to accept or believe that there were two sides to every story. Every outing I had was an opportunity to show my intellect and bombard others with facts and assertions over my new discoveries. I continued to push people away. I mean, who the hell would want to be around someone like me? No one, absolutely no one. It was around this same time that my relationship with my mother began to suffer. My mom, who had been my rock, my confidant, my everything, began to distance herself from me. It seems 2007 was the year that I began isolating myself from the whole world around me.

5
JONATHAN COMPLETES OUR FAMILY

"There is nothing more rewarding than watching your child born right in front of you and having the opportunity to love and care for them, as you once hoped others would for you." -Frankie M Powers-

It was now January 26, 2008. Yvette, one of Yari's closest friends, was celebrating her birthday with dining and dancing on Saturday night at Amnesia in South Beach. Yes, that is right, the same Amnesia where I had my going away party to the Marine Corps almost 12 years earlier. We drank; we danced. I really liked Yvette and her husband Norbert. I have not spoken to them in years. I miss those two. Anyhow…as the night came to an end and Yari and I arrived home, I was ready to have a nightcap drink and drift off to sleep. Well, my wife had other ideas. After trying to resist her advances, I caved in and we made love.

Nine months later, on October 8, 2008, my family was complete. My son, Jonathan Frank Lopez was born. To this day, Yari still says that Jonathan was all her doing. Although Jonathan looks very much like her, I think what she means, is that Jonathan would not be here on this earth if she had not convinced me to be intimate. She is absolutely, 100% right. Boy, am I glad that I obliged.

On a warm summer day in May at the doctor's office, the doctor came to us and told us, "It's a boy." I asked, "It's a boy? Are you sure?" They then proceeded to show me the sonogram and said, "Well, you see this?" I nodded. They continued, "Every boy that has ever come out of a mother's womb has one of these." I burst out in laughter and then I began to cry. So many emotions ran through me at the time. I never expected to have a son. I somehow believed that God was going to gift me two daughters. It never occurred to me that I would be gifted with my very own son.

I cried tears of happiness; I cried tears of fear. I wanted to make certain that I could show my son what it means to be a man, to lead by example, so he could follow in my footsteps.

Now the search was on for a name...we asked for suggestions. It was also around this time that Yari and I sat with our daughter and told her she was going to be having a baby brother. Although for a moment, she stated she wanted a baby sister, she was elated to have a baby brother.

Summer 2008 was coming to an end and we had yet to pick a name. Most people around us were encouraging me to name him Frank, after myself. I was never too drawn to that idea. I always believed doing that takes away some of their own individuality.

In the meantime, we had discovered a theme for his room...Disney sports. Yeah, the wife was not too keen on Disney Christmas. Just teasing. The problem was that although there were a lot of sports room décor, and quite a bit of Disney room decorations, we had a really difficult time finding a Disney sports theme.

In the beginning of the summer, I had just finished watching the HBO documentary series on John Adams. I began to think, hmm...Jonathan? John Adams was a man of honor, a man of compassion. John Adams was a man of God. I thought of John the Baptist. Jonathan, I continued to ponder. As I write this, I just finished ordering John Adams HBO documentary series from Amazon. I want my son Jonathan to know the man he was named after.

Here we are walking along Disney Springs in Orlando, known as Downtown Disney at the time, and we come across a small store front booth on the way to have lunch at Rainforest Café. As we stopped at the booth, I noticed they had different Disney characters that could be made into a nameplate for a child's room. Example, "Frank's room." I looked at my wife and said, "Babe, what do you think? Jonathan?" She looked at me with her palms facing up and said, "I don't know." We had previously discussed the name Jonathan, and she seemed to kind of like it. I looked at her dead serious and told her, "We need to make a decision. We need the Jonathan's room sign." I laugh immensely now, 12 years later, how we came to that decision. That booth sealed the deal. The movie John Adams kind of did it. We never considered John, so Jonathan it was, and just like that, our son had his name.

Truth be told, he did that name justice. At least he has done so to this very day. My son is 12 years old as of this writing. I have never met a man or boy with as pure a heart and such a loving soul as him.

As the due date quickly approached, we were ready. My wife was ready, I was ready, or so I thought. On October 7, 2008, as I arrived home from work and came through the door, I said hello to Yari and Nori and gave them both a kiss. I then walked over to the bar to serve myself a drink. I remember being excited to watch the Vice-Presidential debate between then Senator Joe Biden and Governor Sarah Palin when, all of a sudden, my wife says, "Frank," with her eyes open widely. I looked at her and said, "What happened?" All I remember is seeing liquid everywhere. She tells me, "My water broke." I remember being frantic and upset saying, "What? What do you mean your water broke?" I then told her, "This is not supposed to happen." She then calmly told me to call my parents so we could drop off Nori and go to the hospital. She was calm as a cucumber. I, on the other hand, felt like Fred Flintstone.

I shamefully realized that the reason I was so upset that her water broke was because I never got to even sip my drink, and I was going to miss the Vice-Presidential debate.

Nori was born after her due date. The doctor had to induce Yari's labor. Somehow, I had convinced myself that the same thing was supposed to happen the second time around.

On October 7, 2008, we arrived at the hospital. The next morning, October 8, my son Jonathan Frank Lopez was born. My son, Jonathan Frank Lopez. I remember the emotion that came over me when the doctor handed him over. I almost collapsed. Somehow, I felt more pressure to be a great parent with the birth of my son, than I ever did with the birth of my daughter. I suppose since I was a man and he was male, I believed that he was to emulate me. I remember telling my wife how exhausted I was. I swear if I could capture the look on her face when I said that…if she had a baseball bat, I think she would have clobbered me over the head with it.

Jonathan was born with an infection. For precautionary reasons, he was required to stay in the hospital with Yari for ten days. Never once, out of those ten days, did I spend the night with my wife and newborn son. I always stated that my reasoning was so that I could stay with our daughter Nori. However, I have never fully admitted the truth to anyone, until now. The truth was that being home, with my daughter, would give me the liberty and ability to drink alcohol at night.

My mom spent every single one of those nights with Yari. I do not think I ever really thanked her for her sacrifice. You see, my mom had severe back pain. Those evenings in the hospital must not have been very comfortable for her.

Just as Nori looked like me, my son looked identical to his mom. He had clear white skin, blond hair and beautiful green eyes. He loved his room, as I did. Truthfully, I do not know who enjoyed it more. Jonathan had frequent ear infections his first year. There was a moment I recall his doctor, Dr. Ruiz-Casteneda, telling us that if he had one more ear infection, an operation may be in order. Luckily, that never happened.

Nori, on the other hand, was filled with joy. I will never forget the look on her face when she first laid eyes on her baby brother. It was priceless. I believe she fell in love with him the very first moment she saw him. Nori took great pride in being a big sister. She took it upon herself to look after him, almost like a second mom. Now, 12 years later, she still looks after him, more so than she could have ever anticipated.

After ten long days, Yari and Jonathan finally arrived home. Our family was now complete. Yet, here I was, still seemingly so unhappy. Nevertheless, the holidays were right around the corner. And God knows how much the thought of Christmastime being near, would do for me emotionally.

Before we knew it, the year was coming to a close. While the country was still suffering from an economic crisis, we were not spared from the recession. We had done a condo conversion on the 100-unit property that I managed in Opa Locka. My brother-in-law Gus and I were part of the conversion. Once the units were sold, we would each get a percentage of the share. As you can see, we had an extremely close, vested interest in selling, but just as the country was broke, so were its people.

My relationship with my family, specifically my mom, continued to deteriorate. My drinking got gradually worse. I did not know it at the time, but I continued picking fights and arguments with all those around me. My parents would often take care of my children. I did not value or appreciate all they did for me, especially my mom. I remember one specific day getting into a volatile argument with my mom who had just gone to Costco and picked up a case of Vienna Sausages. I don't know what happened, but I became so angry that I slammed the case of sausages on the ground. One of those cans ricocheted off the floor onto my mom leaving a huge welt on her leg. My anger got the best of me that day. My anger got the best of me for the better part of 43 years.

It was June 2009. I was outside, it was around 7pm. I was having my daily cocktails and smoking a cigarette when Nori came outside and told me, "Papi, I know what I want for my birthday." I said, "Okay, Chi-Chi." Chi-Chi was a nickname I had given her since she was a baby. I love giving people nicknames. I always found it another way to show endearment or love to those people I care about. Mimi is another nickname I often call her. Anyway, I asked her, "So, what is it? What is it that you want for your birthday?" Here I am thinking a barbie house. Perhaps another trip to Disney World. It would not have even had to be my idea.

Her answer came completely unexpected. She said, "Papi, I want you to quit smoking so you can spend more time with me playing inside the house." Wow, I was caught completely off guard. Nevertheless, I answered without hesitation, "Okay, Mimi, for your birthday I will quit smoking." She smiled and yelled yay! She opened the sliding glass door, closed it, and excitedly ran inside to tell Yari and her baby brother. In that split second, I knew without a shadow of a doubt that I was done. I knew that I would honor my promise and that for my daughter's birthday I would, in fact, quit smoking. As I write this, I realize our whole life can change in just one moment. A moment of decision can shape our destiny.

I had tried to quit smoking dozens of times to no avail. However, I knew, I just knew, that failure this time was not an option. On June 30, 2009, I drove about 40 miles to Miccosukee Indian Village and bought ten cartons of cigarettes. Enough, I calculated, to last me through the weekend of her birthday. The reason I purchased the ten cartons on June 30th was because on July 1, 2009, cigarettes would be taxed an extra dollar a pack. So, in essence, I would be saving $100.00.

I remember a few days later commenting to my mom about Nori's birthday wishes. My mom responded, "Frankie, how can you make her that promise. If you break that promise, she will never believe anything that comes from any man." I looked at my mom lovingly and said, "Mom, I know. That is why I have no choice but to keep that promise."

My daughter's birthday was on a Wednesday that year. We celebrated it that Saturday, September 12, 2009. I told her, "Nori, Sunday, September 13, 2009, the day after we celebrate your birthday, I will smoke my last cigarette." I did, exactly eighteen years to the day from when I had first started this terrible habit, I left it. Eleven years later, I have not even contemplated picking one up. . Soon after, I realized that in all the years I had been smoking, I had never had a drink without a cigarette. I associated the two hand in hand, like oil and vinegar, like salt and pepper. I then vowed to quit drinking… and for a while, I did.

I stopped drinking for roughly two and a half months, until one December, while in my garage going over Christmas decorations, I opened the refrigerator and opened up an ice-cold Miller Lite. For the first time in my life, I had a beer without a cigarette. Better yet, cigarettes did not cross my mind. I had no cravings; I was elated. I felt a great sense of achievement within me. So, what does one do when they reach a goal? Let's celebrate, of course. My drinking started again and for nearly a decade, rarely, if ever, came to a stop.

My young daughter Nori's wish had been granted. Papi did quit smoking. However, her true wish, which was for me to spend time with her, was short lived. I did not realize that as her wish at the time. Truthfully, I did not realize it until I began writing this sentence. So back to my escape, my sanctuary, I found myself, once again sitting outside watching political commentary, occasional sports, with my forever companion, Captain Morgan, by my side. It was now late September 2009. While at work, I got a call from Yari telling me that Jonathan said his first word. I was so excited. "Really? Really? What was it? Mama? Papa?" Nope…neither. My son's first word was touchdown. "What?" "Yep, touchdown." How in the world this occurred, I have no idea? Jonathan was born an athlete. He is the most athletic kid I have ever seen. Both my kids are. Nori and Jonathan are both phenomenal, natural born athletes.

The year 2010 was upon us. Adjustments were made at work. We decided, since we were unable to sell the condos and money was getting tight, we began the process of renting out the units. Renting was a challenge. The units were completely remodeled. These were military barracks built during WW2 right across the street from Opa Locka Airport. We redid everything…I mean everything, including roofs, electrical, bathrooms and plumbing. The only thing we kept was the shell, which were built with solid masonry, concrete blocks. Housing sure is not constructed the way it used to be. The buildings foundations were as solid as they come. To use the slogan, they were "built Ford tough" was an understatement. However, due to the original intent (military barracks) for the units, they were quite small. They were two bedrooms and one bath, ranging from 585 square feet to 610 square feet. We began asking for $1,000.00 a month for rent, with water included. Yet, it took quite a bit of time to find our market. The monthly costs of our loans, insurance, and expenses had us feeling overwhelmed and anxious.

At home, family life also was difficult. My relationship with my mom had become distant. My parents continued to take care of Nori and Jonathan on Wednesdays and Thursdays, those being the days that Yari was at work.

Me with my Mom

With my Parents in Their Backyard

My proverbial pattern would be to come home from work sometime between 4 and 5 pm, serve myself a couple of Captain Morgan's, and take some extra stock of the Captain over to my parents' home, in case their inventory of rum was running low. I would say hi to my mom and the kids and head on over to the kitchen to see what was available to satisfy my appetite. I never thought to ask my mom, I would just serve myself some food, always assuming, there was enough. I thought to myself, "It's my mom. I shouldn't have to ask." I now realize, although there always was enough and my mother has never limited me to what I could eat or take home, I still never bothered to think perhaps she did not make enough for leftovers. Truthfully, I was selfish in that regard. It never even crossed my mind. So, as I ate some rice and whatever protein was available, I would serve myself another drink and head to the front of the house and just glance at my surroundings.

To this day, I cannot figure out why the front of their house appealed to me so much, considering they had about half an acre of a beautifully decorated and maintained backyard patio. I continued sipping my Captain Morgan's until my dad came home. I would say hello, talk a bit about work, and as 8:00 pm would come around, we somehow would manage to get into an argument about one thing or another and I would grab the kids and go home.

I was miserable. My relationship with my wife was really non-existent. We acted more like roommates than partners. By the time the holidays came around, I slept more on the couch than in the bedroom. My excuse was that I was tired and had fallen asleep. The truth was, there was no connection, no love. I never told her that because I did not want to hurt her feelings.

Today, I recognize that oftentimes we do not necessarily need to say anything because our loved ones can feel everything.

There was no intimacy in our marriage. There was no physical, mental, or emotional connection. We were completely detached; however, I continued to believe, and had convinced myself, that somehow, someway, everything would sort itself out.

It was now summer, 2011. My aunt, Tia Yoly, my only aunt, was very sick. She had been suffering from cancer for a few months. It took hold of her real quick. My aunt was a difficult woman. She never had children and was only married for about five years before she lost her husband. She was extremely lonely; the only person she had in her daily life was my grandmother, who lived with her. My grandmother was her best friend, her only true friend. My aunt was my grandmother's best friend, as well. Tia Yoly loved me. She loved me dearly. Between my sister and I, I believe I was her favorite. I remember feeling guilty about it because I am sure my sister felt it too.

Shortly after Nori's 7th birthday, in September, my aunt passed away. My grandmother was devastated. It was always a difficult situation throughout our lives. My aunt, Tia Yoly, was my father's only sibling. They had a tumultuous relationship. There was always constant friction in my childhood home, that was ever present as far back as I can remember.

My dad deeply loved his sister. My mom, on the other hand, did not fancy her much. During the holidays, it was always an extremely stressful time at home for my father. Feeling a sense of loyalty to his wife, but an obligation to his sister to spend time together.

Nevertheless, her passing, in a way, brought a small sense of peace. My aunt suffered all throughout her life with mental health. It was a battle she could not win. Mental health is a constant battle in all of our lives. Many of us, however, never become aware of it.

*****

Before Jonathan turned three, we decided to enroll him for a few weeks at Red Berry's Baseball camp. Red Berry was a former major league baseball scout and University of Miami Hurricane's baseball coach. Red opened the baseball camp for youths from the early ages of two through twelve. He taught sportsmanship, fun, and good old traditional American values. This would be Jonathan's first crack at sports and boy…was he a natural. In his first week, he earned the best player trophy award and a patch and was declared, "A Nasty Boy." Now, as far as the term "Nasty Boy" goes, it was referenced to him for having played so well, that he was deemed nasty good. The following week when he arrived at school and informed his teacher, Mrs. Trujillo, of his weekend, he told her, "Teacher, teacher, you know what? I am a Nasty Boy." With a wide-eyed expression, she said "No, no, Jonathan, you are not a nasty boy." He looked at her, nodded his head and said, "Yes! Yes! I am a Nasty Boy," and explained to her his accomplishment and being proud to be deemed a "Nasty Boy."

It was now December 2011. Nori is seven years old; Jonathan is three, and I am planning the biggest, greatest, Christmas party I had ever done. As the kids were getting older, I could no longer pull off the Santa suit attire. The suit was not the problem, it was the eyes. Shakespeare was right. "The eyes truly are the windows to the soul." As adults, we often forget, but children don't, they know.

For that year's Christmas party, I hired face painting elves, Christmas carolers, an Italian catering company making fresh pasta sauces, made to order and, of course, how could I forget, but none other than, St. Nick himself.

Now it was not just any ordinary St. Nick. The Santa that came to my home was the actual Santa Claus of a Coca-Cola commercial being televised throughout the country.

The party exceeded expectations. I will never forget a friend of ours, Illiana's face when she saw Santa. She looked at me and said, "Holy c***. Frank. He looks like the real one." I looked at her with a grin, "Of course, that is because he is." She immediately realized what she had said and we both burst out in laughter. My famous hurricane punch was a smashing success, of course. For the first time in her entire life, on her final Christmas on this earth, my grandmother, Abuela Yolanda, whom just a few short months ago went through the pain and heartache of burying her best friend and daughter, took a picture sitting on, none other than, good old Santa's lap. I had never in my life seen my grandmother so happy. It was a very precious memory that I will carry with me for a lifetime.

It was now February 2012, and my grandmother was very sick. She had tuberculosis and got an infection. She was hospitalized. It did not help matters that she was suffering from heartache, depression and loneliness. She was also 94 years old. My grandmother was a fighter, she was tough. I believe that when my aunt died, she lost her desire to live, her purpose. I firmly believe that she was more than happy to depart this earth to reunite with her daughter.

The loss of my grandmother affected my dad in more ways than I think he realized. In a span of eight months, he lost his only sister and mother.

In the meantime, my parents had just purchased a beautiful cabin home in Piney Creek, North Carolina, where many of their friends also had secondary homes. This truly was a beautiful escape for my parents, especially my father, after the difficult and tumultuous year he had experienced.

On the work front, things had picked up. We had adjusted our rents and had filled over 50% of our units. We surely were not where we wanted to be, but thankfully we were not where we used to be either. I, on the other hand, did not seem to have missed a meal, no matter the circumstances. By December 2012, my weight hovered around 330 pounds. Big was an understatement. Here I am, 5 foot 8 inches, 330 pounds. No matter how I tried to shape it, no matter what my body type was, I was obese by anyone's measure. I think if I would have been put on a scale in space, I would still far surpass the weight standards for my body.

It was now December 27, 2012, and our white Dodge Durango is loaded up and ready to go. Yari, Nori, Jonathan and I woke up early that morning for a fourteen-hour drive to Piney Creek, North Carolina, to visit my parents and enjoy our first New Year's, in their cabin home.

My wife was the driver. I could not stay up for more than 30 minutes without dozing off. I suffered from sleep apnea at the time. My weight was having severe effects on my health. I was diagnosed pre-diabetic. I was suffering from high blood pressure. Now, with sleep apnea, I would stop breathing in my sleep. One would have thought that getting into an accident by hitting a fence while I had fallen asleep would have been the wakeup call that I needed (pun intended). But, apparently, not. I either believed I was invincible, or I was just a simple fool.

I remember week after week telling myself that I will start dieting and exercising on Monday. Monday turned to Tuesday, and then it never happened. Every morning, I would wake up too tired and lethargic from the heavy drinking of the night prior. Anyhow, on our way to Piney Creek, the kids were overzealous, hoping to see snow for the very first time.

We arrived around 8pm. It was breathtaking. Our cousins had also joined us for the getaway. The cabins were exactly what one would anticipate a cabin to be. It had a large, open porch in the front, a beautiful, warm, inviting fireplace as you entered. My mom had made one of her specialties, fabada. Fabada is a hearty, white bean stew, filled with pumpkin, smoked ham hocks and Spanish sausage. To this day, the kids still talk about that dish. Talk about food coma, it was spectacular. I am not quite sure if it was that warm pot of yumminess that they enjoyed so much, or if it was the feeling of the last trip of when their parents were last together.

The cabin had an open kitchen with two bedrooms and a full bathroom on top. Downstairs, in the basement, were another two bedrooms, bath, as well as a game room for us to enjoy. We had a blast. We went trout fishing and enjoyed the beauty of God's natural wonders. It was serene, it was tranquil. It was peaceful.

A few days before we were set to depart, we were planning on going snow tubing on Thursday, January 3, 2013. I never made it. The night before I had a huge argument with Yari. I was mad…no, I was livid. I honestly cannot remember what the fight was all about, however, I was distraught. I let my anger get the best of me and it carried over to the next day. In the morning, Yari somehow managed to put the prior evening to the side and said, "Come on, let's go." I couldn't, I wouldn't. I stayed in my emotion, in my anger.

I spent most of the day just thinking, playing over and over in my head the previous night's argument. I blamed her. I began thinking of what I could have done differently. I beat myself up all day and had a little assistance from the Captain. I decided to have a couple of drinks, believing I would feel better. Of course, I did, for a little bit, until …I didn't.

The kids came back excited to tell me all about their snow tubing experience, wishing I could have seen them. I missed out on that moment. Truth is, I missed out on a lot of moments. I just did not consciously realize it then like I did this time. In that moment something hit me. Damn it, No! I am going to do better. I am going to try to make this work. I need to. I had to, for the sake of the kids, or so I thought.

It was early Saturday morning, on January 5th. We loaded the car and began our drive back home to Miami. Winter break was soon coming to an end, and the kids had to be in school at St. Kevin's Monday morning. I remember an hour into the drive back, I turned to my wife, who was driving, and told her I was sorry. I want to make this work. I want us to have a strong and happy family. She listened, nodded her head, and seemed to agree to give it a shot. However, although I believe that her heart wanted to, part of her was done. She was finished. For years we were roommates. There was no intimacy, no friendship, no communication. I never really knew what her triggers were or how she felt. I prided myself in being a good listener and friend to anyone. However, could I have ever truly listened if she spoke to me? That is a question to which the answer I may never really know.

Needless to say, I tried, I really tried. I mean, I tried the best that I knew how at the time. For a few weeks, things were going pretty well. On January 12th we had a great family date.

Family dates were something I prided myself in doing for our family. A few times a year, I would plan a full day of events for us four. On this one particular day, it started with an 11am show at Ringling Brothers Barnum & Bailey Circus at the American Airlines Arena, also known as, the home of the NBA's Miami Heat basketball team.

We started our day at the circus, which the kids and I really loved. I am not quite sure if Yari liked it though. She was always just happy to get out of the house and be entertained. It did not really matter much the event or the affair. After the show, we walked over to Bayside, which we would frequent a few times a year. We had a small bite to eat and walked by the marina. As we walked near the shops, I sighted my favorite and much anticipated go to spot, Fat Tuesday's bar. How can I miss the opportunity to have me a couple of 190 octanes?

As the evening progressed, one of our final stops at Bayside, before our staple dinner at Los Ranchos Steak House, was, none other than, the adrenaline rushing, Thriller boat ride. The Thriller boat ride is a 40-passenger speed boat, with a narrating captain, a fast and furious excursion and tour of the homes of the rich and famous. We had a blast. Once we exited the boat ride, a photographer had taken a picture of us. I purchased the picture. That was the last photograph we ever took as a family. The very next morning, for the first time in over a year, my wife and I made love. That day was also the last semblance of any romance between the two of us.

A week later, on Sunday January 19th, at approximately 7pm, while at my parent's home, watching the New England Patriots playing the Denver Broncos in the NFL playoffs, Yari received a phone call. It was her sister Yami. Yami's house had caught fire and the firefighters and police officers had arrived. We immediately headed on over. Upon arrival, we saw Yami along with my niece and nephew, Kazzandra and Kyle, outside near the fence. My father-in-law, and his significant other, were there as well. Fortunately, everyone was safe. The house, however, was uninhabitable for quite some time.

After realizing the magnitude of what had happened, without hesitation and without conferring with my wife, I said to Yami, "You and the kids are more than welcome to stay with us as long as necessary," and so… they did.

The first few days went well. However, just like any house guest, everyone's patterns of behavior became a nuisance, not unlike my behavior would become a nuisance in anyone else's home. None of us are immune to that. Small discussions became arguments. Resentments and ill feelings began to develop. Our honeymoon period for Yari and myself was short lived.

By Presidents Day weekend, Yari and I were worse than what we were on winter break. During this time, I had begun an exercise routine in the afternoons. I would bring the kids, Nori, Jonathan, Kyle and Kazzandra with me. We would go for a long walk. I remember telling Nori, "Honey, your mom is not talking to me. I need your mom to talk to me. If she does not talk to me, I am going to leave the house." What an A-hole I was! What a freaking jerk! How dare I put my eight-year-old daughter in that position, with that pressure, with that fear. Regardless of my pleas to Yari to speak to me, never should I have put my daughter in the middle, yet, here I did. Shame on me.

On March 2, 2013, I had enough. A huge argument broke out in front of my kids. I told Yari I was leaving. I remember reading her a letter I had written that spoke of the great husband I was (what a laugh). I cannot believe that after reading her that letter of how great I was, I then told her that I did not want to go. I remember pleading with her to please say something, anything, to convince me to stay. Her eyes, watery, she picked her head up, looked at me, and gently says, "Just go, Frank. Just go." I did.

I drove to my father-in-law's house. As soon as he opened the door, most probably expecting a surprise of some sorts considering it was his birthday the following day, well, a surprise he got, just not the one he expected. I talked and talked and talked some more. He nodded and listened and did not speak much. I then went to my parent's home and explained to them what had happened. I began parking my car in the back of their house in order for it to be out of my wife's view. I wanted her to be wondering of my whereabouts. It was stupid and immature. I recognize that I put my parents in a very difficult predicament. However, I really had nowhere to go. In addition to that, for three days, not once did I pick up the phone to call my children. For three days, my children did not hear from me.

As I write this, a feeling of guilt and shame arises inside of me. On that fourth day, Yari calls me and tells me that the kids want to talk with me. I spoke to Nori and Jonathan for a bit and then hung up the phone and bawled my eyes out. Every evening, I would walk outside and take a peek at my old house, seeing if my sister-in-law was still staying there. I drank myself to sleep every single night. I felt so alone. Well…almost alone.

My dear friend Lisa was everything to me during these difficult times. I do not know where I would have been in those moments without her. She was a bright angel at some of my most troublesome times. My relationship with my dad was civil. Truth is, it was probably the best it had ever been. He, too, was a constant presence during those days, as well as he knew how to be. My dad has a big heart. His biggest problem is that he has convinced himself all his life that feeling his emotions, that being vulnerable, and that being kind is a weakness. Truth is, it is quite the opposite. More on that later.

I remember seeing my father's face during those moments, seeing a desperate son who was lost, clueless and in distress.

My mom, on the other hand, was scared, upset and angry at me. I am not quite sure what it was. Was it me? Was it the pain that I had initiated all those years? Was the emotional and mental anguish I had put her through too much for even a mother to bear? I wondered. Were the disappointments, her sacrifices, the unmet expectations from her first and only son too much for her? At the time, I remember longing for her during those difficult days.

On April 1, 2013, Easter Sunday, I had asked Yari if I could go over to see the kids open their Easter eggs and spend the day together. She agreed. I told her I would bring over breakfast. I had put together a breakfast taco bar, eggs, sausage scramble, diced ham, shrimp, as well as an assortment of sauces and cheeses. The kids were running around the house excitedly searching for and finding the hidden Easter eggs. They seemed so happy. I am not sure what made them the happiest. Was it getting their Easter eggs or seeing Mom and Dad both together? God, I love my kids.

On that day, Yari and I had a long conversation. I remember telling her just how sorry I was for many of the things that I had done. I told her I wanted to make things right and had asked her to speak to the therapist she was seeing. She gave me her information. Her name was Martha Lauren. About a month after our separation, I spoke with Martha and began to see her. I saw Martha quite often. Many of our sessions lasted two hours. I held nothing back.

I find it interesting how often times, people who do not feel well will go to a doctor, tell them their symptoms and then lie to them about their eating habits, physical activity, or lack thereof. I also find it amusing how people will go to a doctor when their body is not feeling well, however, they refuse to go to a therapist when their mind is ill. Keep in mind, scientific studies can prove that 80% of our diseases and sicknesses culminate in our mind. Why is it taboo in western culture to seek mental health help? We are taught to suppress our feelings and emotions, and somehow, we are to will our way into wellbeing and safety.

Anyhow, a few weeks after beginning to see Martha, it was Nori's first communion at St. Kevin's Catholic Church. We celebrated her communion with a brunch at 94th Aero Squadron, Nori's favorite restaurant. 94th Aero Squadron is a beautiful brunch restaurant with a pianist and a cozy, homey feeling to it, right next to Miami International Airport. From the windows in the restaurant, you can see the planes taking off and landing. The kids and I have traveled the world in those restaurant seats. It was a beautiful day. Not many people in our family at the time knew what was going on within my relationship with Yari. On this day, we played it off without a hitch. To be totally honest, if I would have been a gambling man, I would have bet the house on that day that we were going to get back together.

About a week later, I received a pamphlet as I exited church on a Saturday evening. The pamphlet read, "Emmaus Men's Retreat," coming up. I looked at the flyer and asked Mike, the gentleman passing it out, some questions. Remember, faith was always a deep part of me. I was born with Christ inside my soul. When I received that flyer, it was as if God was calling me to Him once again. I signed up. It was a three-day weekend retreat of men connecting with other men, allowing one another to be completely vulnerable and allowing the love and fellowship, as brothers and followers of Jesus, to reside in us.

I was in a dark place at the time. I remember arriving at the parking lot at St. Kevin's church. The retreat was to take place in the school cafeteria and in the church. I sat in my car in the parking lot for about an hour, contemplating whether to go back home or to go to the retreat. Finally, I gave in and got out of the car with my suitcase in tow. As I asked the gentleman if I was in the right place, a welcome embrace was given to me by about a dozen men, none of whom I knew, except Mike.

Mike, the man who I had just met a few short days ago, gave me a loving hug, like a longtime family member who had been gone and was now coming home. Home…I had been searching for home all my life. Truthfully, I did not realize it then. Honestly, I just realized it right now.

I have been searching for the feeling of home since as far back as my memory can take me. The love and warmth that was given to me by all these men, was so pure, so noble, so …real.

There were no hidden agendas; nobody wanted nor sought anything from me. All they asked of me was to surrender my heart to Jesus. It was a surreal weekend experience. As the retreat came to an end, I had met some incredible men from all walks of life, just doing their part to serve one another as best they could, as Jesus served us.

Serving our fellow man is the key to life. I, without a shadow of a doubt, believe that the key to life, to having fulfillment, is serving one another. Most people never recognize this. Their innate sense of self-worth can never be attained in seeking for oneself. That weekend a new seed was planted in me. One that took years to grow, but it took ahold of me. It was also the first time that I can remember a day that had gone by without alcohol or drinking, or it even occurring to me.

For a few weeks, I was on a spiritual high. I had begun exercising again. I began believing in miracles. I was convinced that Yari and I would find a way, where there was no way. I continued to see Martha Lauren, the therapist. During this time, I would see the kids whenever Yari worked, which happened to be every Wednesday and Thursday, as well as every other weekend.

Sometime mid-summer 2013, Martha had asked Yari to join me for a marital counseling session. I was hopeful. I believed that this was the beginning of a turnaround for both of us. It was not. As I look back, I often wondered, as did Martha, as to why Yari even went to the marriage counseling sessions, because it was apparent to Martha, as well as myself, that she had no desire to attempt to work things out.

Every session was avalanche after avalanche of attacks. I remember feeling baffled. I was clueless as to all the anger and vitriol she held inside. I was angry and upset that she never had expressed any of these feelings, thoughts and emotions. In hindsight, I really do not think it would have made much difference if she had. Well, I say it would not have made a difference; what I mean is, it may not have made a difference for our relationship, but it would have been a relief for her to free herself from the anger, resentment and deep-seated pain she had been carrying inside. Those five sessions with Martha did not do anything to help our relationship. In fact, I believe, they gave her added fuel, to build her fire.

It was Friday, May 10, 2013. I left work early and picked up the kids from early dismissal. I had a surprise in store. I was taking them to CB Smith Paradise Cove Water Park. I was excited. I was excited for them. It had been years since my parents took me to that waterpark. As I picked the kids up from school, Jonathan, only four years old at the time, got in the car and told me, "Papi, I got really mad at mommy." I asked him, "What happened, Macho?" Macho was a nickname I gave him since he was a little boy. He told me, "Papi, I yelled at Mommy because I told her it is your fault, it is your fault that Papi is not home anymore!" I looked at him, eyes watery and I lost it. Uncontrollable tears streamed down my cheeks. I was crushed. I was devastated.

Thank God, CB Smith Park was a 45-minute drive. It was going to take me a full 40 minutes to compose myself. As I looked at him, I pulled his face close to mine, I gently rubbed my thumb across the left side of his cheek and told him, "I am sorry. I am so, so sorry for the pain I have caused you." I was broken. I was not sure if anything could lift my spirits up; however, as soon as we got to the waterpark, everything changed. The kids began jumping for joy. As we entered the park, Nori and Jonathan went running towards the slides. "Can we go, Papi? Can we go?" I said, "Go for it." As soon as their bottoms hit the slide and they entered the water, they were rejuvenated. I could not help but smile, despite the pain I was feeling inside, at the joy my beautiful daughter Nori and my loving young son Jonathan could always bring to my heart. For a few hours, everything was okay. No...it was better than okay. For a few hours, everything was great. The kids enjoyed their time at Paradise Cove so much that just a few short months later, Nori, decided to celebrate her 9th birthday there.

That summer was hard. That summer was really painful for me. Every once in a while, it seemed Yari was nice, was kind. Then from one moment to the next, she was like a completely different person. My life was spiraling completely out of control and I had no idea the direction in which I was heading. I hated that feeling that I needed to control everything. I prided myself on being a planner, on being ultra conservative. In looking to see how everything needed to be done and in what order. I did not realize then that life, in and of itself, was uncertain. There is no certainty.

I remember every trip we would go on as a family. I needed to plan everything. I needed to plan the time, the place where we would have breakfast, lunch and dinner. I would plan the breaks in between. There was never any room for spontaneity or adventure. Everything was stoic. Every detail planned to perfection and boy…I was damn proud of it.

The problem was, I was miserable. Here I am, in essence, being damn proud of being miserable. I cannot help but laugh at myself now. Yes…I learned it is okay to laugh at myself. I remember when one plan or detail would fall out of place, everything would spiral out of control. In trying to control everything, I controlled nothing.

During this time, a deep-seated friendship was blooming with Jessie and Noel Barrera. Jessie and Noel are the parents of Gabi, Dani and Christopher, who are Nori and Jonathan's best friends. We all met at St. Kevin's as our children attended the same school. They instantly became friends with both Yari and myself. As I take an observer role of our relationship, I feel for Jessie and Noel. I have realized for quite some time, all the talk they must have heard from both of us through the years, of us bashing one another, must have been unbearably taxing for them. Heck…they could probably write a book about us, themselves. It would be called, "Chaos, in Miami. The Lives of Frank and Yari Lopez. The Insider Edition."

I have to say though, one of the best things that happened for me throughout those years, was the unwavering friendship I developed with this family. Jessie has become my sister. There is nothing that I would not do for her and her family. As you may have noticed by now, I gravitate towards women in my life. I always have. Although anger was my emotional home for much of my life, my heart has always been the size of the ocean. I have always allowed myself to feel my emotions, so, naturally, I have always understood and connected with women more so than any man I have ever met. I have many male friends, but to deeply connect with people you must be willing to get vulnerable. I did and I do. It is liberating.

I was always a safe guy friend, too. I never looked or sought anything from my women friends other than a dear, loving friendship. In the summer of 2013, a new friendship with the Barreras began to blossom.

6
DIVORCE AND THE DOWNWARD SPIRAL

"Life is like a trampoline; you have to hit rock bottom before you catapult to the top. - Frankie M Powers-

It was Christmastime 2013. Wow, what a year, I thought. After hope of reconciliation with Yari seemed out of reach, I needed to move out from my parent's home. For the first time in my life, I was out on my own, alone. I rented a two-story, two-bathroom, two-bedroom apartment in Kendall. I loved it. The kids loved it too. I would have never had found it if not for my dear friend Lisa. That year, those holidays, the lonely nights were really difficult for me. When feeling lost and lonely, there was only one person who would not let me down…that was the Captain. I always had the Captain by my side. Captain Morgan and me, together forever.

That Christmas morning, waking up without the children, was becoming all too real. The decorating was not the same. The sights, the sounds, the smells of the holidays lost some of its luster. The life I had always dreamed of was going up in flames and I did not have a hose to put out the fire. That Christmas, I went to Yari's house to visit the kids. That was one of the last times Yari and I were on speaking terms.

It was now 2014. I was in the dumps. My weight continued to skyrocket. I now weighed over 400 pounds. My two-story apartment was on the second floor, and it took me several minutes to climb up the steps. My apartment was a mess. I struggled to take a shower. I was forced to order clothes online. At work, I park in the grass right next to the office, to avoid a fifty-step walk from the parking lot. I had papers scattered everywhere, clothes laid all over the house. From my second-floor apartment, I would go upstairs to where my bathroom was to shower and wash, about three times a week. While I was in the room, I made sure to bring down some clothes for the remainder of the week. I went to visit my doctor so that I could receive an authorization to receive a handicap sticker.

At this point, I was unable to walk a few steps without experiencing shortness of breath. I would order food from restaurants, and they would have to deliver curbside, to my car, before curbside became such a thing. My ankles were swollen, my whole body was swollen. I began to have problems with my knee, so I began wearing a knee brace. Everything pained me. My sleep apnea was worse than ever. I would fall asleep on my desk, on my dining table, at restaurants, everywhere. I began to need one of those electric carts every time I went to Publix or any other department store. I do not know how I was alive.

During this time, I was taking Lisinopril for my blood pressure, Xanax for anxiety, Prilosec for my heartburn, Ambien to sleep, and Captain Morgan for companionship. I was not even able to see my daughter's soccer games; the walk was far too long for my body to absorb. When I could, I would watch with binoculars from the car.

It was now July 31, 2014. Yari comes to pick up the kids at my apartment. The usual routine is she would call from the security gate and I would buzz her in. The kids would give me a kiss and then head downstairs to go home with mom. On this particular day, I heard a sudden knock on the door. When I opened it, Yari looks at me and hands me a sealed manila envelope. She said to me, "This is for you." My eyes widened as she turned away and I knew immediately what it was. I could not believe it. My wife served me our own divorce papers. I lost it. I kind of knew it was coming; nevertheless, I guess you are never really prepared until it happens. As I look back, the truth was that I was not in love with her and I was not happy with my life, yet, her serving me those papers had me completely distraught. I believe the significance of that moment was that the dream that I had envisioned all my life, was dead. I would never have the life I always wanted. So, what did I do? Well…I opened me up a bottle of Captain's and ordered myself some food from my favorite Mexican restaurant, El Rancho Grande.

Oprah Winfrey often shares a story about the moment she was able to get over her heartbreak from her first marriage. It took me years to understand this. Oprah's aha moment came when she realized that the heartache was not from the loss of the relationship, but in the loss of the expectations that she had for the relationship. What I did not realize then was that, in fact, my dreams were not over. What was over, was the idea of what my dreams needed to be, that were, in fact, extinguished.

On August 1, 2014, I called Martha to meet up with her. I sat in her office for two hours and she calmly and soothingly assured me everything would be okay and everything with Yari would work itself out. I interpreted her words to mean that we would end up back together. I convinced myself of this. I thought, well, she knows her, she talks to her, she must know something that I don't. But what happened? What do I do? I was a mess. I was a big, fat, drunken… mess.

By mid-August, I had Nori and Jonathan seeing Martha, as well. I was deeply concerned about the psychological and emotional burden our pending divorce would have on our children. I reminded myself, that this, in fact, was the reason that I married Yari. It was for fear that if I did not, it would cause irreparable harm to my daughter. In my mind, this was a fear that seemed to be coming to fruition. What I was thinking in those moments, I recognize now, was a limited belief that I had about the pending divorce. The kids really liked Martha. She did a really great job of connecting with them and meeting them where they were at emotionally.

On August 18, 2014, I walked into the office of Christina McCarthy, my first divorce attorney. I had no idea what was in store for me. I hired her on the spot. Christina was a young, extremely kind, aspiring attorney. I remember her having just found out that she was pregnant. I remember giving her a laundry list of things I would desire from my divorce. I had wanted all sorts of ridiculous rules and enforcement of wishes I deemed necessary for my children, most of which were all fears having to do with my children's emotional well-being.

I convinced myself that if I could just get my soon to be ex-wife to agree to these things, then, maybe…just maybe…my children would have a chance to be psychologically spared from the breakup of the family dynamic.

Just as I had done after the events of September 11th, I immersed myself head on with book after book relating to parenting and the effects of divorce on children.

In between meds and drinking, and the occasional presence (being mentally present) at work, because my body may have been there but the rest of me was elsewhere, I was reading and consuming anything and everything that I could get my hands on, as far as bettering myself as a father. While at work, I began notifying the office (my father), that I was intermittently waiving late fees from the tenants. I lied. I was stealing. I was stealing from my parents, to have some extra cash to help me with some of my legal and counseling expenses. I was stealing from the two people who had always given me the opportunity to have anything and everything I ever desired and wanted, the two individuals who had always provided for me.

I was feeling down and distraught. This was the one time one would have thought I would turn to faith. Faith always being my center or safety net. But this time… I did not. I was miserable. Like most people insanely do, I wanted to continue to stew in my misery. Lisa was a steady presence in my life during these days. She would spend hours upon hours listening to my rants, hearing my self-destructive thoughts and hopelessness. I can never thank her enough for the role that she played during those dark hours. I am so grateful to God for bringing her into my life. I continued to see Martha, roughly twice a week.

As the summer came to an end, Nori's birthday was right around the corner. Yari had planned a party at the beach for our daughter. I remember feeling too hurt, too emotionally beaten up, to get myself to attend. On the day of the party, I drove to the beach, gave Nori a kiss and a present and I left. I had forgotten about this birthday. I have never asked my daughter how she felt about it. Damn it, I failed her this day, big time.

A few weeks later, the weekend of September 19th arrived, and I took Nori and Jonathan out of school for a few days. I was taking them to our favorite, or perhaps I should say, my favorite place, the most magical place on earth, Walt Disney World. By this time, between Yari and my divorce attorney, we had loosely planned our time sharing with the children. This particular weekend was my time and Yari was livid. She was furious that I decided to take the children out of school that day to go on vacation. I had let her know my plans beforehand, but it did not matter. I believe that Yari believed then, as she believes now, that going away on vacation while there is school, is irresponsible. Although I respect her beliefs, I had different views on that matter.

As we arrived at our hotel, the Disney All-Star Sports Resort, the kids were ecstatic. Nori and Jonathan both loved sports, they loved Disney, so they were in paradise. We checked into our room and then proceeded to take a bus to downtown Disney. I received my electric cart to get moving around. The next morning, we awakened extremely early and headed to Epcot. Immediately after riding my favorite ride, "Soarin", I began feeling ill. I was having heart palpitations and shortness of breath. I walked up to a staff member and told them how I was feeling. He had me sit down and gave me water. My heart was racing, and I was continuing to have palpitations. I had not walked that much in months. Heck, I couldn't walk. I was obese.

I remember feeling afraid, afraid about my heart racing, but more so, I was afraid about the children. "What if I have to go the hospital? What would happen to the kids?" I thought. I knew that Disney would be safe, but I was still concerned about them. The paramedics arrived and took my blood pressure. They told me I was okay. Disney staff sent a private driver to take myself and the kids back to the resort. Upon arrival, I began feeling chest pains again. Once again, the paramedics were called. Once again, they told me everything was clear. After contemplating for a few hours on what I should do next, I looked at the kids and told them, "I'm sorry guys. Papi is not feeling well. We have to go back home. I do not want to risk something happening to me and you guys being left alone."

As I look back, I wonder what they must have been feeling during those days. I wonder if they were frightened about something happening to their daddy. Did they think that I was going to die? Were they disappointed, after just riding one ride, having to go all the way back home? I vowed, on the drive home, that the very next day I would start dieting and stop drinking. At this point in time, it was nothing but wishful thinking.

A few weeks later, it was October 5, 2014, and I purchased tickets to the One Direction concert at Sun Life Stadium. My daughter was filled with joy. She had a huge crush on Zane. Nori, Jonathan, and I would attend with my closest friend, Lisa, and my goddaughter Gianna and Gabi. We rented a limo to arrive in stylish fashion. The event was sold out. As we arrived, moving, or better yet walking, was extremely difficult. I could barely breathe.

After entering the stadium and taking a few steps, I motioned for assistance. I could not walk. The staff called medical personnel and they requested a wheelchair. I was embarrassed; I was exhausted. I had told Lisa to take the kids with her and I would get to our ground-level seats once they brought the wheelchair. She agreed. After a few seconds had passed, I looked towards my right and I noticed my son Jonathan had tapped me on the shoulder. He then said, "Papi, I am staying with you. I am going to help take care of you." In that moment, I cried myself a river. I replied, "Okay, son, thank you." God gave me a son with such an incredible heart. There is so much magic in that boy's core.

After about 20 minutes, the wheelchair arrived, and we entered the stadium. Wow, I thought, I cannot believe the amount of people in that place. Amongst the thousands of individuals, there must have been less than thirty men. Let me tell you, that was the place to be if you were a single man looking for companionship. Within a few minutes after arriving at our seats, none other than the Ice Man, came walking towards us. Vanilla Ice walks right on by me as I shout, "Ice, Ice, Baby." He looks at me, puts his hand in the air giving me a high five, winks and says, "Word to your mother." I remember saying, "Cool, man." Brought me back visions of my high school days.

Shortly after the concert started, within approximately 45 minutes, I had to go. I was hot, I was uncomfortable, I was sweating, and Jonathan had dozed off. Medical personnel helped escort Jonathan and I to the limousine, until Lisa and the girls joined us once the show was over. I recall once again feeling sad, disappointed, frustrated and angry at myself. As I sat in the car with Jonathan being sound asleep in my lap, I told myself, I cannot continue to live this way. I knew that if I did not do something soon, I would die. I realized that my greatest fears I had ever had, leaving my children without a father, would come to fruition.

As the holidays came around, I could barely move. Amazon was my saving grace. Amazon…and Armando. Armando was an employee that worked for my dad and I for many years. He was a handyman…well, not really. Armando was so much more than that. Armando was like the brother I never had. He helped me put up Christmas ornaments, he helped me bag the children's gifts, he helped me through some troublesome and heart wrenching moments.

As 2014 came to an end and 2015 began, I had an outpatient appointment at Jackson South Hospital in Miami, Florida on January 7, 2015. God was looking after me that day. Truth is, God has always been looking after me. In fact, He has not only been looking after me, He has been carrying me for many years.

As I checked in for the appointment, a nurse came over to check my pulse. He immediately called another nurse and told him, "Can you please check his pulse?" They looked at one another, looked back at me and asked me, "Hey, man, are you okay?" I remember feeling remotely concerned at their question as I replied, "Sure, why?" They replied, "We are going to bring you in for some further examination." They then asked me again, "Are you sure you are okay?" My reply this time was, "I think so. Why?" I answered apprehensively. Immediately a head female nurse came over to me and told me, "Mr. Lopez, your resting heart rate is 160." At this point there were four people in the room and from the looks on their faces, I knew this was not good.

They rushed me to emergency. This gentle and kind female nurse held my hand and told me, "Mr. Lopez, you are going to be okay. We are going to give you some medicine through your IV." So, she did and…nothing happened. I took a quick peek at the monitor at my heart rate, and it read 162. She repeats, "Mr. Lopez, it is going to be okay. We have to give you some more medicine." She then called something out loud and before I knew it, I was surrounded by medical personnel. They began talking and whispering amongst themselves. The kind nurse, gently looked into my eyes and told me once again, "Mr. Lopez, we are going to give you a little more medicine and your heart rate should slow down." She did and…nothing happened.

Now I was beyond frightened. Tears began to flow down the sides of my cheeks. I started thinking of my parents, who were away at the cabin in North Carolina, not having any clue as to what is going on with their son. I began to think of my children. I grabbed the nurse's hand and pleaded to her, "Please, help me. Please, save me. I have two children. I cannot leave my children without a father." I looked up at the monitor and noticed that the medication was not working. Before I knew it, she called someone, and a medical staff member came near my bedside with the machine that I had always seen in movies but never witnessed in real life. The one with the two "X's." It was the device used to revive someone. I believe the medical personnel saw my face and responded to my facial expressions. They said, "Mr. Lopez, no need to panic. This is standard procedure." Now look, I have been to enough emergency rooms and hospitals before to know, that what was happening to me, at that moment, at that time, was not standard procedure.

A few minutes later, a gentleman came by and introduced himself. "Hi, Frank, my name is Dr. Mendoza. I am a cardiologist." He then proceeded to tell me that the medication they had been giving me was not working and they were going to have to do a special procedure. He then informed me they were going to give me some anesthesia that would put me to sleep. He explained the procedure to me as such, the heart is like a clock and it is off rhythm right now. We just have to give it a little jump start to get it back in sync. I remember him being so nonchalant about it, as if this was perfectly normal. My mind was saying, hey, look Doc, I sure as hell know it is not perfectly normal to have to jump start my heart. I am 40 years old and in all these years, I have lived without getting a jump start. Finally, I signed some papers and the next thing I knew, I opened my eyes and the procedure was done. It was over. He looked at me with deep compassion and empathy and told me, "Look, son, you have to lose weight. You were having cardiac arrest. If you had not come into this hospital, there is a good chance that within 24 hours, you would have been dead."

I immediately contacted the offices of Dr. Moises Jacobs and within a few weeks, I was scheduled to have the gastric sleeve operation. The day before the surgery, as I walked into his office and jumped on the scale with my father next to me, I could hardly believe my eyes…448 pounds, 448 pounds. How I ever reached that weight is unfathomable to me. What I can tell you is this, I sure as hell did not get that way eating salads.

After having the gastric sleeve operation, the doctor began giving me a list of what I was able to eat and what I needed to do in order to get my health back on track. He also told me I needed to refrain from alcohol for at least a year, because the lining of my stomach was extremely sensitive. After the operation, I stayed with my parents for about two weeks. My mom was really great during this time. She fed me, bathed me and took care of me. I cannot fathom the heartache and pain that my mother and father must have endured during those moments, having to see their son so helpless and hopeless.

In less than two weeks, I was down 50 pounds. In exactly one month, I had broken the office record. In one month, I lost 100 pounds. Literally 100 pounds, insane. I felt so much better. My stomach had shrunk immensely. I mean, it is 100 freaking pounds. Well, what do I do to celebrate? I must celebrate, I thought. What is one or two drinks going to do to me anyhow? So, I poured myself that first drink. I looked at it for a few minutes, sipped it, drank it and...I never stopped.

Two drinks became three and three became four. Having had the gastric sleeve surgery, I could no longer turn to food to deal with my depression and to deal with my pain. I gave that job back to the Captain as I poured all of that into my body. I stayed stuck on my weight loss. I hovered near 335 pounds for quite some time. I continued to see my therapist until...all of sudden, she was arrested. She was indicted for conspiracy to commit Medicare fraud. What? What, I told myself? God, help me.

By the end of the summer, I started seeing a psychiatrist named Dr. Guerrero. What a deeply loving and caring man. He too had the gastric sleeve procedure done. He was deeply concerned about my drinking and told me so. He also informed me that if I did not watch myself, that my stomach would expand again, and I would be able to eat like I did prior to the surgery. However, what I did not know at the time, and truthfully so many people are unaware of, is that the surgery does not fix the problem. The problem with weight, with obesity, with drugs, with alcohol...these things are not the problem but mere symptoms of the real problem. The problem lies in the mind. So, in the meantime, Dr. Guerrero put me on some anti-depressant drugs.

It was now August, and I was having difficulties getting any traction on my divorce, so I sought other counsel and hired Anastasia Garcia.

In the meantime, there was friction between Yari and me. And I did something that lit a fuse in her to this very day. I threw Nori a small birthday party gathering of approximately twenty to twenty-five family members and friends and did not invite Yari. I have not lived it down ever since. I was wrong, I admit it. I wish there was some way I could take it back, but I cannot. I realize I cannot change what I did. And worst of all, here I was putting Nori, once again, in the middle between her mom and me. I was dead wrong.

On December 15, 2015, my divorce papers were finalized. It was done. My marriage was over. I did not make it to court that day, there really was no reason to go. By this time, the final divorce proceedings actually gave me a sense of relief. I had already accepted the fact that my marriage was irreparable.

It was now Christmastime. Although Christmas had lost a little bit of its charm in the past few years, I was feeling somewhat better. I had recently found out that Disney's Hollywood Studios, Osbourne Festival of Lights would be coming to an end as of December 2015. There was no way I was going to miss out on this last Christmas extravaganza. I mean…Disney? Christmas? So, on December 18, 2015, the kids and I drove off to Disney World and stayed at Disney's Port Orleans Resort. We immediately took a bus and headed to Disney's Hollywood Studios. By this time, there was no way that I was walking into a theme park without my Captain Morgan.

I began to fill up two 20-ounce bottles of Lipton Iced Tea with the Captain and took it with me in my travel bag. It was a simple and inconspicuous way of getting my fix at discounted prices. Although I fooled the Disney employees, I sure as heck did not fool my kids. By this time Nori was 11 years old and Jonathan was 7. We had a really beautiful weekend. We enjoyed the lights, the sounds and the beautiful Christmas cheer. Our weekend culminated on Sunday at the Magic Kingdom with Mickey's Very Merry Christmas Party. We rode rides, we laughed, we ate and we had hot chocolate. It was really an extraordinary time spent with the children and I did not need to be assisted by medical personnel this time.

*****

As 2015 came to an end and 2016 began, my drinking got progressively worse. How bad? Bad. By springtime, there were days that I was drinking around the clock. I had purchased a 32-ounce Yeti silver cup. Yeah…every single time I see one of those, I wonder what is it that they are drinking? Hmm. When I realized that there were moments that my drinking just would not stop, and I ceased to have control over when and how much I drank, I switched to vodka. I told myself, you cannot smell vodka. While that is partially true, it is also true that if you have been drinking for 20 of the last 24 hours of the day, even vodka comes out of your pores. There were times I would show up at Jonathan's basketball games at Tamiami Park and gargle with Listerine, thinking I could fool all those around me. The truth was, I was fooling no one. On second thought, maybe I was fooling someone; I was fooling... myself.

It was now, September 2016. I decided to coach Jonathan's basketball team with the assistance of my godson and nephew, Gus Rodriguez. Gus was great. That young man is such a loving and caring soul; he always has been. He helped me out quite a bit. I remember several days showing up to practice drunk. As I look back in shame, I cannot help but wonder what the hell was wrong with me? I realize now that I was a sick, sick man.

It was also around this time in November 2016, that my psychiatrist, Dr. Guerrero, had a heart attack and died. Wow, what a shocker to me. To make matters worse, my therapist, Martha, was convicted and sentencing was to begin soon. I had developed a deep affection for my psychiatrist but more so for my therapist. I really cared for her and her family. I believe that I used those instances as excuses to convince myself that these were more good reasons to continue my reckless path and journey.

As 2016 ended and 2017 came around, I became dangerous. I mean...I was dangerous. I was a danger to everyone who was near me. I was a danger to my parents, my children, whoever was out on the street, and myself. I had also taken this time to mix and match my drinking. I would drink seven days a week. I was drinking Grey Goose for five days of the week, and the good 'ole Captain for the other two days. I was drinking almost a jug of liquor a day. I would drink six of the 1.75-liter bottles of vodka or rum in a span of six days. I was a walking canister of gasoline ready to explode. As for the few friends who remained in my life, I have no idea how they managed to stay close to me. It was Ralph, Mari, Armando, Ivan, Lisa and Jessie and the Barreras. I do not know why they put up with me. I do not know why they cared for me. Hell, I didn't even care for me. I hated myself. All this time, I was a solo drinker. I did not need anyone to accompany me. I would drink primarily at home, alone, for the last several years.

Around springtime 2017, my counselor was sentenced to prison for five years. As soon as that happened, I lost complete control. My car became a moving bar. I had a small cooler that was always filled with ice, tea, water, diet coke and cranberry juice. Now, as you can well imagine, those bottled waters were vodka. And the tea...yeah, you guessed it; it was rum. My 32-ounce Yeti cup and I were a team. You know what cell phones mean to people (never leave home without it). That is what my Yeti cup and alcohol were to me. If I had to go to Publix, I took my Yeti cup. In the mornings to drop the kids off at school, I was with my Yeti cup. I would drive to work, get to the office, and I was hammered. I was drunk. I made mistakes, countless mistakes.

Several times I would wake up in the morning and open my refrigerator to find food from restaurants or bags from Publix; I would have no recollection of having been there. Every now and again, I would hear a knock on the door, and I would panic. I would often think to myself what if it is the police? What if I killed somebody? I am going to jail for manslaughter, I would think. Fortunately, most of the time, the knock on the door would be an Amazon delivery or a neighbor letting me know that I had left my car door or window open. I was a danger. I was a threat to everyone and anyone that entered my path. I would constantly get into heated arguments with people everywhere I would go. It is a miracle I never hurt anyone, or anyone hurt me. As I sit back and reminisce, I think of my poor children and what they must have gone through, what they must have witnessed. Many times, I must have shamed them. They must have felt unimaginable fear. I was sick.

By the end of summer 2017, I began to have delirium tremens (shaking). I was not able to do simple tasks. I could not even sign a check. As I write this, I remember my dear friend Noel (Jessie's husband), asking me several times if I was okay, helping me fill out forms that I was unable to fill out on my own. I would miss countless days of work, in which I was unable to even move. My body was immobile, I would throw up white foam-like bile. I was destroying the lining of my stomach.

On the days I was with the kids, on school mornings, Nori would often have to make herself and her brother breakfast and bring me a hospital bed pan so I could throw up. I do not believe Yari ever really knew what the kids truly went through. I do not think anyone really knew. Truth is, I am certain that I do not even know.

On the weekends when I had the children, about 75% of the time, quite an accomplishment for where I was during these days; I was able to get through the morning and afternoon without a drink. The problems would arise when I would wake up in the middle of the night, and if I was still intoxicated. If I still had some liquor in me and it was three in the morning, I would be off to the races. I could not stop. Alcohol was my master and I…was its slave.

It was October 2017. A friend of mine, Mari, had rented a room for the weekend of her birthday at the Margaritaville Resort in Hollywood, Florida. She invited me to go. It was the weekend of Jonathan's birthday. On Sunday, October 8th, I was scheduled to pick him up and take him to his favorite restaurant, Benihana; however, on the night before, October 7th, after consuming only God knows how many vodka drinks, as I stood, or better yet hobbled, on the 17th floor balcony, I do not know what happened, but I apparently fell, hit my mouth and almost flew off the balcony to what would have been my untimely death.

As I opened my eyes, there were paramedics and blood everywhere. I busted my mouth open and had to go to the hospital to get seven stitches near my chin. I was beat up. My body was in severe pain, but the pain I felt the most, was the realization of what I had just done to my son. I had to call my son and wish him a happy birthday and cancel our plans. I lied to him. I made up some crazy story that someone slipped into me and that I lost my balance and hit my mouth on the bar. I was embarrassed, I was ashamed. That day I told myself that this is it. I am done. No more drinking. I quit, and I did…until six days later…I started my adventure again. Alcoholism is a disease, yet I did not know it then. I believed it was about will and that I lacked the will power to quit. It is really hard to explain. I will attempt to do so later on in my story.

View From the 17th Floor Balcony

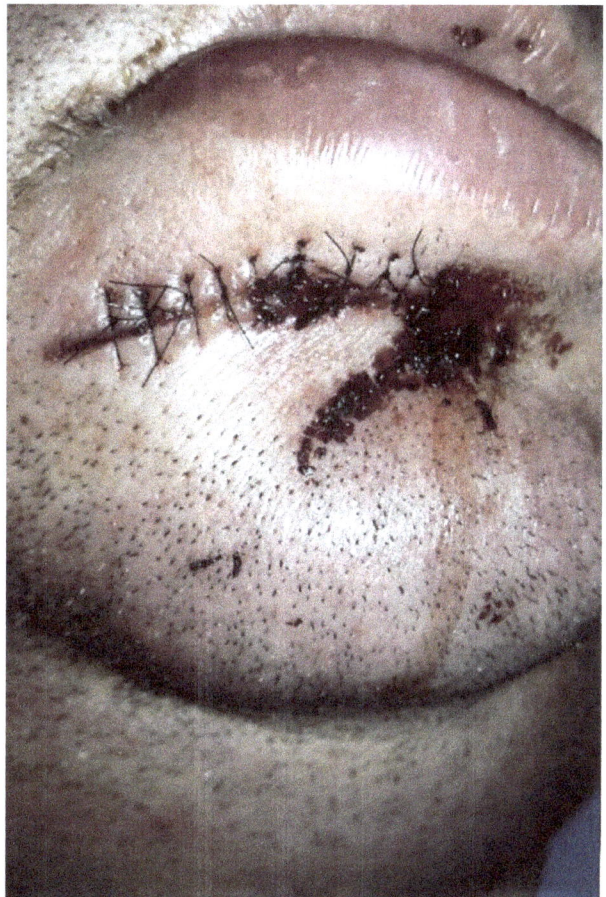

My stitches

It was now October 22, 2017. The kids, myself, and my buddy Ralph and some friends had purchased tickets to the Miami Dolphins versus New York Jets football game. A friend of ours, David, had a Winnebago, and we tailgated and partied hard with him before game time. Truth is, I started way before. Actually, I had not stopped from the night before. I was hurting; I was really intoxicated. Somehow, others did not seem to notice. I guess I pulled it off, or, at least, I thought I did.

I did not drive to the football game on this particular day. I left my car at Ralph's house. After the game, we went to his home to pick up my car. On the way home, I do not really know what happened, but what I do remember is getting into a huge argument with my daughter, Nori.

Let me tell you something about Nori. Nori does not raise her voice. Nori does not cuss. Nori has never talked back to me. Whatever it was that happened that night, Nori had decided she had enough.

As I arrived at my parking spot in my apartment complex, Nori called her mom and told her to pick her up. I remember yelling at Nori and condemning her for calling her mom. I then looked over at Jonathan and asked him, "Are you leaving me too?" He cried and said, "I am sorry, Papi. I am sorry. I cannot leave Nori alone." As I write this, tears stream down the side of my face. My poor son and the inner turmoil I must have put him through that night. My poor daughter and how she must have felt to have gotten to that point to call her mom.

The following Wednesday morning, Yari dropped the kids off at my house, as was the norm, so that I would drive them to school. As I opened the door, I noticed it was only Jonathan, Nori was nowhere to be found. I asked Jonathan where was Nori? He told me, "Nori does not want to come spend time with you for now. But I told her that I was not going to leave my daddy. I wanted to be with you, Papi." Oh, my God. I was crushed. I was torn up inside. What have I done? What the hell have I done? For a few weeks, it was only Jonathan and I. Nori would not even talk to me on the phone. That year when Christmastime came around and it came time for pictures with Santa, there are none of Nori. They are of Jonathan, all by himself.

Around Thanksgiving, I finally spoke to Nori on the phone. I remember asking her, "Are you not going to spend time with me anymore?" Her response was, "Are you still drinking?" I could not lie to her, I responded, "Yes." At that moment I felt embarrassed, ashamed and defeated. Nori must have felt that I was choosing alcohol over my own precious daughter.

It was now December 1, 2017. My friend Mari and I had tickets to go see comedian Gabriel Iglesias (also known as Fluffy) at the Miami Arena. I showed up at Mari's house and had one drink after another. The next thing I recall, is waking up in my apartment with the same clothes that I had worn the night prior. I had zero recollection of how I got home. I immediately called her and said, "What happened? How come we never made it to the show?" She replied, "What are you talking about? You even entered the Fluffy Dance Contest. I said, "What? You are lying!" I exclaimed. She said, "Frank, you got on stage and entered a dance competition. And not only that, you were runner up…you should have won." I did not believe her, I thought she was pulling a prank on me, until…she sent me a picture. I was stunned. I had no memory of this. Oh, my God, I thought, as I poured myself another drink.

That night, as I walked up the stairs to shower, while in the shower, I do not know what I did, but I stuck my finger so deep into my ear that I hurt myself so much, that I saw stars. My left ear was in severe pain for several weeks. After a few weeks, I went to get my hearing checked. The results were that I had lost 50% of my hearing in my left ear by damaging my ear drum. For a while, I would joke around, "It was too bad I did not lose it while I was married." Truthfully, on Yari's behalf, she never spoke. Part of our problem was she never really expressed any of her feelings and emotions to me. Anyhow, by Monday morning, December 4th, I was beat up. I could not take it anymore. I realized I could not continue to live like this anymore.

On December 5th, 2017, I called Armando between 7:00 and 8:00 pm. I had a Captain Morgan's drink in my Yeti cup on my end table near my recliner and a 9-millimeter in my hand. I was bawling. I told myself, and him, "I cannot do this anymore. I cannot live like this anymore, Armando." I do not remember what he told me that evening. What I do remember is that he immediately came to visit me. After several hours of listening to me shed my tears, he managed to convince me to give him the gun.

In that moment, I believed that by ending my life, I would end all the suffering of those around me. I felt like I was a burden to all those who cared for me. Thank God for Armando that day, or I would not be here.

The next day, Wednesday, December 6th, I called the law offices of Barry Yablen, one of the top divorce attorneys in all of Florida and made an appointment. I was desperate to get my daughter back. His assistant, Martha, notified me he did not have an opening until Monday. However, hearing the desperation in my voice, she put me on hold and after a few minutes told me, "Come tomorrow. Tomorrow, December 7th, at 10am." I agreed.

That night, Jonathan had a basketball game at Tamiami, and I saw my daughter and assertively told her, "You are coming with me this weekend." She looked at me and fearfully said, "No, Dad, I am not." Know that I have never been physically violent with either one of my children. Till this very day, I have never raised my hand and physically hurt either one of them. However, God only knows that the emotional scars that I have given them have been more than any child should ever have to bear. After the game, Jonathan came home with me. He showered and went to bed. I poured myself some vodka, and it was game time for one more night.

It was now Thursday, December 7, 2017. I am level-headed, or as level-headed as I could have been at the time and took Jonathan to school. After I dropped him off, I parked my truck by the school cafeteria near a shaded tree. The same cafeteria that was a church almost thirty years prior, where I used to pray for that love I had always yearned for. I pulled my seat back to take a short nap. My appointment with my new attorney would not be for another 2 ½ hours.

At 9:15am I woke up, fixed my seat and exited the school by the church. As I made a left on 127th Avenue and SW 40th Street, about a half block away, I sat idle, stopped in traffic. I suddenly saw a white dove flying near my front windshield. The dove flew left, it flew right. I was puzzled. For a moment, I remember hearing my inner voice saying, "God, are you trying to tell me something?" I nodded my head, side-to-side, telling myself, "Frank, you are going crazy." Suddenly, the dove flew circling around my truck and got back towards my front windshield, looked right at me, and flew away as the traffic dissipated. I swear I smacked myself on the left side of my cheek wondering if I was dreaming. It was almost unreal. It would be hard for me to believe anyone if they were telling me this story. Heck, I had a hard time believing it myself.

Anyhow, off to Coral Gables to meet Mr. Barry Yablen. As I walked in, I had the tremors. Martha opened the sliding office window, introduced herself and then shortly thereafter, called me in. As I walked in, a tall but gentle looking fellow introduced himself and said, "Hi, Frank. My name is Barry Yablen. Nice to meet you." After introducing myself, he proceeded to tell me, "You know, Frank I was not supposed to be here today. I had a wake this morning. But Martha told me you sounded really bad, and, I don't know...I felt like God told me that I needed to see you." Immediately I got chills, goosebumps. I told him to wait one minute. In that moment, although I had gone to Catholic school all my life and had gone to hundreds, if not thousands of services: in that particular moment, I could not believe what I was hearing. I immediately did a Google search for, what is the symbol of the Holy Spirit? The answer...a white dove. I broke down again. I looked up to the ceiling and put my hands in prayer position, and said, "Thank you, God."

I do not know what must have been going through Barry's mind at the time, but he must have thought I was going crazy. Barry has been my attorney for over three years. I had not realized it until this moment, although I have mentioned my faith in God many times in our interactions, I believe that that has been the one and only time that I have ever heard him mention anything about faith. Truth is, I do not even know what his faith is.

I began telling Barry about my whole situation. He leaned in, he listened, and then he looked at my divorce case number. He looked at me and said, "You know, you have a court hearing." I said, "What?" He said, "Yes, you don't know about it?" I replied, "No." He then continued, "I have a pretty good feeling it has to do with your drinking." As he began looking over the case, he told me, 'Frank, Yari is seeking full custody of both of your children." I said, "What?!" I then yelled, "No! No! No!" I begged him, "Help me. Help me, Barry. Please help me. What do I have to do?? Please tell me what I have to do!"

He replied, "Frank, I will represent you under one condition." I said, "Yes, anything. Anything." He said, "Frank, you must stop drinking right now." I looked at him and told him, "It is done." He told me, "I need you to begin to attend AA meetings and to make sure that someone signs off on worksheets that you were present." He then told me that he wanted me to see a substance abuse specialist named Charlie Horner. He also required me to go see another counselor named Susan Wilder.

He then vowed to do whatever he could do so that I could spend some time with the children during the Christmas holidays. He just had me guarantee him of one thing. "Frank, I need you to promise me that no matter what, you will not drink." In addition, he also required me to take frequent random urine tests to make sure that I was not drinking. I did not hesitate; I needed my kids. As I mention needing my children, I cannot help but think of Robin Williams from the movie Mrs. Doubtfire. I was Mrs. Doubtfire. I hired Barry immediately.

Barry then proceeded to contact Yari's attorney. Thankfully, Yari agreed to allow me to take the children with me to my parents' cabin in North Carolina for the New Year's holiday. It was the first time in several months where my whole family was going to be reunited. It was my nephews, my parents, Nori, Jonathan and myself. It was also the first time, in what seemed like forever, that I was going to have time to spend with my precious daughter. There was absolutely nothing I was going to do to jeopardize that.

On December 8, 2017, I walked into Sabal Palm Alcoholics Anonymous room in Kendall, Florida. I walked in and for the very first time in my life I stood up and admitted, "My name is Frank, and I am an alcoholic." I remember feeling skeptical, insecure and …frightened.

I attended a meeting every day for the next five months or so. I actually attended various meetings on the same day on many occasions. On Christmas Day I attended three. On our winter break trip with the children in North Carolina, I had my parents drop me off at several meetings, often an hour or so from where we were staying. While in the cabins, I thoroughly enjoyed my first nights having both of my children present in over two months, which had seemed like an eternity to me. We laughed, we ate, we made smores and saw snow. We had a great time getting away and spending time together. It was also the first time since I was 16 years old, now over 27 years, in which I spent the holidays sober.

I read thoroughly the Big Book of Alcoholics Anonymous every morning and every single night. I read those twelve steps of the Big Book over and over again. The first step is to admit that you were powerless over alcohol and that your life had become unmanageable. That was an easy check mark for me. I was hopeless. The most important and vital check for myself, and for what I believe to be foundational to life and to staying sober, was the third step, which was…made a decision to turn our will and our lives over to the care of God, as we understood Him. In a nutshell, it is to recognize that in life there are things that we can control, however, most things, we cannot control.

If we are doing our best and things do not work out for us, it is having the discernment to recognize that that was God's will. It is the realization that life does not always work out the way we desire it to and there is not a damn thing we can do about it. It sounds simple, right? Well, …not really, I chuckle, not so fast. The way Alcoholics, or Narcotics, or Overeaters Anonymous works is, they are a 12-step program for one to live by; in following those 12-steps, one will be able to live a full and transformational life, a life of real freedom. A life free of dependency of anything or anyone. A life filled with compassion, with love, with acceptance and humility.

Alcoholics Anonymous (AA) meetings start with an introduction, a set of rules to follow, an explanation of who we are and a short welcome for newcomers. The meeting begins with the serenity prayer:

> *God grant me the Serenity to accept the things I cannot change, Courage to change the things I can, and the Wisdom to know the difference.*

Shortly thereafter, the chosen speaker of the day choses a story or passage from the Big Book on how to stay sober and live a full life, while maintaining their sobriety. After the speaker shares their experience, strength and hope, they begin to tell us that freedom from drinking is not only possible but attainable, if you follow these 12-steps:

1. We admitted we were powerless over alcohol—that our lives had become unmanageable.
2. Came to believe a Power greater than ourselves could restore us to sanity.
3. Made a decision to turn our will and our lives over to the care of God as

we understood Him.
4. Made a searching and fearless moral inventory of ourselves.
5. Admitted to God, to ourselves, and another human being the exact nature of our wrongs.
6. Were entirely ready to have God remove all these defects of character.
7. Humbly asked Him to remove our shortcomings.
8. Made a list of all persons we had harmed and became willing to make amends to them all.
9. Make direct amends to such people wherever possible, except when to do so would injure them or others.
10. Continued to take personal inventory and when we were wrong promptly admitted it.
11. Sought through prayer and meditation to improve our conscious contact with God as we understood Him, praying only for knowledge of His will for us and the power to carry that out.
12. Having had a spiritual awakening as a result of these steps, we tried to carry this message to alcoholics and to practice these principles in all our affairs.

I remember at first feeling quite intimidated. As I watched and listened to the people introducing themselves in many of the rooms, with over 30 years of sobriety, they were still coming to meetings every day. I remember thinking, oh, my God. Do I have to do this every day for the rest of my life? Funny thing is, in western civilization, we all want a quick fix. Okay, tell me, what I have to do, and I will do it, but we want anything and everything and we want it, now. That, in and of itself, is the problem. That is why you will often hear a catchphrase or a common thread in the rooms of AA that says, "One day at a time."

The meetings are generally run by two people. One is a speaker, the other…" the bartender." Yes, you heard that right, the bartender. The bartender stands behind the coffee bar and serves coffee, snacks, and sells water and soda. There are no fees in AA. Donations are encouraged to keep up with the costs, however, nothing is asked for and nothing is pushed. A basket is passed around the tables near the end of the meeting and much like the baskets at church people pitch in whatever they can. After the speaker of the day shares his story, a microphone gets passed around and others share their thoughts and/or experiences. No one is required to speak; you chime in, if you feel you have something valuable to say. At the end of the meeting, a member is chosen to pass out chips for those that have attained a certain timeframe of sobriety.

A white chip is the most important chip you can get. By grabbing a white chip, you admit that you are ready to change your ways and commit to one full day of not drinking. A green chip commemorates 30 days of sobriety; a blue chip 90; a red chip 6 months; a gold chip 9 months. At a year of sobriety, there is a monthly gathering for all members having achieved the yearly milestone during that month. That particular month there is a party…it is called birthday night. You receive a gold medallion. The evening culminates in a celebration, where cake and soft drinks are served.

AA is a gathering of people from all walks of life, where everyone realizes that no matter how different we may seem to be, we are all one and part of the same human race. It does not matter if you are rich, poor, black or white. Addiction does not discriminate in any shape or form. In AA, sponsorship is encouraged. A sponsor is a fellow AA member who has done the 12-steps and now offers their guidance by being a mentor to another who struggles with addiction.

AA is what it claims to be…anonymous. Nothing that is said or that happens in these meetings is to be spoken of outside the walls of the room. No one is to disclose anyone's identity. It is an unwritten rule, a code of conduct. Integrity is paramount, there is no judgement. If you mess up or relapse, you are welcome the very next day, or, truthfully, the very same day. In a way, it is like one big family. For many people, it is their only one.
Meetings are held seven days a week throughout all hours of the day. Meetings can start anywhere from 5:30 am all the way to 10:00 pm.

AA taught me a lot. Funny thing though…when I walked in, I thought I knew everything. Within a couple of weeks, I became certain of it, until…later on, I realized, that was the problem. You cannot will yourself to sobriety. Will power only works for so long.

At the end of every session, everyone locks hands and says the Our Father, The Lord's Prayer:

Our Father, who art in heaven,
hallowed be thy Name,
thy kingdom come,
thy will be done,
on earth as it is in heaven.
Give us this day our daily bread.
And forgive us our trespasses,
as we forgive those
who trespass against us.
And lead us not into temptation,
but deliver us from evil.

*For thine is the kingdom,
and the power, and the glory,
for ever and ever. Amen.*

For a long time, I did not realize the significance of that prayer. The key to the Lord's prayer is the following words: "Thy kingdom come; Thy will be done."

The History of AA

The first ever archived report on the effects of alcohol and it being thought of as a mental disease, was in 1784 by, none other than, Benjamin Rush, founding father and signer of the Declaration of Independence. In 1784, he published a pamphlet entitled, "An Inquiry into the Effects of Ardent Spirits on the Human Mind and Body." He described how alcoholism was a disease. Benjamin Rush today is viewed as the father of American Psychiatry. He wrote about alcoholism, "The use of strong drink is at first the effect of free agency. From habit it takes place and then from necessity."

In 1935 in Akron, Ohio, home to future NBA Hall of Famer, Lebron James, a chance meeting between a New York stockbroker, Bill W., and one of the most anonymous legends of all time, Akron surgeon, Bob, began a fellowship that for the next 85 years has saved millions of people across the globe. Bill W. and Dr. Bob began Alcoholics Anonymous in a desperate last call for hope in their personal struggles to survive alcoholism. In 1935, Alcoholics Anonymous was born. It is a fellowship that emphasizes universal spiritual values in daily living based on biblical institutions from Oxford groups in America. Members of the Oxford group began, possibly the first self-development program in the history of the world, that would soon serve as a catalyst for growth, empowerment and personal freedom.

It was a formula based on taking a self-inventory of who you are and who it is you desire to be. It is focused on having integrity and character and admitting one's wrongs and wrongdoings. It detailed the importance of putting ego and pride aside and instead showing humility by making amends when one is able to do so. It made adamant the importance of using prayer and meditation to surrender to the powers that be, whether it be to God, or the universe. In conclusion, it was showing that the key to finding fulfillment in life was by carrying the message to others in service and in love. These tenets became some of the principles and values for AA and proved to be an invaluable resource for those seeking freedom in the only place where one can truly be free, "freedom from within."

It is the freedom of accepting oneself with all our faults and imperfections. It is in giving compassion and empathy to oneself and to others. Bill W. and Bob were wise beyond their years. They realized that AA could not be monetized or offer memberships because if it did, it would sooner or later be monopolized for power, control and greed. They realized that if this happened, the message would be evaporated.

What most of us never realize, or come to terms with, is that every single one of us suffers from doubt and fear and are often imprisoned by our minds. While imprisoned in his small cell in a German concentration camp, Victor Frankel, survivor and New York Times best-selling author wrote, "Man's Search for Meaning.". The one thing that he recognized while he was imprisoned was that no matter where he was, no one was able to take away his thoughts.

"I can go anywhere in the world I want to go and live wherever I want to live. No one can take away my imagination." Imagine that…we can all go back to who we all were at one time, the dreamer, the believer, inside every one of us before life and our subconscious mind imprisoned us all.

AA and the 12-step program are a blueprint for a life that values the sentiments of human beings and our basic human needs of love/connection, contribution and growth over our selfish desires of significance, greed and material accumulations.

*****

On January 6, 2018, my mom's birthday, the kids and I awakened in my parents' cabin in Piney Creek, North Carolina. We had a big breakfast and a few hours later headed back home to Miami. The big week was coming up; on January 10, 2018, I would finally have my court hearing. Yari was seeking full custody of our children. I was prepared and willing to take full responsibility for all my failures and wrongdoings.

I woke up early that morning and went straight to a 5:30 am AA meeting. I had asked my fellowship friends for well-wishes and prayers. After the meeting came to a close, I drove to St. Kevin's Catholic Church to attend the 7:30 am service at the chapel. Father Sardania held the service. Once service was finished, I kindly asked him for a special prayer. He put his hand on my shoulder and without thinking twice, prayed with me. I have always had tremendous faith, but on this very day, I was frightened. As I got into prayer and my knees hit the floor, I called out to Jesus, "Jesus, please help me."

I remember being dressed in a navy-blue suit, a color that has psychologically proven to show stability and confidence. I walked into the court room with Barry and truthfully, Barry held me that day. Opposing counsel was Barbara Queens. She threw everything she had at me. As you will see throughout my story, I have tried to give my best efforts to take full responsibility for my life and to make amends to those whom I have hurt and who have suffered by my actions. Needless to say, I can say without hesitation, Barbara Queens is not a decent human being. The anger, hate, and vitriol that spewed out of her mouth throughout my court appearances is downright shameful for anyone towards someone who she does not even know. Facts seemed unimportant to Barbara.

Anyway, after careful consideration, the judge ruled in my favor and I was extremely grateful that I did not lose my children. Now…there were a multitude of things I had to agree to do, such as, continue to go to AA meetings, take random urine tests, and use Soberlink twice a day.

Soberlink is a breathalyzer test used to determine a person's alcohol levels. You place a straw in a hole, turn the machine on with the press of a button and you exhale your breath. After several seconds, it would measure a reading and the reading would be transmitted to the Soberlink station, where a report would then be sent to all legal parties. In addition, I had to continue to see Charlie, my substance abuse therapist.

As I exited the courtroom, I looked at Barry and shared a warm embrace. I looked into his eyes with my hands on his shoulders and said to him, "Barry, thank you so much for everything you did for me in there. Thank you for the way you handled yourself in that courtroom. I want to tell you, no matter what my ex-wife's attorney ever says about me, it is okay to go after her fairly, but do not ever disrespect or put down my ex-wife in the courtroom. If you were ever to speak to her the way that Barbara ripped into me, I would have to dismiss you as my counsel." I do not know why I felt the need to tell Barry that. I didn't have to. That was not in his nature. Barry was a class act. I must say, he and I have had a few disagreements and differences at certain moments, but that man is a man of honor.

It took me a few years to figure out why some people would do the kind of work that Barry does; people who make their livelihood, oftentimes, by destroying one another and by breaking up families. Well…that was not Barry. I believe that for Barry, being a divorce attorney was not a career choice but a vocation. It is a vocation to do whatever he could to help people going through difficult circumstances and in doing so, providing children hope of a more promising tomorrow. I personally do not know what Barry's opinion of me is, but I cherish that man and his entire staff. If this world had more people like Barry and Jessie (other counsel), we would be living in a world closer to utopia then dystopia.

I got into AA, went to court and got sober. Life was perfect, right? Well, not so fast. I managed to stay sober for a little while. Meanwhile, I had also packed on quite a few pounds, although nowhere near as heavy as I once was. On February 5, 2018, I made a decision to lose weight and hit the gym. I went all out. As I stated earlier, I have been an all or nothing guy most of my life. I would either give all that I have or give very little. There was never a halfway point with me. If something was important to me, you were going to get everything that I had.

Around the same time, a Jamaican gentleman named Randy, came by Opa Locka, sharing an interest in buying a few of our apartment buildings. He invited me to lunch at Shula's Steak 2. After several lunches, we quickly became friends. I told him we were not interested in selling a few of the buildings. If we were to sell, he would have to purchase all 24 of them. After talking it over with his business partners, he was all in. I could not believe it. I remember feeling excited for my parents, whose long days in the office were becoming burdensome. I felt it was time for them to relax and enjoy a little bit of the hard-earned fruits of their labor.

In the meantime, I continued to hit the gym and engage in a high protein, low carb diet. The pounds started to melt off. I decided to double dip on the cardio. I would exercise beginning at four in the morning and then, again, in the early evening. I also decided to sign up to coach Jonathan's basketball team. My day was jampacked. It was, wake up, go to the gym, go to a meeting, go to work, and in between, coach Jonathan's basketball team or go to my daughter Nori's soccer practice and make certain I saw Charlie once a week. Fortunately for myself, I established tight friendships in the soccer community. The deepest of those friendships was Jessie and the Barrera family. They have become as close to me as any family I have ever known. I love those people with all my heart and soul. They have loved me through thick and thin. Not once have they ever judged me about my past. They have done so much for my children and myself. In fact, they have done much more than anyone could ever wish or hope for. The most important thing about our friendship is that not once has anything come as an obligation from them; it has always come from unconditional love. I will forever be grateful to them and their family.

As April was coming to an end, I went for my typical cleaning visit to my dentist, Dr. Jose Bushdid. The doctor was a high school friend known to me not as Doc but Pep. Pep was the older brother of my high school crush and dear friend Dunia. Pep is just one of those people, much like his younger sister, who exudes warmth, care and compassion. He knew of my difficult journey and that there was something missing in my life. He then mentioned The Landmark Forum. Okay, now Frank, Randy told you about Landmark, well, better yet, Randy hasn't stopped talking about Landmark, I told myself. I had done a bit of homework and researched Landmark. However, as I started reading the countless reviews, many of them described it as a cult, an anti-God religious cult. So, faith, being such a huge component and foundation of my life, that was the one thing I was unwilling to compromise or put into question.

It was now the first week of May 2018. In less than three months, I had dropped over 100 pounds. I was looking primetime. As things progressed on the possible sale of our 100-unit complex in Opa Locka, Randy had been telling me about a self-development program that had been transformational in his life, called the Landmark Forum.

There was definitely some hesitancy in me. In knowing Pep as being a strong man of God and having such an unyielding and strong conviction about his faith, I asked him about it. Pep assured me there was nothing in the Landmark Forum that would contradict or put in question our deep-seated faith and values. You know, I didn't realize it at the time that I began writing this book, but upon editing it and talking to my dear friend Dunia, I realized had it not been for Pep's testimony and assurance that my faith would not be in question, I do not think I would have ultimately done the Landmark Forum and without the Forum I would not be writing this book or have become the man that I am today. Randy cracked open the door and Pep had me busting right through it. In late April, I made my decision and signed up for the Landmark Forum for the month of May 2018.

A few weeks before the workshop was to begin, I was advised that the children would be taking their basketball team pictures on one of the evenings of the four-day workshop. I remember being strongly advised that I could not miss any part of the event, so I had to postpone it until August. In the meantime, May 2018 was crazy. After nineteen years of managing Michelle Village Condominiums in Opa Locka, my parents were getting ready to sell and my next court hearing was upon me. On Tuesday, May 29, 2018, I walked into the court hearing with a folder two inches thick filled with all the AA meetings that I had attended. Barry provided proof of all the Soberlink tests I had passed, and I had the testimony of Charlie Horner, as well as all my urine tests coming back clean. Upon completion of the hearing, we won. We won…well, almost. I had been seeking co-parenting classes for

Yari and myself for quite some time to see if perhaps, we would be able to put our disagreements aside and find a way to settle our differences and make peace. After the conclusion of the hearing, the judge took me off Soberlink, restored all my parental rights and provided co-parenting classes for Yari and myself.

It was now mid-June and Opa Locka was sold. I was still working at the property, giving Randy and the new owners a little of the play-by-play of how to manage the property. Simultaneously, Yari and I were going to co-parenting counseling on Friday evenings in Coconut Grove. After a few sessions, things had gotten pretty heated between Yari and me.

Before the session on Friday, June 29, 2018, I asked Nori if there was anything that she wanted. Nori said, "Yes. I want you to talk to mom about doing a "15's" birthday party together. So, in the session I asked Yari what we were going to do about Nori's "15's" birthday. Yari exclaimed, "You have yours, I'll have mine!" I was angry, livid and red faced. "How are you going to do this to our daughter?" I said. In the discussion, the lady running the coparenting program had me step outside. Yari refused to compromise. And I was emotionally and mentally spent.

I left the session. I was irate. I had had it! After 5 years of trying to make peace with her this is where I ended up.

The next morning, we had a championship basketball game for Jonathan at Tamiami Park at 9:00 am. For one reason or another, the administration kept changing the allocated time for the game. The children's parents were getting visibly upset. After having several words with Yari and upset over the continuous changing of the time slot, I stopped at a liquor store on my way home and bought a bottle of Grey Goose vodka and did what I did best. I took down over half the bottle of Grey Goose on the night before I was to coach my son's championship basketball game.

The following morning, I was exhausted, beaten up and extremely dehydrated. Seven months of sobriety gone just like that.

The evening prior to the game, I had a disagreement with the opposing coach that resulted in a few choice words exchanged that night and throughout the course of the game. As far as the game was concerned, I was for all intents and purposes hung over. But the fact was that we had a much better team. My son Jonathan was far and away the best player in the league at that point in time. Our team was loaded, there was no way we could lose, except…Jonathan and the other kids had the worst game of the season. With three seconds left, down by three, Jonathan had the ball in his hands and took a desperation 3-point shot that got stuck in the rim to give the opposing team the trophy and first place championship. When it came time to shake hands, I refused to shake the other coach's hand and all hell broke loose. Spectators and fans had to separate us. I had always prided myself in being respectful. Well, I broke every rule in my book that day. I was unhinged.

I remember seeing my team, this group of 9-year-old boys, stumped and dejected. I looked at Jonathan, my son, and he is crying hysterically. He looks at me, with tears in his eyes and tells me, "You, Dad, are my father. You are supposed to set the example for me. Look at the example you showed me today." My shoulders shrugged over in defeat and I put my head down. I looked at him and the team and said, "You are right son. I am the leader, and I am your father. Please forgive me. I am supposed to set the example."

I proceeded to tell the young boys how deeply sorry I was and apologized for the way that I handled the situation. No words were spoken by the children. I then went on to each child individually and told them how proud I was of them. I then gave my son and daughter, who was present, a hug and a kiss and let them know I was going to pick them up the following day at noon. On Sunday, June 30, 2018, we were all to head out on vacation for a week. We were headed to one of our yearly traditional spots, South Seas Island Resort in Captiva, Florida, for some good 'ole family summer fun, until…

I left Tamiami feeling angry, frustrated and beaten. If only my ex-wife wouldn't have gotten me so upset, I exclaimed. If only she would have listened to me, none of this would have happened, I bemoaned. Of course, it was not my fault that I relapsed, I begrudgingly told myself, it was hers. All of a sudden, I came up with a wonderful idea. "Well, Frank, you still have half a bottle of Grey Goose at home, and you don't have any responsibilities until tomorrow when you pick up the kids for Captiva," I told myself. I had convinced myself this time that somehow, someway this would be different. I convinced myself that I had figured out a way to control my drinking and that once Sunday morning came around, I would be able to stop drinking and go on vacation with my children. Yeah…that didn't quite turn out as I anticipated.

I got home, served myself my Grey Goose and cranberry in my Yeti cup and stopped at the liquor store to pick up another bottle, just in case I ran out. I drove to my friend Mari's house to have a few drinks and vent about my horrible life. Wah, wah, wah, wah, wah. Victim, victim, victim. As I look back at myself, I feel bad for that guy, that guy who could not see that in life we can experience certain situations and turn them into lessons or stay stuck in them and continue to experience suffering. I chose suffering because in doing so, I did not have to take any personal responsibility for my actions.

It is now noon on Saturday, and I am. "off to the races" (term used for binge drinking). Mari and I poured drink after drink. Before I knew it, it was 7:00 am Sunday morning. All of a sudden, I realized I had to get home and pack my bags for Captiva. I remember looking at the Grey Goose bottle and noticing that there was still quite a bit of vodka left in it. So, I poured myself another drink, thanked Mari for the company and went home to get my bags ready.

While I packed, I would pause, serve myself another drink and continued indulging. Before I knew it, it was well-past noon. Actually, it was closer to 2:00 pm and I was running late. I arrived at Yari's house, put on my sunglasses and took a swig of my blue Listerine to mask the smell of alcohol (the kids will never notice, I thought). Nori sat behind the passenger seat and Jonathan was seated behind me. Next stop, Captiva, I imagined.

About a mile and a half from Yari's house, Nori said, "Papi, take us home. We are not going to Captiva." I said, "What? What are you talking about?" Jonathan, puzzled by Nori's words, said, "What happened Nori? What is going on?" As Nori tried to dodge the question, I proceeded to try and reason with my daughter, but I knew. I knew…that she knew. I could feel her eyes piercing me through the back of my skull. Finally, after asking his sister several times what was going on, she responded, "Papi is drinking again." He loudly said, "What?! What?! What do you mean?" Jonathan, then, feeling dejected, cried, "Why? Why Papi? Why are you drinking? Take us home. We want to go home," they said. Tears begin flowing like a bathroom faucet as I write this. This hurt, this really hurt. I told the kids, "I am sorry, guys. I am really sorry. I will take you home." When I opened the passenger side door for my son, he looked at me in the eyes and told me, "Papi, you need to go to a meeting. You need to go to an AA meeting." Crushed is how I felt in that moment. As I took down their luggage, I told them how sorry I was and drove off.

Damn it, damn it, I did it again. How could I have done this to my kids? After waiting all year for summer vacation, bags packed, in the car driving off and I do this to them. Damn you, Frank. What a pathetic piece of crap you are. You are such a horrible father; I told myself. You blow up at the basketball game and act like a complete jerk and now you pull this on your kids?

At the same time, I cannot help but recognize how mature, responsible and courageous my daughter was in that moment. In the last 24 hours I had witnessed my son standing firm to me after I exploded at the basketball game and now my daughter, telling me to go home when we are on our way to vacation in Captiva. I am blown away at the strength and character my children showed in those moments. As I write this, I realize that we are all students in the game of life. We are never too old to learn, and we are never too young to teach.

As I exited the turnpike on Kendall Drive on my way home, feeling angry and sobbing uncontrollably, I remembered that I was out of liquor at home. Oh, my. What do I do? I must get another bottle, of course. I mean…look at this horrible weekend and all that has happened to me. I never once took accountability or responsibility that all these circumstances were the direct result of my actions. As I exited the liquor store with a bottle in hand, I headed home. I climbed the steps to my apartment, served myself a drink and told myself, again, "I cannot do this anymore. I do not want to live. I cannot do this to my kids anymore." Since I did not have a gun, I realized that I did have pills, I had lots and lots of pills.

I then called the gentleman from the basketball game who I had had an altercation with 36-hours earlier. As I dialed his number, I heard a voice, I told him, "Lars, I am so sorry man. I am sorry about yesterday. I am an alcoholic and I am a mess. Please forgive me. I have destroyed my family and my kids' hopes and expectations of their father," and I told him, "I do not want to do this anymore, man. I want to tap out." He then told me, "Frank, don't worry about it, it's okay. Come on Frank, you are a great father. I see you. I see how you are with your kids." He offered me beautiful words of encouragement, but I couldn't believe him.

In hindsight, that call to Lars was a cry for help, a desperate plea for help. Thank God he answered and thank God…for what he did next.

About 15-minutes later, there was a knock on the door. "Frank Lopez?" I heard a gentleman ask. I replied, "Yes." "This is Miami-Dade Police Department. Can you please open the door?" I obliged. I instantaneously knew what had happened. Lars must have called 911. Damn it, Lars. Thank you, Lars. Damn it, Lars, I remember thinking to myself. How in the world did he know where I lived? I still don't have an answer to that question. The police officers asked me a multitude of questions and after roughly ten minutes they told me, "Mr. Lopez, put your hands behind your back." I was confused. I asked why, what is going on? I still do not understand why I had to put my hands behind my back. I never raised my voice at the officers. I assumed it was standard protocol.

As I entered the back of the police vehicle, once again I asked, "What is going on? Where are you taking me? What have I done?" They replied, "We are taking you for a mental evaluation." "What do you mean?" The police officer replied, "You are going to be having a psychological evaluation and possibly Baker Acted." I began screaming, "What? What do you mean Baker Acted? There is nothing wrong with me!" I yelled. Who the hell was I kidding? Everything was wrong with me. After several hours of being questioned, I was finally released to my father. I remember feeling relieved that I was not Baker Acted. At the moment, I remember believing I fooled the psychologist. Truth was, I was the fool. I needed help; I needed help desperately.

I remember the look of great concern on my father's face. As he drove me home and got out of the car, he walked me upstairs and stayed with me for a little while. I remember wanting him to leave, so I could have the remainder of the vodka that I left under the kitchen sink. My father asked me if I had any alcohol left? I lied, of course. "No, Dad, they threw it all out." My father asked me if I wanted him to stay with me. I told him no. I saw the love in my Dad's eyes that day. I saw the heart in the man who had spent his entire life seeing love and vulnerability as a weakness. I loved that moment of love that I captured from him that day. However, I still could not wait for him to leave so I could get to my stash and pour myself another drink.

As soon as my father left, I did just that. I finished the bottle of vodka that night and told myself, I have had enough. This is it Frank, you are done. I was…well, for a little while, at least.

As I write this, I realize that very few people ever knew that I was hospitalized, almost institutionalized and Baker Acted. The truth of the matter is, if or when Yari reads this book, she will have just found out.

Surprisingly, Yari was sympathetic to my relapse. She kept Nori and Jonathan away from me for a week and decided not to take any legal action. I remember calling Barry and advising him of my relapse. He told me to take a "wait and see" approach. On Tuesday, July 3rd, I walked into my next AA meeting and told myself I needed to find a sponsor as soon as possible, and I did. I found one a lot quicker than I anticipated. Actually, I believe God found him for me.

That Tuesday evening, I went to a late, men's only AA meeting at Sabal Palm. I remember staying in the parking lot of Miami-Dade Community College, talking to this gentleman I had just met, for nearly three hours. This man was so full of wisdom and knowledge. As a bonus, he had seven years of sobriety. It was nearly 1:00 am. As I was saying goodbye, I called him and said, "Hey,

Mark, will you be my sponsor?" He chuckled, smiled and said, "Of course. But one thing Frank..." I said, "What is that?" "He told me, "Frank, you are not that important." I remember having a confused look on my face and asking him, "What? Excuse me?"

He then proceeded, "Frank, you see, most people spend their entire lives thinking the world revolves around them. That people are either out to get them, talking about them, or attacking them." I nodded, "tell me more." He continued, "You see, people are not out to get you. People project the reality of what is going on inside of them. It has nothing to do with you." As I listened, I was having a difficult time understanding what he was telling me. He then continued, "In life, you cannot control those things that happen to you. You can only control how you react or better yet, respond to them." He then shook my hand and wished me a good night. As I opened the car door and sat on the seat, I remember saying to myself that Mark was exactly what I needed. For several days, I pondered his words of wisdom.

A week later, I saw my kids for the first time since my relapse. I apologized profusely, once again, for disappointing them. They readily accepted my apology, as they always have. I mean, they love their dad. I remember letting them know that I would make it up to them; that next month we would go back to Captiva.

I have to say, I was extremely fortunate that the management at South Seas Island Resort did not penalize me for not showing up and allowed us to return in August without incurring any fees. I was determined to not let the kids down this time. But would determination be enough?

It was now, July 28, 2018, and my dear friend Manny the Magician came to Miami to visit me from Puerto Rico with his wife Nery and his children Richie and Eddie. We decided to meet up for brunch at none other than Nori's favorite restaurant, 94th Aero Squadron. 94th Aero Squadron had an incredible brunch buffet; among the items were eggs Benedict, freshly made to order omelets, oyster bar, snow crabs, paella, prime rib, amongst many other specialties. They also had unlimited champagne and mimosas. (Although, I was done with alcohol at this point, or was I?)

Anyway, as we all sat at the table, Manny looked at me, looked at his wife and said; "Frank, you have a gift." You have an incredible gift." I looked at him trying to understand what he was trying to tell me. He then looked at Nery, grabbed her wrist, gazed at each other and then simultaneously looked at me; nodded and smiled. He proceeded, "I can see you on stage, speaking to audiences. You are inspirational. You were born to be a Motivational

Speaker. I see magic in you Frank." I was…. I was at a loss for words. I was humbled. I had forgotten about that conversation. I had forgotten about that conversation for quite a while. Manny has always believed in me. He saw in me that day, once again, the man that I have discovered today. His words stuck. His words stuck with me.

It was now August 5th, and we are off to South Seas Island Resort in Captiva, for good this time. Nori and Jonathan were extremely excited to arrive. Although we were excited, red sea tide had contaminated most of the Gulf of Mexico's waters. Yet, we were prepared to make the best of it. As we exited our vehicle, we could not help but breathe in the horrible stench of dead sea life. There were thousands of dead fish all around us and it permeated the air that we breathed. Okay, so the beach is a no go, at least we have the pool, we thought. The first day we arrived, we had checked out a golf cart and kind of just settled in. Upon arising the following morning and having a quick breakfast, we headed on over to the main pool. Before leaving the room, I breathed into the Soberlink machine.

You see, although legally the court had told me that I was able to get off the Soberlink, after my relapse, my ex-wife had demanded that I get back on board and I agreed.

We spent the day in what looked more like paradise than it smelled, but we were determined to enjoy our experience. I remember being by the pool bar and wondering if it was such a good idea being out of town with only a month of sobriety in me at the time. "I am good," I convinced myself.

It was now day three, August 7th. I remember listening to calypso music near the pool, looking at beautiful women in bikinis. I looked over at the kids and told them, "Hey, I am going to get myself a non-alcoholic beer. I will be back." My intention truly was to get a non-alcoholic beer. However, once I got to the bar, I reasoned with myself. "Heck…I am not a beer drinker. I can have one regular beer. Bartender, get me a Corona please." And he did. I poured my Corona into a plastic cup and entered the pool. As I placed my plastic cup on the edge of the pool, I slowly took a sip, exhale, ahhh…so refreshing, I thought. Heck, I can have one more, I told myself, and I did.

After having that second beer, I convinced myself that I could get myself a small bottle of vodka and when the kids went to sleep, I could have a couple of drinks. Once morning would roll around, the kids would never notice a thing. I bought myself a small bottle of vodka and hid it inside the beach bag. After a long day at the pool and a nice seafood dinner, everyone was off to sleep. Well…the kids drifted off to sleep. I, on the other hand, had a whole party for myself planned. I remember checking in on them to make sure they were sleeping. As soon as I knew they would not be awakened, I opened the bottle of vodka, added some cranberry juice and began the festivities. After finishing the small bottle, I dozed off to sleep.

The next morning, upon awakening, I remember feeling good. I remember telling myself, "That was great. Look how good you did, Frank." However, I remember feeling fearful about breathing into the breathalyzer. I began doing the math. I stopped drinking around 2:00 am, it is now 9:00 am, the mathematical equation seemed to work out for me, so I decided to give it a shot. As I blew into the Soberlink, it read….000. "Yes!" I exclaimed. "I did it, that was great." I figured out a plan. Gosh, I want to drink again. I came up with a great idea. I would break the plastic straw and if the straw was broken, I couldn't blow into the machine. I knew if I could not blow into the machine, I would be able to drink without any consequences.

Breathalyzer

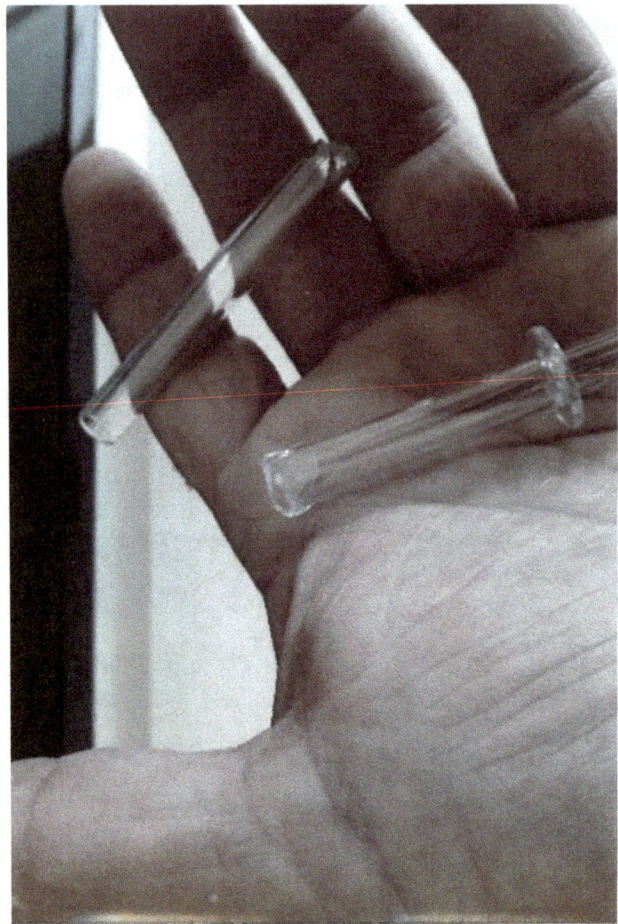

Breathalyzer Tube

Nori and Jonathan at Captiva

I then drove the golf cart to the pool. While at the pool, I told my kids to stay near the shallow area, that I had left something in the room. I told Nori to make sure she looked after Jonathan. Nori was 13, almost 14, at the time and Jonathan was 9 going on 10. I got in the golf cart and went to a small liquor store just outside the South Seas Island Resort. I purchased a few small bottles of Grey Goose vodka and dropped them off in the room. By the time I got back to the pool, Nori asked me why it took so long. I don't quite remember the excuse I gave her, but she bought it, I thought.

Here I am, away vacationing with my children, my treasures, everything that is most precious and dear to me, and yet, alcohol took precedent. Alcohol was my master, it owned me. I had absolutely no control over the power of the drink. All my children wanted was their dad, all they wanted was a fun day to laugh, play and smile with me. They wanted to play catch, they wanted for me to just be present with them. I…I don't know. I really don't know how to explain it, but I just could not stop going for the drink.

Later on, that day, I decided to push the envelope. I had bought some pork chops to throw on the grill. I convinced the kids to hang out at the pool at night, next to the room and have a nighttime barbeque. "Awesome, Dad, sure." As I prepared the food, I discretely poured myself a drink. I hid it, or tried as best I could to hide it, from the kids view. As the kids played in the pool, I began to play music. I continued telling the children that I had left something in the room. So, I would go back up, pour myself a drink and return to the pool area. Each time I would leave and return, I would come back with a little extra pep in my step.

After a few trips, Nori whispered to Jonathan, "Dad is drinking again." At around 7:00 pm, my son bashfully came up to me and asked me, "Papi, are you drinking?" Oh, wow. I could not look him in his eyes and lie. I shamefully said, "Yes." I apologized and stopped, right? Nope. I asked him, "How did you know?" He said, "Nori could tell." Nori then looked at me and softly said, "I called mom." I freakin flipped. I said, "What?! How can you do this? How can you do this to me? Your mom is never going to let me see you again. She is going to take you away from me."

As the children began packing their bags, my rant continued. Nori and Jonathan gathered together in one of the bedrooms. I continued yelling at Nori, blaming her for all the things that were going to happen to me. I kept telling her it was her fault. I write this with such a heavy heart. I understand now that everything in life happens for a reason. That I needed to go through all these things in order to get the help that I needed. But man…my kids deserved better. Nori and Jonathan deserved better from their dad.

I told Nori all sorts of things, including that her father was done with her. I told her she had betrayed me. Till this day, Nori has never ever raised her voice at me. She has never disrespected me. My daughter Nori and my son Jonathan are two angels that God has sent my way. He sent them, to save me from the wreckage of myself.

A few hours later, Yari arrived. She drove from Miami to Captiva, a nearly three-hour drive, to pick up our children, in essence, to save them from their very own father. Yari despised me, she has despised me for quite some time. First, I neglected her for all those years as her spouse. Now, I was showing disregard and neglect to our very own children. In hindsight, I guess I cannot blame her for the way she felt, and/or feels about me. My behaviors propelled those feelings from her. Perhaps, one day, that will change. The truth is that

I created Yari's perception of me.

I awakened on the morning of August 9th and continued my reckless behavior. I poured myself a drink and then asked myself what the hell happened. I packed my bags and checked out of the hotel. I, this intoxicated drunk, got behind the wheel and began to attempt to drive three hours back home to Miami.

Frankly, I do not really know what happened, but at some point, I picked up the phone and called my parents. They drove roughly two hours to wherever I was at and met me at a Longhorn Steak House. After having a discussion, words of which I have no recollection, the police soon arrived. The police officers spoke to me for a bit and left me alone. The next memory I have is being at the bar at the Longhorn Steak House near Fort Myers, drinking a Grey Goose and cranberry, I have no car, a few hundred dollars, and an Uber app on my cell phone. I called an Uber. The Uber driver picked me up and drove two and a half hours. As we were getting near my apartment, at roughly 9:45 pm, I asked him, "Hey, can you do me a favor?" He said, "What is it?" I said, "Can you stop at the liquor store so I can get a few bottles of alcohol and I will give you an extra twenty dollars?" He replied, "Absolutely, no problem." So, the party continued, once again. As I walked up my apartment steps, still dazed and dumbfounded as to what had just happened over the course of the last 48 hours, all I knew was that I had three 1.75-liter bottles of Grey Goose and a 1.75 liter bottle of Captain Morgan, which was all that I needed.

By the time I sobered up some, it was the morning of August 11th. I talked to my dad. It was one of the few times in my father's life that I noticed he was frightened. He had no idea what to do with me. My dad looked like he felt helpless. I was…hopeless.

I knew that when he came to see me, he would be scoping out my home for alcohol. So, being that I was an alcoholic, I was an expert at concealment. I hid alcohol everywhere. I would hide it under the sink, inside the toilet tank, I would hide it in vases.

As my father sat beside me and spoke, he saw how beaten I was. I was defeated. As he looked at me, his eyes would veer off to the ceiling as he searched for words. My dad, with his eyes watering, looked at me and said, "Son, whatever you need, please, how can I help you? Please. Please. Frankie, look at Nori, look at Jonathan, look at your kids, your beautiful kids, do it for them." For anyone who is reading this, what I want you to know is that unless your loved one has gone through addiction, it is not possible for the rational mind to comprehend. One has absolutely no control over the drink. To the alcoholic, alcohol is undefeated. You cannot win, unless…unless…

The very next day my father and I called Barry. Barry had been waiting for my call. He already knew. On the morning of August 14, 2018, Barry met with my father and me. I was a shadow of the man Barry knew. As I entered his office, I was stumbling and slurring. I was drunk. Barry looked at my father and told him, "Frank needs to go to rehab." He told us that Yari was not going to let me spend time with the kids and there was nothing he could do at this time. I remember telling Barry no way, there is absolutely no way I am going to rehab. Within 24 hours, I changed my mind.

On August 15th, I called Barry and asked him where the rehabilitation center was. Charles had recommended The Hanley Center in West Palm Beach, Florida to Barry. The Hanley Center is a rehabilitation center for alcoholics and drug addicts. It is a 30-day treatment facility. After several days of going back and forth with the insurance company, it was done. I had agreed.

7
HELLO ROCK BOTTOM, MY NAME IS FRANKIE

'The gateway to freedom, is found in your ability to surrender."
-Frankie M Powers-

On August 18, after several days of not seeing the children, in actuality, after not having seen them since the day I relapsed, I managed to sober up long enough to go visit them. My father had given me my car back under one condition, that right after I saw them, I would return the car back to him. I agreed. As I saw my two precious children, I was in deep despair. I told them that I was sick but that I was going to get the help that I really needed. I remember seeing the look of fear on their faces. They were greatly concerned. As I left, I gave them each a big, gentle hug and a kiss. That was the last time I saw them until September 23, 2018.

After spending some time with the kids and before I dropped off the car at my father's office, there was just one last stop I needed to make. That's right, my bread and butter liquor store. I remember doing the math in my head, telling myself, okay, today is the 18th, I'm going to rehab on the 24th. 18…19 (counting), so I need to get myself six bottles of liquor just to be safe. Over the last year of my drinking career, I had kind of pushed the Captain off to the side and had been going for the Goose. So, for old times' sake, I told the clerk give me four bottles of 1.75 liters of Grey Goose, one 1.75 liter of Tito's vodka, and one of the good 'ole Captain.

Me at Rock Bottom

I quickly dropped off the liquor at home and went to turn in my car to my dad. As he drove me back to my apartment and took my vehicle with him, we had agreed that on Friday, August 24, 2018, my mother and father would drop me off at the Hanley Rehabilitation Center in West Palm Beach, the day before my 43rd birthday. I remember telling one of my closest friends, Ralph, when it was I was going for treatment. He responded, "Frank, why don't you just wait till Monday, August 27th? Why go in the day before your birthday?" I will never forget my response. I said, "Brother, I have been drinking for 27 years. The quicker I get in, the quicker I get out."

In the meantime, I drank. I drank all day and all night, for those six days using short naps as breaks in between.

On August 23rd, my dear friend and co-worker Armando, came to see me. He picked me up and we went out to have a few drinks at Outback Steak House. I then asked him if he would be able to take me to Ralph's house, and he did. When I arrived to see Ralph, he was pleasantly surprised to see me. We hung out for a bit and shared our final drink together. I love that man. He and I never shared the same interests or hobbies, but what we did share and have in common was something far greater. We both have always had the same sized heart.

After spending a couple hours at his house, he invited me and his wife Daisy, to go to a late dinner at Bonefish Grill. After the meal and a few more cocktails, they lit a candle and sang me happy birthday at the table. Ralph and Daisy drove me home. When we arrived at my house, they asked if they could come in. I replied, "Of course." As they entered my apartment, something prompted either Daisy or myself to put on my wedding video. We watched; I cried. I remember wondering, "How did I get here?" As it got closer to 1:00

am, they had to leave to go home, I thanked them both and gave Ralph a big hug and a kiss and told him, "See you in a month, my brother."

It was the morning of August 24, 2018. I had only slept an hour or so that evening. It was nearing 7:00 am and the kids are on their way to school. I called Nori and Jonathan and told them, "Guys, I don't know what is going to happen while I am gone, but I am going to get well. I am going to come back better than ever. I promise you, believe it." I think they smiled when they heard that. I think somehow, someway, they knew it. They felt it in their dad's whisper. I remember not having any idea of what was going to happen. I remember being extremely inebriated. I still knew that somehow, someway, deep in my core, that my life was on the brink of a huge turnaround. I was getting ready for my come back.

I then called Jessie and thanked her for her friendship and asked her to please look after Nori and Jonathan while I was away.

In the meantime, I served myself a few more drinks and awaited my parents to come pick me up. We had agreed to go to Shuck 'n Dive to have my last supper, before what I deemed psychological boot camp. Shuck 'n Dive is my favorite restaurant. It is a New Orleans themed restaurant in Fort Lauderdale. They have Cajun specialties such as shrimp po boys and andouille sausage gumbo, red beans and rice, jambalaya, and my favorite item on the menu, blackened gator. Now to finish it off, I would have what I deem to be the best bread pudding in the USA. I love that place. When we arrived, I was pretty juiced, to say the least. I then ordered myself a couple more Grey Goose and cranberry drinks. My parent's eyes opened wide as they looked at me in disbelief. I smiled and said, "Mom, Dad, this is it, my last drink ever." They shrugged. I mean, what could they do? I was going to rehab.

At roughly 7:00 pm on Friday night, August 24, 2018, we pulled into the parking lot of my new home for the next 30 days. I swear I felt like Marty McFly in Back to the Future. I really felt like I was back at boot camp. The difference was that here there were no drill instructors; however, there were no phones, no leaving the property, no distractions. As they went through my belongings, they took away my hair spray, my mouthwash and my cologne. I remember asking, "Hair spray? Hair spray? Who the hell would drink hair spray?" I thought. I guess I thought I was a high-end, classy alcoholic, whatever that is. I then hugged and kissed my parents goodbye and notified them that I would not be having any access to the telephone for at least two weeks.

I then entered the facility, proceeded to fill out some paperwork and was called to blow into a machine to see my alcohol content. I blew a .019, more than twice the legal limit in Florida. I just realized right now, perhaps .019 is my number, as that is the exact same number that I blew, when I got my one and only DUI. As they proceeded to walk me to the detox center and show me my sleeping quarters, they handed me a bookbag, a notebook, and a Big Book. The Big Book being the bible for Alcoholics Anonymous. It is a testament to living a life free of alcohol, and has been in circulation, using the same content, since 1939.

As I got comfortable, I decided to nap for a few hours. I awakened Saturday morning, my birthday, August 25, and my first day sober. They began giving me a medication called Ativan. Ativan is a medication used for people with addictions in order to detox safely. For people battling addiction, quitting cold turkey can be fatal. I remember hating that stuff. For some reason, Ativan did not affect me. It seemed everyone who was taking Ativan was sleeping 22 out of the 24 hours in the day. Not me, I could not sleep. I was ready. I was ready to do whatever I needed to do to beat this damn disease.

As I reminisce about those days, it brings me back to the moment I made the decision to stop smoking. I knew in that moment, something came in me, and I knew this time it would somehow be different, I just did not know what it was. I grabbed that Big Book and ate it. I read page after page. I immersed myself fully into those words. I took notes. We would have an examination that we had to study and prepare for. After each and every chapter of the Big Book, we were tested. It was a hand-written test and then an oral examination to make sure we understood the meaning behind it. After finishing two chapters and passing both tests, I asked for the next one. They told me I would have to wait until I was transferred to the men's building, after I was fully detoxed, before getting any further into my work. I remember feeling disappointed. I wanted more; I was hungry. I read chapter after chapter. This all occurred within 24 hours.

By Sunday morning, I met my first roommate. His name was Jerry. Jerry and I hit it off right away. He had attempted to get sober for over 10 years, but the drink continued to get the best of him. Nevertheless, he guided me as best he could. Jerry was a brilliant man, an Ivy league grad, I believe. As I said before, alcohol does not discriminate. It could care less about your skin color, background, or education level. It gets every one of us, every single time.

By Sunday afternoon, my counselor Caesar came to introduce himself. He told me he would be here throughout my stay for anything I needed. I immediately took a liking to him. He was genuine. He was real. This was not his job; it was his way of life. Being a counselor gave him fulfillment in his vocation.

Monday morning came around and everyone around me seemed to be continuously sleeping. I had kind of had enough. I somehow began hallucinating. I went to the nurse's station and I said, "Look, man, I don't know what you guys are up to, but everyone here is acting like zombies. I am not buying into this; I am out of here." I have no money, no phone, no identification. Where the hell I did I think I was going, or how I was going to get there? All I knew was that I was out. I put my shoes on, grabbed my bookbag and my Big Book and began to walk. I remember the puzzled look on the faces of the nurses in the detox center. They must have been saying to themselves, "This guy is nuts; this guy has gone mad."

As I started wandering around, looking for a way out, I ran into Caesar, my counselor. Caesar looked at me aghast and said Frank, "Where are you going?" I responded, I don't know, man, but I'm out of here." He looked frozen. In hindsight, I laugh about the incident. The poor guy had no idea what to do., However, he looked at me and said, "Frank, wait just a minute," so I did. After a few minutes, one of the heads of the Hanley Center, a former United States Marine named Michael, walked up to me and said, "Hey, Frank, why don't you come with me, sit down and have a talk," And I did. Michael then proceeded to ask me, "Look, man, what can I do to get you to stay in treatment? I replied, "I want to go to the men's unit. Look Michael, I did not come here to sit in a detox center, I came here to get to work and to learn how to get sober." He then looked me in the eyes and said, "Okay. If I take you to the men's unit, you'll stay?" I replied yes, excitedly. He said okay, you have yourself a deal and we shook hands.

You see I did not know what rehab was. I had no idea what I had in store for me, but I prepared as if I was heading to Parris Island, South Carolina, United States Marine Corps boot camp. I mentally psyched myself up for it and I was ready. I took that same attitude in with me into the Rehab Center as well. The problem was that in the military, there are two primary objectives. One, mission accomplishment; two, troop welfare. However, in rehab, it was an every man for himself mentality and I was not nearly ready for that. Actually, I was not prepared for that at all.

You see, all my life, I have loved everyone. I have put everyone's thoughts, wishes, and desires well above my own. In essence, I always put myself last. Yet, in rehab, I could not help or save anyone, because first I needed to save myself. The best analogy I could give you is like when you are on an airplane and they tell you that if something happens, when the oxygen mask drops, you have to first put the mask on yourself, before you can put it on your child, because you cannot take care of anyone if you do not help yourself first. Rehab had the same mentality. If you cannot take care of you, you cannot help others. This, my friends, would become my biggest challenge, the challenge of self-love. I remember asking what the hell is that? I mean, I know that I am a good, loving person, but love myself? Hell no, I hated myself. I hated myself for all the things that I had done to the people I loved the most: my sister, my parents, my loved ones, and most importantly, my children. I did not know how to love myself. Along the way, surrendering to what is, to God's will and learning self-love, became the most intricate components for me to achieve sobriety.

That first night was rough. I was an emotional wrecking ball. I remember there was a guest speaker at the rehab center that evening and he brought the house down on me that night. Truth is, although every part of me was dying to get to the men's unit, I was not ready to leave detox. I just…wasn't. I wanted to. I thought I was ready, but that night showed me differently.

Once the speaker was done sharing his experience, strength and hope, my heart rate was through the roof. Some of my newfound friends were quite concerned for me and walked with me over to the nurses' station. After taking my blood pressure, it was a staggeringly high 190/120. The nurse gave me some blood pressure medication and told me to stay still; if my blood pressure didn't drop soon, I would have to return to the detox center so they could continue to monitor me.

Luckily, within a few hours, I was okay. As Tuesday morning rolled around, I was a new man. I got up, got down on my knees and said a prayer. Then I got dressed, and was ready to get to work, whatever that meant. To give you an idea, wake up was at 7:00 am with a hard knock on the door. We would have 15 minutes to meet up in the lounge. The lounge had a large television, several comfortable sofas throughout, a large, beautiful kitchen with marble countertops, coffee machines, soft drinks, water and the like. The refrigerator was filled with hummus, cheese, guacamole, yogurt and other snacks. We had ice cream, chips and popcorn. We were definitely not going to be going hungry during our stay. I immediately changed my breakfast of cranberry and vodka to several cups of coffee. In all honesty, it was actually a pretty seamless transition.

At around 7:20 am we would read a small book of spiritual inspiration and proceed with a short prayer. Afterward, we would head out to breakfast and have some free time before 9:00 am, when there would be a Big Book study class. We were also given several exercises, called experientials, that would teach us the value of teamwork and working together with one another. In between, we would meet with small groups and the therapist in charge, then lunchtime would come. After lunch, there would be some alone time and then we would meet for some more class instruction. At 5:00 pm we would have an hour for wellness, if we chose. Dinner was set for six o'clock, and then our nightly gratitude meeting amongst ourselves, stating what we were grateful for that day and rating the day on a scale of 1 to 10. Every night, by 7:30 pm, there would be a speaker meeting, in which they would share their story of experience, strength and hope, for a life free from the obsession of drinking.

Most people have no idea of what a rehabilitation center is. Hanley Rehabilitation Center was not limited to alcoholics. Amongst my new brothers were people addicted to benzos, cocaine and heroin. My new roommate was nicknamed "Ice Man" for his addictive drug of choice, crystal meth. Contrary to what most people believe, there was no difference between any one of us. We were all equal, we were all the same, we were all one. We had Native Americans, Anglos, Blacks and Hispanics. We were from all walks of life and all parts of the country, yet we were brothers and sisters. We had attorneys, judges, pastors, major league athletes. Addiction does not discriminate. Believe it or not, meetings were not mandatory, they were optional. But I, myself, did not come here for a 30-day vacay or get away. I came to get the tools I needed to survive.

After the third day with my boys, which we called ourselves, "F-Troop," I spotted a desk and chair in the hallway of the building. I immediately used that as my writing place, to study, to do my work. Every day, I would do a chapter of work, every night I would turn it in, and every single morning, I was tested to make sure I knew the material and not just copying down the answers. There were no certificates, no accolades, it was a self-fulfilling accomplishment. The only person I was up against in that building was myself. Well…Jerry too. You see, Jerry had also joined me in the F-Troop building, and he had started a competition with me as to who would finish first. We both finished tied at the end.

It took me a number of days to get acclimated. We had a large television set along with a blue ray player that was available every day after 6:00 pm and all day on Sunday to watch, none other than NFL football. Every night it was lights out at 10:00 pm. The curfew didn't matter at all for me. I wasn't there to watch television. I went in for self-development 101, which for me was how to learn to deal with life on life's terms and not on mine.

My alarm was set for 5:00 am. I would wake up, make my bed and get on my knees and pray. Why on my knees, one might ask? There is something about getting on your knees that quickly humbles you. With that, I will share with you how my prayers went, which were something like this:

> *"God, thank you. Thank you for all you have given me. Thank you for my wonderful kids, Nori and Jonathan. Thank you for my parents. Thank you for Yari, the mother of my children. Thank you for my friends, Lisa, Auri, Gianna, Gabi, Jessie, Noel, Gabi, Dani, and Pipa. Thank you for Kyle and Kazzandra, my sister, my nephews Gus and Chino. Thank you for Ralph, Daisy, Mari, Ivan, my cousins and all those that I love, and countless others that need help. God make me a better man today than I was yesterday. Guide me in the direction that You want me to follow in life and let me do Your will."*

I would follow these words with the Lord's Prayer, then do the sign of the cross and I was good to go. I would stand up, brush my teeth and off to the track to exercise. I would do cardio for an hour and fifteen minutes, then head inside the F-Troop building, just in time for a spiritual prayer and head on over to breakfast. After breakfast, I would take thirty minutes and go to the chapel to read the bible; then, continue the day's activities after that.

Once lunchtime would hit, I would sit with my peers and then go back to the track for another hour of exercise before the meetings began. I would spend the wellness hour lifting weights. Every single minute of every day, I squeezed the zest out of every second of it. No time was wasted.

After about ten days, Caesar called me in to talk with him. He told me, "Frank, you cannot save everyone." I remember asking him, "What are you talking about. He told me, "Frank, you just can't. Not everyone in here is going to get sober. Truth is, not everyone in here cares. You really have to do you. In observing you, what I have realized is that what you need to learn most of all is to love yourself." I struggled with that. I struggled with that for quite some time.

As week three came around, I began to feel better about myself. I was dedicated, determined and disciplined to become the man that God intended me to be. I was focused and at peace. Twice a week, I began to partake in nightly meditations that calmed the anxiety that had been affecting me. On Sunday, September 9th, Nori's birthday, I attended Christ Fellowship Church in Palm Beach Gardens with Pastor Todd Mullins. All my life I was raised Catholic, but there was always something inside of me that seemed a bit amiss and I was eager to find it.

Now, a week or so before I went to rehab, something came over me. I knew that my life was going to change tremendously. At the time, I did not know if it was innate wisdom, or conscious awareness. Today, I realize it was none other than the direction of the Holy Spirit. I reached out to someone that I had not spoken to in about twenty years. I reached out to Jackie Villa. Jackie was my ex-fiancée, Ari's, sister. Now, why in the world would I reach out to Jackie? I have no idea. All I know, or all I knew, was that Jackie was a Christian and, I guess, I was searching for guidance.

As I spoke to Jackie, I let her know I was entering a treatment center. I remember asking her which church she was attending in Miami, so perhaps I could check it out some time. She replied, "Christ Fellowship Church, Palmetto Bay." On September 9, 2018, the morning of Sunday service, on the board there were two options for church services that we were allowed to be bused to. Option 1, St. Marks Catholic Church and option 2, Christ Fellowship Church in Palm Beach Gardens. As soon as I saw Christ Fellowship, my eyes opened widely. A huge smile emerged, and I looked up to the ceiling and said, "God, thank you." Nothing against St. Marks, but it didn't stand a chance. I have no doubt in my mind that as I looked at the board and saw Christ Fellowship and smiled, God was smiling right back at me.

In that Sunday service, when Pastor Mullins asked the attendees to raise your hand to all of those that wanted to surrender and accept Jesus Christ as Lord and Savior, something came over me and I immediately raised my hand. I don't know what it was, but it felt like A Welcome Home, son; it has been a while, I've been waiting for you. I remember one of my newfound friends from F-Troop named Chris telling me afterwards, "Frank, it looked like you had a halo over your head, man. You were glowing." I smiled at him and I felt it. I believed it.

The next day, my brother from another mother, came to join F-Troop. His name was Edzo. Edzo was a firefighter and a former marine. He was, and still is, the epitome of high energy. He is my brother to this very day. Now truthfully, I would have never imagined that the first time I saw him, though. I remember one day on my way to get breakfast at the cafeteria…by the way, let me tell you, those folks preparing food; they weren't cooks, they were chefs. What a group of great people. Not only did they serve great food, but they served it with love, man. Every dose was served with pride and a gracious smile. Anyway, as I am walking by the cafeteria, I could not help but hear this loud, tall, Anglo, white dude just yelling and yapping all over the place. I remember thinking, damn this guy is annoying as hell. Well, lo and behold, here we were just a few weeks later and Edzo and me are hugging, sharing and just allowing ourselves to be completely vulnerable with one another over our life's struggles.

Edzo and I would get up every morning and get our workout going. Man, Edzo was loud. That never changed. As we would do our 5:00 am cardio and walk near the women's building, I would always have to tell him, "Hey, Edzo, lower it down, you're going to wake up the girls." Now to put that in perspective; in 1993 in high school, I was voted loudest in my class. So, for me to consider someone loud, let's just say, he was over the top. Well, he was, but that guy is still my man, my boy, my "Devil Dog."

Before I knew it, my time was coming to a close at the Hanley Center. I had finally begun to learn to love myself. The day before I left, the men in the F-Troop building had some kind words for me. I remember some of the things that they said that stayed with me most…they told me, "Frank, you want it, man. You got a fire inside of you that just won't let up. Frank, man, you love your kids. You absolutely adore your children."

That last day, after church services, on September 23, 2018, my parents came by to drop off my car, give me a hug and show me some love. I remember sharing some warm hugs and embraces as I left, wondering what the next chapter of my life was bound to look like.

As I left the Hanley Center, it was roughly 1:00 pm, and I was making a beeline for one place and one place only. I needed my kids like a man needs air. My daughter, Nori, had a soccer game and I vowed to get there before it ended. I did. I remember playing the scenario out in my head on the hour and a half drive. I would show up at her game and almost like slow motion; my kids would see me, and they would run towards me. We would share a big hug and a bigger cry. Well…let's just say, the story didn't quite go as I envisioned it. I can't help but laugh about it now. Although I'm sure they were happy to see their father, perhaps they were also frightened. I mean, I missed my daughter's 14th birthday, and the last time I saw my children, I was a mess, a drunken mess. But, man, was I so filled with gratitude at just the thought of holding them in my arms again.

8
VISUALIZING THE MOUNTAIN TOPS

"Faith cannot exist without trust. Trust cannot exist without belief. You cannot have one without the other. Believe in the unseen." -Frankie M Powers-

I got home to a boat load of mail. Thankfully, I was not behind on any bills. I had prepaid all of them. Home sweet home, I thought.

The next day, I called South Miami Outpatient Rehab Treatment Center, since I had another six weeks of outpatient therapy awaiting me. But this was way different. The schedule was Monday through Thursday, 9:00 am to 1:00 pm. Truthfully, I absolutely loved it. I felt like a veteran in there. I had tools that I had learned at Hanley and I was giving them away. I was a sponge, though. I was a sponge for information, and I was soaking in everything that they gave me.

Now while rehab at Hanley was Big Book AA intensive, this was a bit different. This was more cognitive behavioral therapy or CBT, which is changing the way we think and perceive things. Cognitive Behavioral Therapy is a psycho-social intervention that aims to challenge beliefs that we hold to be true. It focuses on challenging and changing cognitive distortions and behaviors, improving our emotional responses and developing personal coping strategies to change our way of thinking. This was where I first learned of Brene Brown, who I perceive as a rock star in my book.

Brene Brown is a powerful speaker, author and professor. She has spent countless years studying the concepts of courage, vulnerability, shame and empathy. After hearing a few of her talks, I was hooked. I purchased her best-selling book, "The Power of Vulnerability," and it just blew me away. In the short span between the Hanley Center and now outpatient rehabilitation, I began to recognize that there was a huge gap in our educational system.

In essence, I learned that our educational system is quite broken. We do not really learn about emotions, but as human beings, emotions are everything.

Emotions drive action. We all deal with loss, but we are not taught how to cope. Everyone seeks connection with others; yet we're never taught how to communicate. How do we integrate intuition, mind and heart into our lives? When faced with indecision, what do we do? Our brains are but a 5-million-year-old tool that is conditioned for protection, for fight, flight, or freeze. You see, in a moment in our lives, something happens. Our minds record the event and the feeling associated with it. Was it pain? Was it joy? Was it fear? That information gets stored in our personal database or hard drive (our subconscious mind).

Neuroscientist, David Eagleman, explains that 95% of our decisions are made by our subconscious mind, throwing our fundamental beliefs as humans, or as westerners, that we have the decision of free will out the window. So, based on our experiences in life, or what we believe to be those experiences, will fundamentally alter or prescribe to us the lie that we end up living. I will explain more on this shortly, as I will explain in my experience in the Landmark Forum; which, after three attempts, I finally arrived there. This idea fascinated me. As the weeks in South Miami Intensive Outpatient came and went, I came to realize that I actually miss that place. It gave me a small preview of a new realm of possibility that can be taught to the human race.

I had a thought. "What if, we could change our subconscious mind?" Hmm…more on that later. On the final week of my time at South Miami, we had a class that partook in a small exercise that was about none other than self-love. Now here I am, excited. I am actually elated. Here, I had a test. Here I would be tested to see if my counselor Caesar, from The Hanley Center, was able to get me to tap into some real self-love. The assignment was, "I want you to ask yourself, do you love yourself? Are you worthy of love? I also want you to find something kind about each one of your classmates. When you finish the assignment, you will tell them aloud something positive that you see in them."

This is it! Did I pass? Was I worthy of love? My friends, the answer was a definitive yes. After a few minutes of writing down our thoughts, Carol, the instructor asked, "How many of you found this exercise of self-love difficult?" As I looked around me, everyone's hand was raised. Well, everyone… except mine. Carol, while grinning at me asked me, "So, you did not find it difficult to love yourself?" I looked at her unabashedly and said, "Truthfully? No. You see,… just a few weeks ago, while in rehab, self-love was my Achilles heel or greatest challenge. And truthfully, I was not quite sure if the self-love process had worked." In that moment, I remember feeling like a kid who had just won the state baseball championship (guess my subconscious mind gave me that one, wink). "It worked! The affirmations worked," I said excitedly. The class smiled and chuckled. I then went around the class telling everyone what it was that I saw in them, what it was that I found so great about them as a human being. There were quite a few teary eyes during that exercise, however, none more so than mine. It was time for my classmates to describe me.

This group of people, in just a few short weeks described who I was, who I am and who I pride myself to always be, deep beneath all the pain, hurt and anguish. They repeatedly said, "Frank, you want this bad man. You are determined to never drink again." I remember nodding my head, smiling. They then proceeded to tell me, "Frank, you are a man of remarkably strong faith." I tilted my head, and a soft gentle smile came up over me. And then they told me, "Frank, wow, there is no question of your devotion and/or love for your kids. Your eyes speak it." A few tears rolled down my eyes in that moment, as I nodded in agreement. Then, the instructor said one thing that poured the waterfall of tears from inside my soul.

Carol looked at me and said, "Frank, you are all those things, but the one thing I see in you exhibits everything everyone here has said and more." She said, "Frank, you are all heart." I lost it. I completely and utterly lost it. That was who I was. That is who I am. My heart runs the show; it is the show. Let me tell you; to all my dear friends, families and others, that is one of my greatest blessings and not a curse. One of my favorite spiritual verses in the bible is the one that says, "In order to reach the kingdom of heaven, one must enter with the heart of a child." In my life, have I suffered? Absolutely! We all experience pain; we all experience hardship in life. That is without a shadow of a doubt, a certainty. However, what I did not know then, that I know now, is that most pain is experienced by the stories we tell ourselves based on falsehoods we feel, as if they are our reality.

The First Story I Told Myself

It was now Friday, October 26, 2018. I finally made it. After two unsuccessful attempts at registering for Landmark, the third time proved to be the charm. As I entered that morning, I was quite apprehensive and cautious about the upcoming four days of what Randy described as life transforming. Although I had only known Randy for a little over a year at this time, I really trusted him. Randy was an easy going, really loving man. He had an energy about him that was infectious. I really love Randy. However, little did I know then, that everything happens for a reason. I needed to be at Landmark on this October weekend; not back in May when the basketball pictures prohibited me from doing so; and not in August when I was too drunk to drive, much less sit in a classroom for several days in a row. It was predestined for me to be here on this particular weekend in October 2018.

As soon as I entered, the first person I met was Terri. Gosh, I love Terri. Terri was dealing with some struggles in her marriage, and we immediately hit it off. It has been two years now and we have maintained our friendship until this very day. As I looked around, I told myself, "Okay, no weirdos yet," or at least people looked normal, whatever that means. What is normal anyway?

The class consisted of 106 people, each recognizing that there is so much more to life than what we are taught in schools, at home, or amongst our peers. As day one began, the instructor, Ori, begins with a statement, "There are things that you know that you know. There are things that you know that you don't know, and there are things that you don't know that you don't know." I remember looking around the room to see if everyone was as puzzled as I was. A few hours into the class, a beautiful blond woman walks up to the microphone to speak. Her name was Norma and we immediately connected. She had a great energy about her that was infectious. Every time someone had a question or something to say, they had to get up and address the class. Little did I know then that we would establish a deep friendship, the kind that seem to come along so rarely in this life.

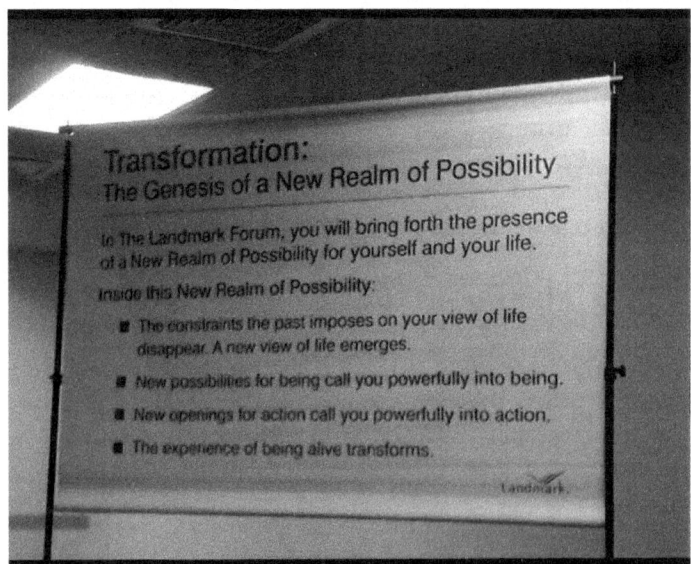

Landmark Forum

By the end of day one, I was lost. Not only was I lost, but I was also confused and frustrated. On the drive home that evening, I remember having a conversation with myself, asking myself if I should go back. Should I? Shouldn't I? I remember my conscious mind asking me, what are you going to tell Randy? So, I bargained with myself, I say chuckling. I told myself that if by lunch break something didn't shift, I wouldn't return. I lived in Miami; the Landmark Forum was an hour drive for me. The hours for the weekend were long, 9:00 am to 10:00 pm Friday, Saturday, and Sunday, and Tuesday from 7:00 to 10:00 pm. So, it was a three and a half day intensive unveiling of beliefs that we hold as truths, how those beliefs help define how true our experiences in life are, and whether those experiences that shaped our lives were based on, realities or our perception of our own reality.

Day two started off with a revelation that completely changed a belief that I now know today that I had stored in my subconscious mind, and it has ill-served me for all of my life. For years, I have suffered immensely due to the story that I convinced myself to be a fact. Let me share.

Ori proceeded to tell us, "I want every single one of you to go back and think of the first memory in your life that was extremely upsetting or painful." I remember closing my eyes and doing so. He then told us, "I want you to play it in your head." I remember telling myself okay, I have it, I could see it. "What is it?" he asked. As I played it in my head, I could remember the memory vividly. It was a story that I shared at the beginning of the book. I was in my parents' home; I was two years old, in my Superman shirt, and my parents left me. I was crying uncontrollably. Then, he said something that profoundly changed my life to this day. "Is it possible that the way you remember that story, is not real?" I remember thinking, who the hell is this guy and what the hell does he know about what happened to me? He wasn't there.

He then proceeded to share his experience. He said, "I remember being a young boy in Asia. I was roughly five years old. The next thing I remember, a woman I barely knew came into my life and began telling me what to do, how to do it and when to do it. That woman was my mother." He continued, "You see, I was raised by my grandmother until the age of five. I remember suddenly thinking to myself, who the hell is this woman telling me what to do? I don't really know you. You are my mother? Well, where have you been all these years of my life? Heck, you left me. "You see class," Ori said, "This is my story. My story is that my mom abandoned me as a child and then all of a sudden, she came back. That feeling…that sense of abandonment was present for me, for about 35 years.

The truth is, that memory would have probably stayed with me forever, if I had not walked into the Landmark Forum ten years ago. That feeling of abandonment made me insecure all of my life. It made me feel unwanted, unloved." He then proceeded, "During one of the breaks in the forum, I remember picking up the phone, 35 years after this incident, and calling my mom. The conversation went something like this, I said, "Hi, mom." She said, "Hello," lovingly. I then said, "Mom, can I ask you a question?" She said, "Certainly." I then said, "Mom, why did you leave me? After a short pause, she responded, "What? What do you mean why did I leave you?" "Yeah, mom, when I was a little boy, you left me. You left me and had grandma raise me. All these years, I felt like you abandoned me." She stayed quiet for a moment, swallowed to clear her throat and with heartfelt emotion said, "Son, I was 19 years old. You were a sick, sick boy. Your father had a business opportunity in which we had to travel overseas. It was supposed to take six months and ended up lasting over 5 years. It was the most difficult decision I ever had to make; not a day goes by that I don't think about it. I thought at the time, that I could not risk your life and who better to care for you than your very own grandma."

My mom wept as she shared this truth, as she shared the real story. Ori was teary-eyed as he shared the story and said, "Everyone in this room that is between the ages of 18 and 25, please come to the front." About a dozen or so classmates did. He then said, "Do you see them?" This is the age of most of your parents when they made that decision. Do you think they meant anything bad, or do you think they meant to try to do their very best?" He then finished by saying, "What I believed for 35 years was a sense of abandonment by my mother was actually the complete opposite. The truth is that what my mother demonstrated all those years ago, was an act of pure, unadulterated love."

In that moment, my whole story changed. As I listened, it hit me. I was two years old. What was my sense of time at two years old? Perhaps my parents were outside for a few minutes, yet, as a two-year-old, it felt like two hours. What if they told me they were going to the garage, but because I was entertained, I didn't hear them? Oh, my God, Oh, my God! This story that I have been telling myself that had such a profound impact in my life, on who I had become and on what I believed, was just a story. I had a fear of being alone all my life. I have sensed the fear of abandonment. For the next few days, my butt was glued to that seat; I needed to hear more. What other stories have I been made to believe were true? Over the next few days, it was one a-ha moment after another.

I remember this other time when Ori asked us, "Where are you in your life?" Are you engaging and interacting with others? Are you living your full life?

Are you in the stands as a spectator, or are you playing full out on the court, engaging?" I was hooked, I loved me some Landmark, I've got to tell you.

By the end of day two, I had also met a young man who was inherently bright, altruistic and exhibited peace. His name was Jonathan. I remember asking him what he did for a living. He responded, "I am a coach." I asked him, "A coach? What sport?" He grinned and answered, "Life." I was puzzled. I asked him "What do you mean, life?" He began explaining to me what a life coach was and how, as a coach, he helps people see the truth, the real truth, without the blinders of stories that we tell ourselves. He then continued to tell me, "All the answers, to all the questions you desire in life are deep within you, you just have to find them. As a coach, that is my job, to help you find the truth within yourself."

I was mesmerized. I have always had a lifelong affinity for psychology. My deep frustrations with psychology, throughout my experiences in life, were that they always seemed to focus on the past, what went wrong and why. I remember feeling okay, I get it… Now what? Now, I understood, that a coach, a good coach, helps you find your path, which can determine your desired future. I was fascinated, intrigued. I felt like a bear that had just woken up from hibernation. I…was…HUNGRY! I wanted more. By the end of the weekend, I cultivated many friendships that I hold dear to this day. Wilbert, Jonathan, Terri, Stephanie and my mentor, Norma.

The last evening, a group of about twenty of us started a What's App group, properly named, "Endless Possibilities," recognizing that the possibilities in our lives are only limited by the stories we create. Every single one of us, are, in fact, limitless. I left that weekend feeling a new zest for life, for friendships, for…endless possibilities.

Every day the What's App chat was exploding with contributions. As I think about it, I think it is time that I send a hello. It has been quite some time since we have spoken. So many connections were established that weekend, so much love shown, so much pain healed.

A few days after Landmark, my new steward and mentor, Norma, said "Hey, have you ever been to a Tony Robbins event?" I answered, "Tony Robbins? Isn't he the guy that does infomercials on TV?" She replied, "No, silly. He is a motivational speaker who holds events in different countries throughout the world and helps transform people's lives. He, is, in fact, the number one life coach in the world." I was like hmm…cool…okay. Sounds interesting, Norma, tell me more.

Now here I am going to AA meetings, trying to go day by day without drinking. However, the truth was, I had no thoughts of drinking, absolutely no desire. I was just told, go to meetings and connect with people to stay sober, and so, I did. I remember in going to meetings I would always have this feeling, this energy from many of the members whom it seemed were just trying to survive in life, and I did not just want to survive. I knew that I was born to thrive. Within 48 hours, Norma got back to me and told me, "Tony Robbins is doing an event in the New York area next week. It is called, 'Unleash the Power Within' (UPW)." Without hesitation I said, "I'm all in." Norma had connected me with a contact friend of hers, to set me up with discounted tickets, and less than a week later, on November 7, 2018, I am walking inside Miami International Airport, taking a flight to New York City. I was jacked up.

The event did not start until November 8th. As I arrived a day earlier, I checked into my hotel, then toured the grounds of where the Twin Towers (which consumed so much of my life for a while) once stood.

After touring the grounds, I headed over to the Prudential Center in New Jersey, the center stage for the UPW event, to pick up my tickets a day early. I remember hearing music blasting in the air. People jumping, dancing, moving. The excitement was palatable. The energy was off the chain. I remember telling a young woman, "Wow, the energy in here is crazy!" The young volunteer laughed at me and said, "You've never been to one of these, huh?" I said, "No." She said, "You haven't seen anything yet, just wait until tomorrow." I was stoked. I was jacked! I was in today's terms, "Lit".

The next day, as I entered the Prudential Center and I found myself a seat, there are no words to describe the feelings or sensations that went on inside of me or the other 15,000 or so others in the arena. It was insane. It was just a surreal experience. You can't do it justice with words. One has to sense it, taste it, feel it.

I could not believe this man. Tony Robbins was a man who was larger than life. This man was living, breathing, taking in every inherent God-given gift that he had been given and not only using it for himself, but the beauty of the man was that he was giving it back, to everyone around him. That Thursday night I did the unthinkable, the unfathomable. That evening, I walked barefoot on 1,000 degree burning hot coals. Walking on fire at roughly midnight was an amazing finish to a gruesomely long, but exciting day. I did it! And wouldn't you know it, no burns, no pain, and no remnants of the fire.

The power of the mind is that it really does what you feed it, what you believe.

The power of one's thoughts and one's beliefs, of what we can do or what we can't do, really does determine who we become. Tony Robbins, I love you man. Norma Aguirre, thank you, thank you, thank you. By God, thank you… By the end of the weekend, I learned more than I would have ever imagined in terms of emotional intelligence and life, living life the way it was designed by God to be experienced. You see, most human beings do not reach even 10 % of their potential. They do not reach their potential in their career opportunities, their life goals and in their relationships. The quote that says, "If you believe you can or you believe you can't, you will," resonates with me at this moment.

One of the most jarring and eye-opening lessons occurred to me on day three of the four-day event. When Tony spoke about us as humans and that we all have six essential primary human needs. They are the need for certainty, the need for uncertainty, the need for love/connection, the need for contribution, the need for significance and the need for growth as a human being. He explained that depending on what your two primary human needs are, that is how you live accordingly. Every single one of us has a need for certainty. We want to make sure we have a roof over our heads, a bed to sleep in, a phone, a car, et cetera. We desire to know everything, or to be able to control and dictate how our lives proceed. The problem with that primary need is that life is uncertain. The only certainty in life is that nothing is certain. Take for example, every morning one gets into the car and drives off to work. The only thing stopping the car coming toward you from crashing into you are the yellow lines painted on the street. However, you must trust the driver of that car not to cross over the yellow line. You trust that the person driving the car is not high or drunk. As far as the need for uncertainty, we all have a need for adventure, for thrills and for surprises. However, to live a life where your primary need is uncertainty means you really can't live as if every day is your last day on earth because…well, what if it isn't? You still have bills to pay; you still have responsibilities to meet.

The third primary human need is the need for love/connection. This one speaks for itself. Biblically speaking, God made Adam, and then He made Eve. As human beings, we all have a basic need for love and connection. The negative here is, if you put all your happiness into another person, they can never live up to your expectations. No one can ever make you happy. Your happiness is your job. A partner or friend can add to your happiness but cannot be the consummation of it. The fourth human need is the need for significance. This is the need to be seen, heard, to be valued. We all have a common desire to be and to feel special. Now the problem herein lies, when that becomes your end all, be all. Is life all about you? Does the world revolve around you? This breathes of selfishness and insecurity.

The fifth primary human need is the need for contribution. This is the need to give, to serve. As I mentioned earlier, we are all here to serve one another. We cannot just take and take in this lifetime because in taking we create inequity and imbalance in our world. Ultimately, it is in serving our fellow man and of giving of ourselves where we truly attain a sense of feeling whole and complete. The last human need is the need for growth. This is the need to learn, to find meaning, to expand ourselves as people. The problem here is that when you continue to search and search, you do not leave room to absorb what it is that you have obtained and to implement it into your daily life.

Over the four-day event, many of the experiences we had were experiential. We would write our notes, write down the emotions that would come up inside of us, and then share them with someone near us. At first, my two primary human needs came up to be my need for love and two my need for certainty. Tony would then have the audience raise their hands depending on what everyone's primary needs were, to get a gauge on how similarly or differently the audience experienced life.

After a little while, Tony mentioned that if anyone's top two primary needs were anything but love, contribution and/or growth, that they will never have a full and satisfied life. He mentioned, "You will spend your life constantly seeking happiness outside of you, instead of discovering it inside of you. He continued to explain to us the pros and cons of our primary needs. He then encouraged us to take some time, based on what he had just opened us up to, and reconsider. I did. At this time, Love became my number one human need and contribution became my number two.

Me and Tony Robbins

*****

As I got back home that Monday morning, November 12th, I was famished. Wow, what an experience. My brain felt like it was going to explode with all the insights and knowledge I had absorbed. I immediately called my newfound Landmark friends and told them about my experience. I made certain to thank Norma and tell her all the details of my weekend.

Meanwhile, every chance I had, I would go to any and all of my children's events, be it at school or any of their basketball or soccer practices or games. Barry continued to attempt to communicate with Yari's attorney, but we were not getting anywhere. Finally, Barry received a court hearing scheduled for December 12, 2018. I had continued doing all the things I was supposed to do. I was working full time with my parents, going to my daily AA meetings, and I was staying in constant communication with Charlie. I was exercising and also getting prepared for an upcoming operation. On the Monday after Thanksgiving, November 26, 2018, after having dropped over 200 pounds, there was quite a bit of excess skin that was loosely hanging, and I needed to remove it. Quite frankly, it was not very pleasant or comfortable to look at. Luckily, I had the financial assistance of my parents to ease any of the financial burdens that would have been thrust upon me.

On November 26, 2018, I was operated on. I was in quite a bit of pain afterwards. I remember taking the precautions of the doctor way too literally. He was adamant about me not staying stagnant; he wanted me to move around. Boy, oh boy, did I take that way too literally. The same day of the roughly five-hour long operation, I had my dad take me to Subway, Publix, and to see my kids in after school sports at St. Kevin's. This was not the brightest of ideas. The truth is that part of me was scared. I still thought of myself, or better yet saw myself, as that 448-pound guy, and I feared ever getting to that point again.

For a few weeks, I was moving quite gingerly. I recall just six days after my operation, my newfound Landmark friend, Terri, picked me up and took me to her church, Metro Life Church near Dadeland. It was a great church with great energy. After attending several times, I chose Christ Fellowship Church in Palmetto Bay to be my primary home church. Now, I am happy to say that I would happily double dip on the church service front. Truth is, I often do. Now let me say something to all those reading who may have strayed away from church. The messenger matters and the way a message is delivered, really matters. I always seem to get a nugget or two of inspiration or wisdom from attending service.

During this time, I had also enrolled in Liberty University to study psychology. All this newfound passion and vigor for life had me wanting more. Not more for myself, no, no. I wanted more so that I could give more, so I could serve others and inspire them to make the best out of their lives. I continued to engage with my Endless Possibilities friends from Landmark. As my court hearing was drawing near, Barry had informed me of how he was planning to proceed. He was going to state to the court that yes, I had relapsed. However, I voluntarily went to rehab and I voluntarily continued outpatient treatment. I was also back on Sober link and doing random urine testing. Barry was quite optimistic that I would get my 50/50 custody back.

At this point in time, I had not spent any alone time with my children since that fateful relapse date of August 8th, which was over four months ago. Well, Barry's optimism gave me a strong sense of hope, maybe too much. The morning of December 12, 2018, I put on my navy-blue suit, attended church service at St. Kevin's at 7:00 am, and headed to 111 NW First Street, Stephen Clark Center, in downtown Miami for my court hearing. Before I walked in, I reached out to my WhatsApp Landmark friends for some much-needed prayer and support. This is what I wrote:

"Hi everyone. Today is a pretty important day in my life. I will take all the prayers anyone can muster. Today, at 10:00 am, is my court hearing.

Whatever happens today, I have got to hand over to God. God's Will will be done. I kindly ask that if I waiver and make this about me, I ask everyone in this chat to hold me accountable. If things do not work in my favor, I must not question Him, for I never question God when things go right. It is not my job to question why.
1 Corinthians 5:7 Live by faith and not by sight."

I, then sent a second message:

"As we embark on our day, may we remember and value all those things that are really important. You see, in actuality, it is not those things, it is those people, those moments. Those are the real gifts, the real treasures that we have, that we have been given. You see, when our time on this earth is up, if we have been gifted the time to reflect, what will we think about, better yet whom? What memories? Did we hold anything back? It is those things and those moments that we will play on our rolodex, on our picture album of life. So, I challenge each of us to treat all the people in our lives today as if it were their last day on earth. Love them, hug them, thank them, don't hold anything back, because truthfully, for some people, today is all they have; cherish one another, each and every day. I love you all today and every day." One last reflection, *"No matter the outcome, I*

already won. You see, I may not get what I want, but as Terri so eloquently put it, God will give me what I need.

A year ago, I was a drunk, obese father, who was bitter and angry at the world and most people in it because my life was not what I hoped it would be. I blamed the world for my shortcomings as a man and as an individual. That is no longer the case. I am not Frank, the alcoholic, I am Frankie, who happens to be an alcoholic in recovery. I am not a victim of things that happened in my past. I am a man who is stronger for having confronted the fears of his past, and I will use this learning experience to strengthen myself and my future. I am a father who has learned to use his experiences to transform his outlook on life and empower my children and those around me. I am a better friend, who will not just agree with a friend for fear they will not like what I will say, but I will say it anyway. For what true friend sees a friend headed for trouble but stays quiet? Now I know what I want today. Yet, I am consciously aware that what I want may not be what God wants. Godspeed everyone. I will let you know what happens."

I entered the courthouse and said hello to Barry. I tried to say hello to Yari, but she was having none of it. Yari had not really spoken to me in several years, outside of those few co-parenting sessions over the summer. Anyway, when the hearing came to a close, I was quite upset and disappointed. I received my time sharing back with my children; however, I had no overnights. I was to have the kids back by 8:00 pm on school nights and 9:00 pm on my scheduled weekends. I had some hard, choice words with Barry, although, the truth is that Barry didn't relapse, I did. He did the best that he could. For some odd reason, this reminds me of a quote by former Miami Dolphins Offensive Coordinator Gary Stevens, which was, "You can't make chicken salad out of chickens***." The truth was that Barry did the best he could with what I gave him. It also gave me a template that I use now and share with my clients, friends, and others as often as I get a chance; if you turn your expectations to appreciations, your whole life will change.

The reality was that I didn't have my kids at all, and now I get all my time-sharing privileges back, except for overnights. As you can see here, I still had a lot to focus on as far as my essential human need of "growth" was concerned. As I walked out to my car, I realized that I am going to finally have my kids alone for a few hours this coming Friday and all-day Saturday and Sunday. I also needed to learn the inherent value of being fully present in the here and now. More on that later.

As I sat in my car and turned the key in the ignition, I took a deep breath and sent the following message to all my friends at Landmark. It read:

"Hi, everyone. Rome was not built in a day. The decision was not what I was hoping for today. I hope to make the most of this new test I have been given. Thank you all for your

thoughts and prayers. There is a quote that resonated with me that I want to send to you all, 'Nothing can stop a man with the right mental attitude from achieving his goal. Nothing on earth can help the man with the wrong mental attitude. President Thomas Jefferson.' My goal was not accomplished today, not today, but I will not be deterred, I will succeed, as long as I continue my path."

The following Thursday, on December 20, 2018, I picked up the kids from school. They changed and off to Santa's Enchanted Forest we went. As I walked up to the ticket booth to pay, I remember Nori telling me, "Papi, just say Jonathan is nine so we can save ten dollars." I was about to do just that and then, it hit me. What is the cost of the lie? Is saving ten dollars worth the price of teaching my children that it is okay to lie, to steal, to cheat? What is the payoff? How can I teach them that sometimes it is okay to take from another? Where would my integrity lie? What would that say about my character, or lack thereof? What would that say about my values? About my faith? I looked at both of my kids and said, "No guys, Jonathan is ten years old. We always say the truth, no matter the price. Be honest, be truthful. Right is always right and wrong is always wrong." That was one of those moments when I realized the example that I set, the values I live by, are ultimately what my children will copy. Something began changing in me…something was happening…I liked it. Actually, I loved it.

Me, Nori and Jonathan

Wow, what a wonderful weekend I spent with the kids. We spent all day Saturday with my parents, nephews, and loved ones. On Sunday, we went to church, then on to Sun Life Stadium to watch the Miami Dolphins play the Jacksonville Jaguars. I loved the heck out of them that weekend. Heck, I love the heck out of them every day, whether they are with me or not. It is all about love, my friends. It is all about loving people.

Christmas came and went, and we shared countless love, hugs and gifts with the family. As far as growth, I continued searching for more. Landmark had an Advanced Course that I was told was so much greater than the original one, so I was on it like white on rice. The only thing was that the next weekend that the Advanced Course was available was the weekend of January 4th through the 6th in Orlando, Florida. I said, "Let's do it. Sign me up." I was all in.

I arrived a day early. On Thursday morning, January 3, 2019, I drove straight from Miami to The Holy Land Experience, in Orlando, Florida. The Holy Land Experience was a biblical theme park, if you will. It had old bibles and artifacts from as far back as 500 BC (before Christ). That day, for me, was incredibly fulfilling. I was moved, I was touched, and I left inspired.

As I left the theme park around 5:00 pm and arrived at my hotel room, I unpacked my luggage and got ready to pack it in for the evening and to rise up bright and early.

9
SEEING THE MOUNTAINS IN THE DISTANCE

"Transformation can only occur when we stop hearing our own minds talk, and start listening to our souls speak." -Frankie M Powers-

On January 4, 2019, I walked into the Forum and sat front and center with my new weekend fellow apprentices. The instructor was a middle aged, incredibly bright, Canadian woman, named Sarah. She was as sharp as they come. She explained that the stark difference between the Landmark Forum and The Landmark Advance Forum was that, in the original forum, it was about diving deep into oneself; in the Landmark Advanced Forum, it was about diving deep in service to others. Like the original forum, the class began with excitement. Prior to signing up for the weekend workshop, there was a questionnaire I had to fill out. It was quite simple. The main question that I answered almost identically the same as I did for the original workshop was, what was it we desired to accomplish by the end of the weekend? The answer was quite simple for me. All I desired, in all these workshops, was to find a way to be able to communicate with Yari, so we could have peace for the sake of our children.

Much like the Tony Robbins UPW event, there were many opportunities for experiential sharing with one another. One other requirement of the workshop was, in between breaks, to call someone you have had a difficulty with and take full responsibility for your actions and seek peace. In the original forum, as well as in the advanced, my first call was to Yari, but she never answered.

As the day continued, came the core question of discovery of the weekend workshop. Sarah told us, "In your life, there was a moment, an event or an incident that occurred. And in that moment, you felt inept or afraid, and immediately a question of doubt arose in you." She paused and then continued, "That doubt, that fear, is a question that has been running your life ever since." She then gave a five to ten second pause and said, "Your homework for this evening is to find out what that question is and to write out the experience. Tomorrow morning, at 9:00 am sharp, we will open up the forum for sharing." Immediately, you could hear scattered whispers throughout the room. I remember thinking, a question? A question? What the hell question has been running my life? What am I going to have for dinner?" I said jokingly to myself, I'm a fat guy, did it have something to do with food? I was stumped. I was truly stumped that evening. I spent countless hours that night trying to figure out the question to no avail, until I finally just drifted off to sleep.

In the morning, I woke up at 6:00 am, and went to a small breakfast restaurant from the Cracker Barrel chain called Holler & Dash. I ordered an andouille sausage biscuit bowl with an over easy egg and some tater tots and grabbed myself a cup of coffee. I remember saying to myself that this was one of the best breakfast meals I have ever had. Anyhow, it was almost 7:30 am, and I still couldn't think of a question. So, as I began writing about an incident that had occurred to me in relation to a junior high girlfriend, it immediately hit me. Oh, my God, oh, my God. I broke down in tears. I couldn't believe it! How is it possible that she was right? Sarah was right. I had been playing this question, over and over in my mind, for 33 years.

At the beginning of the book, I wrote about my experience with the death of my favorite and beloved grandparent, Abuelo Papo. The day my parents told me to help them get my grandfather to eat, as you may recall, they took me to the supermarket, and I got the packet of Ritz cheese crackers before I went to see him. He looked bad; he looked really bad. He was sick, I mean, he was dying. I offered him the crackers with cheese, and he declined. He smiled, gave me a kiss on the cheek. I can still feel his shrubbery facial hair pinching my face. He told me to give the crackers to my grandmother, so I did, and I left. When I went to visit my grandmother the following week and opened the refrigerator, I saw the crackers. And a question arose in me that has been haunting me ever since. It was, "Why didn't you try harder to get your grandfather to eat?" Then I said to myself, "If you would have only tried harder, he would have eaten and if he would have eaten, he would have lived. You have to try harder. You have to push harder. You have to do the unfathomable, if necessary. You push, go over, or go through it, but go and give it all you got!

The question for every single person in that room had a negative connotation, almost exclusively. In fact, in the Advance Landmark class there were 68 students. I was the only one whose question could actually have a positive spin, except…you can discipline and through hard work and determination, push your way through many obstacles. You can make your way or will your way to success. Now, the problem is, you cannot force yourself or push your way on people, on relationships, on love, which was the number one primary need that I desired in life. So, on one end, the positive aspect is you can push your way to advancement, but on the other end, if you felt all your life that you are not enough, that everything you did was wrong, it cancels itself out. I made myself believe that everything I gave from deep inside of me was never enough to those I cared deeply for. The only one who I felt would reciprocate my love in return was my mom.

Before class that morning, I stopped at a Publix near Celebration in Orlando. I went to the cracker aisle, found the crackers with the cheese spread and that rectangular red stick, and bought a box. I entered my car, opened one up and ate two or three crackers. I looked upwards toward the sky and then kissed the rosary that had magically appeared in my room that fateful day, May 13, 1988, and wept.

I walked into the seminar that day with a packet of crackers ready to share my story. As I walked in, or better yet, glided in, I did not feel like I was walking on the ground that day. I actually felt like I was lifted two to three inches in the air. I knew that people were speaking to each other all around me, yet they seemed so distant, so far away. It was truly hard to put into words. It was like I was in a zone, in my own world. After several people shared, it was my turn. People felt me, they felt my words. My words seemed to pierce their heart. Throughout that weekend, I had several people tell me that I had this voice. They began asking me if I was on the radio? I bashfully smiled and replied that no I was not on the radio. Several others approached me and told me that every time they would hear me speak that I moved them. Sarah, the instructor, herself, told me that I was a natural born speaker.

As the weekend came to a close, we were told to come up with a slogan or catch phrase that we want to share and give to others who walk in our path. When my turn came around, I said, "I want to empower others to pursue their passions and follow their dreams." It was strong. It was powerful. It was heart. It was me. That is who I am, this is my gift. I share from my heart, not being afraid of people judging me or looking down on me. I give everything that I have, not desiring anything in return. I just want to let others know that I care and that they do matter.

God blessed me with a gift of a voice, with a gift of not being afraid to ask or to seek forgiveness if I have wronged someone.

In that moment, the name that I toyed around with at 16 years of age, became who I am, Frankie M. Powers. The joyful pureness and heart of Frankie the child, the adolescent kid in me, M. Powers, my middle initial, and me being lifted up by the grace of God to tell and show others that they can do the same. What a remarkable weekend this was for me. Absolutely transformational.

*****

I continued searching for self-development workshops throughout the state of Florida and the country, for that matter. Anything and everything on public speaking, communication, self-improvement and/or emotional intelligence and I was all in. I was committed to changing the educational system by enacting a class called, "Life," in schools throughout my community, and one day throughout the country. In fact, that became my calling card. As I write this, a quote from Steve Jobs that I have in my bedroom comes to mind, which reads, "Those that are crazy enough that think that they can change the world are those that do." I was off. I was determined. I was…unstoppable!

I signed up for a communications course the weekend of January 19th and 20th. My objective? Quite simple. To better my communication skills with others, especially with my ex-wife, Yari. Throughout the course, I learned that we all have different communication styles and that some of us use manipulation, others aversion, some of us are defensive, some use silence to name a few.

In the workshop, we did an experiential exercise that really blew my mind. They told us; I want you to imagine someone who you have had a difficult relationship with. I thought about it, said okay while he paused. He proceeded; Now I want you to imagine what you believe that individual is going to tell you. Okay, I thought about it. He then continued, I want you to play the role of that individual and say something lovingly to yourself as though that person was saying it to you. Wow, that was powerful. I want all of you who are reading this to stop for a moment and think of a friend or family member that you have had a challenging relationship with and try this. It will blow your freaking mind.

Let me show you my example. I chose my father. I imagined my father coming to talk to me. I immediately visualized him coming, ready to criticize me for doing something wrong. Now as soon as the instructor told me to visualize him speaking to me lovingly or gently, I was unprepared. My body language was already prepared for the negativity and as such, was combative. Truth is my dad never had a chance. I wasn't being present in that moment; I was bringing back past experiences and behaviors to this very moment. I was, in essence, living in the past.

Albert Mehrabian, Professor from UCLA, performed a study in the 1970's that explained the importance of body language in communication. The results will shake the hell out of you. The study concluded that in communication, the importance of body language is 55%, 38% is the tone that one uses, and only 7% is in actuality the words you have to say. Isn't that remarkable? Try it. Can you remember a time when your spouse or partner said some beautiful words with no emotion and a hardened tone? Can you recall certain words (adults only), that may be used in the bedroom, in which they may be deemed okay and used anywhere else would be grounds for divorce. Got your attention now, don't I?

Another important gem that I was taught was the power of asking for forgiveness instead of stating it. Let me give you an example: When apologizing, do you say, "I'm sorry," and expect to be forgiven? Be honest with yourself, do you? If you do, do you not think your body language shows that? Hmmm…I want you to ponder that. Next time seek it. The bible teaches us seek and you shall find. The next time you make a mistake, I want you to try something different this time. I want you to start by saying, I am sorry, can you please forgive me?" Huge difference. Try it, you will be glad you did.

As the weekend concluded, I was elated. I realized I had just picked up more tools for my toolbox.

It was now Wednesday, January 23, 2019. I woke up bright and early. Well, early for most people. I had already become accustomed to waking up at 3:00 am to exercise. At 3:30 in the morning I was off to Tampa, Florida, for a Dale Carnegie two-day workshop on Public Speaking Mastery. Over the course of the two days, I learned the power of the pause, body posture, and how to engage with the audience. While there, I also met up with a friend from Landmark Advanced Course to have lunch and catch up.

In the meantime, in between workshops, I was still working in the office, however, truthfully, not as much as I was being paid to do so. The bold, honest truth was that my parents were pulling my weight. I was filling every moment in my day with substance. Even socially, I would continue to interact with my Landmark friends, Wilbert, Stephanie, Terri and Norma. On a personal level, I began getting close to the Barreras, Jessie and Noel. God, I do not know what I would do without Jessie in my life. The help and shoulder to land on that Lisa had been to me for many years, the mantle was passed on to Jessie. Lisa and I are still the dearest of friends, but our children are in different schools and contact has not been the same.

It was now February 1, 2019, and 10X is coming to Miami Marlins Stadium. 10X is a Grant Cardone event filled with various speakers and entrepreneurs from all over the world. I went with my dear friend Ivan; the event was incredible. I remember my friend Norma had taught me something during this time. She had told me, "Frank, wherever you go, always look for the jewels. Even if it is one nugget or two, look for those gems and hold them dear." Those words stuck with me. Here were two things that stuck with me in this event. Sara Blakely, the owner of Spanx women's underwear, spoke and talked about a lesson that her father taught her as she was growing up. Her father would say Sara, what did you fail at today? At first it would bother the heck out of her. She was often left wondering, why does he always seem to be looking for something negative. On one particular day, she had had enough and asked him. His response was, "Honey, if you failed at something, that means you tried. If you got it wrong, that means you are one step closer to getting it right." That was powerful for me. It reminded me of Thomas Edison, inventor of the light bulb, when his associate said, "Thomas, it doesn't work. You have tried numerous times and it just hasn't worked." Mr. Edison responded, "No, I have tried 1,000 times where it doesn't work," and then, on the 1,001st attempt the light bulb was created. Throughout this journey of my awakening, literally speaking, the lightbulb in me turned on and sent sparks all down my spine and throughout my body.

The second thing that came to me this weekend was Jesse Itzler, owner of the NBA's Atlanta Hawks basketball team. When he spoke, he said, when you are physically tired and working out and your body says you are finished and have had enough, it is only about 40% of what you can truly do. Your mind is trying to deceive you; you still have 60% left inside of you. That message resonated with me. It reminded me of Hall of Fame Head Coach of the Green Bay Packers Vince Lombardi, when he once said, "Fatigue makes cowards of us all." My question from Landmark would have served me well in these instances. Frankie, you have to try harder.

As the weekend came to an end, I was off to my next adventure. Dale Carnegie High Impact Presentations in Fort Lauderdale, Florida, on February 7th and 8th, followed by seeing none other than world renowned pastor, Joel Osteen at the BB&T Center in Sunrise, Florida.

Dale Carnegie High Impact Presentations was what it set out to be (High Impact). It was here that I learned the importance of smiling when speaking. How such a dramatic difference a simple smile makes when you speak to the audience. I also learned that public speaking is the greatest fear that humans have. It is literally the number one fear, even above death, having to give a speech in front of an audience. As far as myself, I loved it. I have always felt born to do it. I mean, oftentimes, I do not really have to think. I have always lived from my heart and when you do that, you do not have to use your mind, you can just feel. When I feel, the words just seem to flow from my lips. I also learned how to change a question. If you do not like the questions that you are asked by the audience, you can repeat the question with a small shift so that it appears you are answering their question, but you are really answering another, one in which you want to steer the conversation to anyway.

As day two of Dale Carnegie's High Impact Presentations came to an end, I did not have time to change, so I went straight to my friend Stephanie's house to pick her up and head out to see Joel Osteen. By this time, my head was spinning. I was getting information overload. Well, Joel was the perfect place for me. A tender voice, a whole lot of God and the theme of the evening, I couldn't help but smile. It was called a Night of Hope. Joel did what he does, and everyone loved him. At the end of the evening, I had the opportunity to shake hands and meet the man with the warm heart and infectious smile.

For the next few weeks, I had tried to conjure up and rehash all I had learned and absorbed. I began listening to motivational speaker, Les Brown "Shoot for the Moon, even if you Miss, you land amongst the Stars". I loved Les. I was listening a lot to motivational speaker ET (Eric Thomas), "When you want to succeed as much as you want to Breathe, that is when you will be successful".

I began reading everything I could by Brene Brown on Cognitive Behavioral Therapy. I began studying Dr. Joe Dispenza and Dr. Bruce Lipton. I started listening to Deepak Chopra and Eckhart Tolle. I was literally soaking everything into my pores, and I loved it. At this time, too, the idea of coaching began to appeal to me even more deeply. I loved it. I loved what it could do, the ability to help others empower and transform their lives.

It was now Wednesday morning, February 20th. At approximately 9:10 am, I received a phone call from Dr. Norman Ruiz-Castaneda, my children's pediatrician. My son Jonathan, ten years old at the time, had recently been at a track meet; after his race he was complaining of chest pains. I remember asking Jonathan a few questions and he told me it had happened a few times during the last week. Being concerned, I called the doctor and he referred him to see a specialist and have some tests done. After getting the results back, Dr. Ruiz-Castaneda called me and told me the results of the x-rays had come back and we needed to take Jonathan to a cardiologist. I remember feeling frantic and asking him, "What is going on Doc?" He replied, "They want to check his heart further." He then stated, "No sports, no exercise."

I, then, desperately asked him, "Is there anything I can do?" He replied, "Pray." I remember freaking out for a bit and feeling overcome with emotions. I gathered myself and drove to his school. That day he had a cross-country practice and I wanted to let him know he would not be able to attend. As I entered the office, I asked to speak to him. They called him over to me and we went to a small room. I remember feeling my heart heavy because taking away sports from him would be devastating. Once I told him, he replied, "I know, Papi. Mom already told me." His mom had told him the day before. I remember being surprised and upset that he knew before me. I gave him a big hug and kiss and told him that everything was going to be okay, and I left.

I immediately asked my Landmark friends for prayer and prayed myself, a little bit, before I drove home. The following day, February 21, I was scheduled to be in Tampa for an NLP workshop. That no longer was on the table. Then I called the hotel in Tampa and cancelled my reservation; I then called the NLP office, explained my situation, and they kindly offered their understanding and well wishes.

What I did next was unfathomable to me. About 12 years ago, before Jonathan was even conceived, I had a conversation with a family friend named Paul. I do not know how we got into that conversation, however, what I do remember is Paul telling me Frank, your children are not yours, they are God's. They are a gift from God to you for as long as He decides to have you care for them. Hopefully, it is for your entire lifetime, but if not, you must be grateful and accept that. I fought with that at the time, I challenged him on it, I argued with his beliefs on it, and now, fast forward, all these years later, his words immediately hit me. It happened almost in the moment as I opened the door and got home. I immediately dropped to my knees in prayer and said,

> *"God, thank you. Thank you for the precious gift of my son Jonathan. Thank you for allowing me to love him and care for him for all these years. I pray and I ask for him to be okay and get well. However, if something is wrong with him, if he is sick or if it is his time to go, thank you for giving me the time that I have had with him."*

I cried me a river. Incredibly, though, it was a peaceful one. I realized, in that moment, that I had truly surrendered. I realized that God's Will shall be done whether I like it or understand it or not. I can fight it. I can reject it. Or I can merely accept it. You do not suffer heartache without having heartfulness. You do not experience loss without first experiencing love. Fortunately, the tests were taken, and Jonathan was okay. As a matter of fact, Jonathan would be just fine. Hallelujah. I remember feeling at peace, grateful, and blessed.

As February was coming to an end, I signed up for an 8-week course that convinced me, with absolute certainty, that I was a coach, a motivator and I was a testament to overcoming one's past in order to have the life that God destined for them.

On February 26th, I started the original Dale Carnegie course. By now, you can see, I obviously love Dale Carnegie. For those of you who are unfamiliar with Dale Carnegie, he was an American writer, public speaker and a master at interpersonal skills. He understood that in order to connect with people, you need to build rapport, and the best way to do that is to recognize people's need to be heard, acknowledged and validated.

In the moment I heard that, I recognized with that simple principle, every single war that has ever been waged throughout human history, every protest and every social movement, is a testament to this. Every individual wants their voice heard. When people's voices are not heard, when they do not feel acknowledged, well, they get sick and tired of being sick and tired. This is how revolutions begin. Every time a politician says forget someone's emotions; it really drives me mad because emotion is what drives action.

Dale Carnegie was also the author of Time Magazine's all-time top 100 books, "How to Win Friends and Influence People." Billionaire investor, Warren Buffet, claims that the best investment he has ever made in his life, that supersedes all others, was his investment in taking the Dale Carnegie course. In fact, with all the degrees and accolades that Warren Buffet has obtained, his diploma from the University of Nebraska and his diploma from Columbia University, he states," The most important degree in my life, and the only certificate and/or degree that I proudly display on the walls of my office, is the Dale Carnegie graduation certificate because it set the tone for my life."

The class was rather remarkable. There were twenty-nine of us in total. Many of them, experts in their field. We actually had an attorney who represented several casinos in Atlantic City, New Jersey. It was quite a group of established professionals all seeking to enhance their skills. We learned that the sweetest sound to anyone's ears is the sound of their name. Let me give you an example. Ever go to a restaurant and the server comes by and says, "Hi, Frankie, how are you doing today?" It gives you a feeling of importance, of significance…it satisfies a basic human need. You realize, wow, they remember me.

The class was every Tuesday night from 6:00 to 10:00 pm. Each week we were to prepare two speeches, as part of our assignment, to deliver in class. Everyone would take their turn and the Dale Carnegie staff would provide us with their feedback. The instructor just happened to be a life coach. Her name was Laine Schmidt. Laine was a breath of fresh air, always smiling, laughing and encouraging. She was one of those people who you just enjoy being around because of her energy.

In speaking about energy, I had also signed up at this time for IPEC University, the top coaching school in the country. IPEC taught core energy coaching, and it involved the seven energies we all carry from within. I was excited. I was excited to follow the man who literally lit me up on fire, the greatest coach in human history Tony Robbins. Tony Robbins coaches over a dozen billionaires. He actually had a seat at the table, or better yet, the plane, and spoke with former Russian President Mikhail Gorbachev, and convinced him to tell him the truth of how the cold war ended. Mikhail Gorbachev! When Bill Clinton was impeached, the first person he called was Tony Robbins to ask him what he should do. Tony's response, "Mr. President, perhaps you should have called me before this incident happened." Tony is a man on a mission. He has provided over 500 million meals to families throughout the world, with a goal to reach 1 billion in the next few years. He helps support and organize efforts to end modern day slavery, the human trafficking of children, and he is… all heart. He loves hard. This man has become an inspiration for me and someone I want to emulate, and no, I do not want to be Tony Robbins. I am me. I am Frankie M. Powers.

Before the weekend at IPEC, Norma had informed me about an event in Broward County with Kyle Cease. Kyle Cease is a motivational speaker, actor and transformational figure. He explains and expresses to others how our minds stop us from achieving those things that we want and teaches people to believe that anything and everything is possible if you can visualize it. He told us that if we visualize what we want and speak it into existence, we get one step closer to making our dreams come true. I decided to purchase a ticket. Norma had agreed to meet me with her daughter Krystal at Shuck 'n Dive. It had been exactly seven months, to the day, that I had last entered and dined at Shuck 'n Dive. That was the day I had walked into rehab, on

August 24, 2018 where I had my last alcoholic drink before treatment.

I then followed Norma to the Amaturo Theatre at the Broward Center for the Performing Arts. The drive took a little longer than expected as we almost ended up on the intercoastal. We parked our cars and walked to the ticket booth. As we pulled out our tickets, Norma asked me, "Where is your seat?" As I looked at my ticket and I looked at hers, I was speechless. Unbeknownst to either one of us, in a 600-seat auditorium, somehow, the seat I purchased was right next to hers. Wow, incredible, I thought. What are the odds?

As the show got underway, we practiced an experiential exercise with a member of the audience we did not know. We played out a scenario where we pictured our dream. We played it out as if we had achieved it, and then the person we had partnered with would celebrate with us, as if they were there when our dream came to life. That exercise was surreal; it was amazing as we watched our dreams come to life right before our very eyes.

Shortly after the exercise, Kyle had asked a few of the audience members to share. Amongst the countless hands that were raised, he chose me. After I shared my dream and passionate desires, I received a loud ovation. It was indescribable. Once the show ended, I had the opportunity to meet Kyle Cease, who told me (Me!!) that I was inspirational. Two other members from the audience walked up to me and handed me their business cards and stated, "If you ever run for office, please give me a call. I will happily contribute to your campaign. We need people like you." For one of the first times in my life, I had no words to say; I was humbled.

As Norma, Krystal and I walked towards our cars, we ran into Jason. Jason was at the show with his wife. Jason was a classmate of ours in the Landmark Forum.

We talked for a little while, and then he told me something that I had begun to hear from several people throughout the different workshops and events I had been partaking in. He said, "Frank, man, you have a gift. You are going to impact many, many lives." I sighed, took a deep breath and said, "Thank you, brother. Thank you so much. You have no idea what those words mean to me."

Before I got into my car, I gave Norma and her daughter a hug and thanked her immensely. You, Norma, guided me on this path. I am so grateful to you and for who you have been in my life. You have been a lantern guiding me to the promised land.

So, this coming weekend, IPEC Coaching University module one, at Florida International University, had arrived. I was stoked. Energy core level coaching, wow. I never realized the depth of inner emotional work. Who are we? Why do we do the things we do? I learned so much about assumptions, interpretations, limiting beliefs and gremlins. These are all the results of how we perceive the things that occur to us in life. In fact, it is only in recognizing where we can see what is real, and yes, what part of it is a story, that we begin to realize what, in fact, is the truth. A Gremlin is a statement that we continue to tell ourselves. It is that negative barrier such as, "I am not enough." It could be, "I am not smart enough, I am not attractive enough, I am not good enough, et cetera." These are beliefs that are not true and do not suit us to enhance our lives.

It was a weekend of friendships, developed and nurtured to this very day. I met some of the most honest and truest individuals that I have ever met in my lifetime in this group. They are friends by the names of Rachel, Fidelina, Aimee, Telanna, Samantha and my dear friend Len. Wow, Len, what a great guy. He is a former psychologist and 20-year Army veteran. Len was a brilliant, brilliant man, but his heart is what is even more fascinating. That man is really dear to me. Love you, old friend.

As the weekend came to a close, we laughed, we hugged, and we even cried a little bit. I have met so many people in all these events, workshops and seminars, in which all of them gathered and shared their deepest fears and insecurities. It is a connection and an openness that we are all taught to suppress instead of express. Yet, only through expressing oneself can we ever fully live.

By this time, the eight weeks of the Dale Carnegie course was about finished. It was now April 16, 2019, and it is our final day of class. After we shared our final speeches, there were several awards handed out. First up, the speech of the day. The second award was the most improved speaker of the class. Finally, was the award given to the person who best exemplified the principles of the Dale Carnegie course and who Dale Carnegie himself would be proud of their achievements. I had my vote, and I believed it was Ray. Then, drumroll…the award goes to Frank Lopez. I… umm…I was…speechless. Here we are in a course on public speaking, and I am speechless…this was the most glorious achievement that I had ever received in my life. It meant more to me than my honor roll in high school. It meant more so than any college accolades or graduating as a Marine from boot camp. After receiving my award, I said a few words and I just felt so extremely grateful and humbled that amongst all these fine men and women, my peers voted for me. I mean, these people were, and are, at the top of their professions, of their fields, and they voted for me…for me…for Frankie. It was just an explosion full of heartfelt emotions.

I remember getting home and lying in bed and just playing the tape of my life; where I was just a few short months ago and where I was now. There were…no words.

I did not sleep that night, not one bit. I couldn't. I kept thinking to myself I have overcome all these battles, all these difficulties. I need to help people. My addiction to alcohol turned into my motivation to help others heal.

Somehow after pulling an all-nighter, I wasn't tired. I had received tickets that day for a Miami Marlins versus Chicago Cubs baseball game. I took Jonathan and Jessie's son Pipa to the game. The Marlin's lost, but we had a great time. I dropped off Pipa, picked up Nori, and went home.

The next morning, we woke up early and headed to Orlando and straight to the Holy Land Experience. It was Easter weekend and we wanted to fully feed our deep-rooted faith. The following morning, we headed home; however, being that it was Good Friday, the kids and I decided to go to Christ Fellowship Church in Palm Beach Gardens on the way to Miami. This was the same church I attended while at Hanley Rehabilitation Center. It was, in fact, the church where I had surrendered myself to God. We were tired. I was exhausted. I had slept a total of five to six hours over the course of the last two nights, and it was catching up with me. After service, we drove straight home.

The following morning, Saturday, we decided to get some rest. Easter was Sunday. The kids and I gathered to make a plan. Growing up, as a kid, I was never really a part of my parent's planning. I think most of us, as children, aren't. We are generally told, well, I am your mom or your dad, you do as I say. Okay, I get it. However, our kids are people. At some point, they are going to make their own decisions. Well, why not involve them in ours?

According to the commissioner for children and young adults and Plan International, children's participation in decision making is an integral part in their self-esteem and how they value themselves as adolescents, then into adulthood. It also shows that a child who feels valued by their ideas and input, generates a stronger connection with their family throughout the course of their life. I asked them, "What do you guys think about brunch at the Rusty Pelican in Key Biscayne?" I showed them pictures of the beautiful ocean views and newly renovated restaurant. They were fascinated. "Yes, Papi, yes!" Now came the most important question. "Do you guys want to go to the

Saturday night Easter Service at Christ Fellowship in Palmetto Bay, or do you want to go to the Christ Fellowship sunrise Easter service near The Deering Estates?" Now the sunrise Easter service was at 6:00 am. We would have to get up at 4:30 am, because we needed to arrive at Christ Fellowship Church, park, and then take a bus to the sunrise service.

Well, lo and behold, both my children said, "Papi, can we do both?" My eyes almost popped out of their sockets. I said absolutely. I remember asking them are you sure? We will have to get up really early, guys. My son said, "Jesus sacrificed his life for us, we can sacrifice some sleep for Him." My eyes welled up with pure joy, with pride, for both of my children. I want to add, at this point in time, it was not only about getting up early on that Easter Sunday morning. It wasn't only about triple dipping at church services (Good Friday, Holy Saturday and Easter Sunday), but Jonathan still believed in the Easter bunny. For him, it meant getting up at 4:30 in the morning, looking around and seeing all those Easter eggs filled with candy and money and saying…I'll pass, God first. I don't have the words to express the emotions that ran inside of me, recognizing the pureness of both of my children's souls. So, we did…service on Saturday night was beautiful. It was a full house.

It was now the morning of Easter Sunday, early, early morning. Nori and Jonathan got up with ease. We quickly got dressed, arrived at the parking lot of Christ Fellowship Church and hopped on a bus headed to service. Before we knew it, we were outside a beautiful estate overlooking the waterway near Deering Estates. There was a full Christian band playing Hillsong and Elevation Worship music. There was a beautiful, large wooden cross near the stage. The children and I had brought blankets to lay on the grass, and we sang and praised and loved on one another. That was without question the most beautiful service that I had ever been a part of. Nori and Jonathan echoed that sentiment.

After service, we went home, had something light to eat and the kids went running around searching for Easter eggs. Both of them actually found the golden egg. We laughed, smiled and took a short nap before our 2:00 pm Rusty Pelican Sunday Brunch.

We arrived at the Rusty Pelican, valeted our car and gave our name to the hostess to check for our reservation. It was a special Easter Sunday brunch. It was a full-on buffet filled with specialties like eggs benedict, Belgian waffles, Alaskan snow crab, fresh shucked oysters and many other specialties. We had a beautiful view of the ocean with a pianist playing music nearby. Nori absolutely loved it. Pavlov was the manager. Pavlov was a good friend of mine that I had met at the Landmark Forum. Pavlov showed us around, we talked for a bit, and as I looked at Nori gazing all around her, there was a sparkle in her eye. Nori was glowing.

*****

It was now April and Nori's "15's" birthday was coming up. I was hopeful that Yari and I could put our differences aside for the sake of our beautiful daughter. When I asked Nori if she was interested in having her "15's" birthday party there, she enthusiastically said, "Yes, yes, Papi." I said perfect. I will send a text to your mom, cover the cost of the whole event and invite her and her whole family. I don't know if I have ever seen my daughter look so happy. Jonathan and I were really, really excited for her.

Nori had been through a lot, more so than what was fair for any child to have gone through. Time and time again, she was put in the middle of many situations between her mom and her dad. She had to go through her father being an embarrassment to her during my years of being so obese, and then having become an alcoholic. Nori having, too often, to shelter and take care of her little brother, having to go through all these emotions, generally, on her own. She would never discuss her feelings with anyone, not friends, not family, not even her parents. I tried countless measures to get her to talk to a therapist. Well, yeah…that's right, even her therapist had left her. I mean, her therapist was in jail.

Despite all this, she was an incredible daughter, a scholar athlete, a girl scout, a loving sister, but better yet, another mother to her little brother. She was loyal, kind, and so adamantly respectful. She was…no is, so beautiful. I mean, she is breathtaking. It is not just her outer beauty but her heart, her faith, her…I could go on and on and write a whole book on my blessed daughter. So here it is, her "15's" birthday party at the Rusty Pelican, or…is it not?

On Monday morning, I called and spoke to Lori from the Rusty Pelican. Lori confirmed they had Friday, September 13th available, or Saturday, September 28th. I reached out to Yari to invite her and her family and the invitation was declined. Yari informed me that she and I would not be present at any of our children's events together, unless it was a graduation or on their wedding day. This upset and angered me; it enraged me. Heck, I don't really care how she feels about me. I mean, do I want forgiveness? Do I desire it? Did I seek it? Yes, absolutely. However, I didn't need it. Nevertheless, my views at the time still stand firm to this very day. Nori and Jonathan never asked to come into this world, we brought them here. They deserve better. Nori's "15's" was a big deal. I mean, it was a big deal to her. Nori has always been a simple girl. She has never really asked for much of anything. My daughter deserved it, no…not only did she deserve it; she earned it.

It was now May 1, 2019. I am on my way to Houston, Texas, to finally take the NLP course (Neuro-Linguistic Programming) that had eluded me back in February of the same year. Norma had raved about it. She told me that I would be immediately immersed in it, and I was. I really, really was.

Over the weekend, I made incredible connections. I still keep in touch, every now and again, with Geoffrey through Facebook. I received lightning bolts of insight that weekend including…that beneath our reasonings and our truths, we must continue to search through the simple question of why. Why ask why? Because the answer to why we want something is never revealed in our first answer. It is sometimes not revealed until our third, fourth, maybe even tenth question of why. The answers to the question of why we believe the things we do are embedded deep inside of us. They live and wander deep in our subconscious state of being.

I also learned about a beautiful Hawaiian forgiveness prayer:

The Ho' oponopono Prayer.

I am sorry.
Please forgive me.
Thank You.
I love you.

As the weekend came to a close and I arrived back home in Miami on Tuesday, May 7th, my trek continued. Advanced Communication Training at Landmark. Eckhart Tolle event. Emotional Intelligence workshop in West Palm Beach; Breaking Bad Communication Habits in Fort Myers; Communicating with Tact and Professionalism in Fort Lauderdale. It was a never-ending journey of aha moments and nuggets, or as my dear friend, Norma, loves to say, "jewels" (jeweled nuggets, I reckon, I say laughingly).

It was now May 17, 2019. After church services at St. Kevin's Catholic Church, the athletic awards ceremony for Nori and Jonathan's school is about to begin. The awards are given in the following order: the primary kids first, followed by the junior varsity and then the varsity athletes. My son Jonathan was in 4th grade and he was up for several primary awards. He won Most Valuable Player for basketball, Most Valuable Player in track and field and most improved runner in cross country. Jonathan is just a natural born superstar athlete. Nori wasn't too far behind. Truth is, it is hard to say for certain who is the superior athlete. Nori is the more cerebral one; Jonathan the more aggressive, passionate one. They each approach their sports differently.

After they finished handing out the primary and junior varsity awards, they began with girls' varsity. The award for best sportsmanship in basketball goes to Nori Lopez; most valuable defender in flag football trophy, Nori Lopez; most valuable player in track and field, Nori Lopez. Funny thing is her best sport, bar none, and the only sport she ever truly mastered was soccer. However, that trophy escaped her grasp. Now came the daddy of all awards, the one that she had been talking about and desiring for over a year now, much like the award that her father had desired decades prior, the varsity "Athlete of the Year" award.

After much anticipation, the award for varsity girl's athlete of the year award goes to "Nori Amanda Lopez". I jumped so high I think I almost touched the ceiling of the church. The award that eluded me exactly 30 years ago could not have been any sweeter, nor the gift been any better. My daughter, my precious daughter, received the award she so graciously yearned for, the acknowledgement she so desired. I, a proud father, took a step back and looked at how the 30-year wait was so very worth it. My daughter, girl scout trooper, honor roll student, young woman of faith, and most athletic athlete of her school. I felt so blessed by my gracious God to hold the title of being her dad.

Wednesday, May 22, 2019 was Nori's final girl scout meeting at St. Kevin's High School. There was an announcement that there would be a guest motivational speaker, psychotherapist and now author of, "Hurt 2 Hope," Dr. Betsy Guerra. Parents had been welcomed and invited to join. Being that I loved any, and all, motivational talks and speakers, I was all in. Nori took a grand liking to Betsy. After Betsy finished speaking, Nori came to talk to me and asked me if I would be able to talk with Betsy to ask if she would see Nori for counseling. I immediately said yes. I then approached Betsy, a kindhearted, compassionate and humble woman. I explained to her some of the circumstances Nori and Jonathan had encountered and asked if she could be of help or guidance.

Dr. Betsy Guerra is a household name in the world of psychiatry and influence. She is a woman who has battled hardships that seem almost impossible for so many to overcome, one is the tragic loss of her two-year-old daughter. In her book, she reveals how she turned her hurt to hope. Dr. Guerra fortunately introduced me to one of the best therapists in South Florida; someone who would be able to connect and be of service to Nori. Her name is Cynthia Tamayo. Cynthia has been a Godsend. There is not a better example of someone who not only understands the teaching of psychology and how to help others, but is willing to go outside the box, if need be, to be of service to those in need.

In my years of having met, interacted with, and spoken with various therapists and psychologists, Cynthia is, without hesitation, at the very top of her field. She is really spectacular at what she does. In working with Nori and Jonathan, primarily Nori, she has been an immense gift and a helpful ear for my so gracious daughter. Her innate wisdom to see things that others in her profession miss, or fear bringing up, has played an integral role in Nori's development. I took mental notes and remembered her when the moment soon came for me, when I felt heartbroken and in despair.

Now May is coming to an end and Nori is about to graduate from St. Kevin's Junior High School. Upon her graduation, I will also finally get my full parental time sharing back. That means sleep overs at Dad's house are right around the corner. It was a great feeling to see the consequences of my actions bringing the results I so deeply desired. But first, one more workshop. It was on to Rhinebeck, New York, and the Omega Institute, a Don Miguel Ruiz and sons' workshop, titled, "The Four Agreements", based on the number one New York Times best-selling book, which is based on the Toltec traditions that we can live by:

1) Be impeccable with your word.
2) Do not make assumptions.
3) Do not take things personally.
4) Whatever you do, always do your best.

These, along with a fifth agreement written by Don Miguel's son Don Jose Ruiz, 5) Be skeptical but learn to listen were five commandments or codes to live by and adhere to. Not only was I excited to attend the workshop, but I also discovered that surprise, surprise, staying in the room right next to me was Don Miguel Ruiz and his two sons. "Awesome," I thought to myself.

The Omega Institute was like a scene of nature's paradise from a movie. It was near the top of a mountain, filled with beautiful trees, benches, creeks and the sounds of nature calling. The weather was perfect. It was mid-70's during the day, and low 60's at night.

It was now five minutes to seven, and the Friday night workshop was set to begin. The lecture was a preview of what to anticipate over the weekend; I was excited. Don Miguel Ruiz, Sr. and his sons, Don Miguel and Don Jose, took turns speaking. These men were brilliant. They had remarkable insights in the Toltec Tradition. One of the highlights for me was when Don Jose spoke about being skeptical but learning to listen, that somewhere in taking a pause and playing the observer role, therein lies the truth.

Often times in society and in culture we are not open to hearing what anyone says that does not align with our way of thinking. A few quotes that resonate with me at this moment are, "No one wants to hear your opinion, they want to hear their opinion coming out of your mouth." Another that comes to mind is, "We are born with two ears, but only one tongue, so we should listen twice as much as we speak." Third, and lastly, "Wisdom is the reward you get for a lifetime of listening when you would have rather been speaking." Truth is, that when we speak, we already know everything we have to say. When we listen, we have an opportunity to enrich our knowledge and gain a different perspective. This was a huge, new jewel. "Norma, are you counting?" my inner voice laughs inside.

During a break, I had the opportunity to meet Daniel Goleman, author of the New York Times best seller, "Emotional Intelligence". In the book, he describes how EQ supersedes IQ in terms of being successful. A grand part in growing a business or having a successful corporation, is building connection with the consumer. If your customers or employees cannot connect or do not feel valued, well, no matter how intelligent you are, it will soon be lonely in your board room or in your bedroom.

The last lecture for the evening was coming. It was Don Miguel Ruiz, Sr. He spoke a great deal about the importance of self-love. He talked about loving yourself more than anyone else in the world. You need to nourish your body, your mind, your heart and your soul. You need to be good to yourself. He taught us that we need to look in the mirror and tell ourselves how perfect we are, how we are perfectly, imperfect. He continued, "You need to stop trying to make others happy or to be something or someone you are not." One of Nori's favorite quotes rings dear to me at this moment, "Be yourself, everyone else is taken." This workshop gave me tremendous awareness to continue on my journey of "Mastery of Self."

I arrived home in Miami on Sunday June 2, 2019 with a busy week ahead of me. School would be coming to a close, and my daughter Nori was graduating from St. Kevin's. The reception ceremony…none other than at the Rusty Pelican.

10
STANDING AT THE BASE OF THE MOUNTAINS

"You cannot create what wasn't already nestled inside of you, so in essence, to build, you must tear down the walls that you once believed were part of your foundation." -Frankie M Powers-

June was another month of breaking new barriers and patterns in my way of living. I attended another weekend of IPEC University training, this time in Atlanta, Georgia, and then on to a second event my mentor, Norma, deeply recommended. It was called, "Spark Your Rock Star," event in Fort Lauderdale, Florida, with Coach and Author Carolyn Rim.

It was a three-day healing workshop, filled in between with meditations, inner healing and deep soul discoveries. I made some wonderful friendships that weekend (Melissa, Lisa T., Brenda, Natalie, Angela and Jay R.).

There was one powerful revelation that came to me this weekend. This occurred at the start of day two of the event. As a young man was speaking to the room, he said three words that caused a roaring thunder inside of me. They were… "I create you…I create you." Yes, that simple. What does it mean? Let me explain. We create the way people treat us. If we are kind to others, they are likely to be kind in return. If we are unappreciative of what someone does for us, over time, people will stop giving of themselves to us. If we allow others to take advantage of us now, they are very likely to continue to take advantage of us in the future. The quote that resonates with me here is, "Be careful what you tolerate. You are teaching others how to treat you." Wow, I thought, this guy hit it out of the park.

As I left the weekend workshop, I went off to meet with my IPEC dear friend Len at Azucar in Little Havana in Miami. Len was down from Tampa because IPEC was having a workshop that weekend. A short while after Len left, I met with a few of my IPEC friends who were meeting at Ball & Chain, which was right next door to Azucar. Ball & Chain was a bar/dance club. There, I met up with Aimee, Dahlia, Preston and Emily.

As they sipped some cocktails, I ordered a tonic water with cranberry juice. I danced, or better yet tried to dance. I had just begun to get my rhythm back that evening. I have always been a really good dancer, however, once I quit drinking, it took me a bit of time to get my rhythm back without the assistance of the spirits. As I took a break from the dance floor, I reached out to grab my cranberry juice, took a good swig…oops, it was Emily's whiskey…pfffttt…spitting it out. She yells, "Frank you spit in my drink!" I was like oh, my God, sorry. I'm not supposed to drink, I'm an alcoholic. I remember the look in her eyes once I said that. Her eyes opened widely in hysteria and panic, as if, oh, my God, what do we do? I smiled and laughed and said "I'm okay Emily. Nothing is going to happen. Please let me buy you another drink." She looked at me, puzzled, and said, "No, you can't!" I looked at her in bewilderment and said, "Okay, why can't I?" She responded, "Because maybe you'll end up getting one for yourself." I remember smiling lovingly at this beautiful, sweet woman and saying, "Emily, I will be okay. I am at a bar, there are drinks everywhere. If I was going to drink, it would not be because I bought you one." Here I had a test. I had taken a sip of alcohol, although accidentally, yet no desire to drink. Phew…thank God.

That very week, I was heading on July 5, 2019, to Captiva once again. I was ready to meet the place that took me down, and I was excited. It was almost like a test for me. I needed to, or better yet, I wanted to prove to my kids, prove to everyone, but most importantly to myself, that I was done. Alcohol and I had gotten a much needed and long anticipated divorce. The papers were signed, sealed and notarized on August 25, 2018, while I was at the Hanley Center.

This should have been an exciting week for me, however, July 2nd changed everything. On July 2nd, 2019, my father and I, while at the office, had a deep-seated misunderstanding and depending on who you ask, let's just say that I was no longer working at the job I was at for over twenty years.

That day, I believe something happened between my parents and I. Perhaps, many years of pain and anguish that I had caused them. Maybe it was the years upon years of Frankie mistreating them, of Frankie not appreciating them, and of Frankie taking them for granted. After so many years of verbal abuse, harsh words and angry outbursts, it had reached a culminating point. The volcanic lava erupted on my relationship with my parents. Although, I do not believe that they realize what it really was that happened that day, there really wasn't much I would have done differently had I had the chance.

Not on that day. Over the years, there was a lot. There was a whole lot, tens or perhaps hundreds of things I wish I could have taken back, things I wish I could have done differently.

As I write this, the truth is, I couldn't have done it differently because I didn't know any better at the time. Anyone who is reading this, I want you to please understand this. Everything that someone does is not done to you, it is done in spite of you. You see, the majority of people walking on this earth are generally good. People are born good, are born pure, are born noble and kind. It is life that hardens them, it is life that brings them down. Most importantly, the thing that I want, that I ask you to please remember, is this…it is the expectations that we put on life that destroys the human experience. It is the expectations of our loved ones, the expectations of our children, expectations of our boss and/or the expectations we have of one another. If we were to learn one simple thing, from this day forward I ask you, to all those that have harmed you, to all those that have hurt you and let you down, to change those expectations you have or have had of them to appreciations for what they have given you. If we as people were to do this, our whole lives would inevitably change forever.

I have often heard that it is easier said than done. Okay, well I ask, what is the alternative? Make them suffer? Really? Well, that is quite a misconception. Let me tell you about suffering. The one who really feels the suffering is the one that harnesses that anger and pain. It is you that is allowing that person to control you. If they have angered you or upset you, you have just handed over your freedom to that individual. You have given away your power, your peace and your serenity. Forgiveness is like releasing someone from prison and once released, you realize that the one who was freed was you. Once you do that, you are taking them off your hook and putting them on God's hook. It is liberating. It is freeing. It is peace.

I have learned throughout my journey that I have no regrets. When living in regret, we stay imprisoned in the past, a past that can never be undone, a past that whatever it is that happened cannot be changed. It is a past that no longer serves its purpose.

Regret is the number one offender for alcoholics and for those suffering. So, what is your favorite flavor of suffering? Alcohol? Drugs? Obesity? Anxiety? Medication? Food? Another partner? Gambling? Shopping? You see, the sickness or disease is our thinking. My thinking kept me drinking. It was learning to let go of what was and surrender to what is and seek a life of that which you want it to be. Surrender is freedom. You must forget what hurts you, but not forget what it taught you.

*****

It was now July 5th and we arrived at Captiva. I checked into the room, rented a golf cart, and headed straight to the bar by the pool. I walked right up to the bar and ordered myself a Diet Coke. As I sat there, I thought about the last time I was there, in that moment, in that very spot. It was a man that looked like me, spoke like me, had my same exact thumb print, but was a shadow of the man that I was in that present moment. I buried that man on my rebirth on my 43rd birthday. His presence still hovers near me as a memory, but I left him for greener pastures.

Sometimes we have to strip ourselves of who we think we are. We come to a point in our lives that what was, is no more. We outgrow friends, we outgrow jobs, we outgrow partners. We can still love those people, but we outgrow the need for these people in our environment and our surroundings. In my journey, I learned that we are a byproduct of the five relationships closest to us. If those relationships are strong, so is your life. If they are weak, then thus is your life. We (You and I) can't control what others think or what others feel. All that we can control is how we treat others and how we think of ourselves. Be the best you available, obtainable and achievable. Don't strive for perfection, strive for excellence. Excellence is obtainable, perfection is not.

As you can see, I did a lot of thinking over these days. One of my three grounding tools for a life rooted in abundance is being present. Unfortunately, for my children in these days, in this trip, I surely wasn't. It was my first getaway with the kids since the relapse and my mind was adrift. My kids would look at me and tell me, "Papi, stop thinking." By the end of day two, I was able to change course and be present most of the time. We watched the sunset; went down the water slides. It was just daddy and his children loving on each other.

Within a few days of arriving home from Captiva, we were getting ready to head out to Disney.

So, Disney here I come, and no more sneaking in Captain Morgan's Rum in Lipton iced tea bottles either. The kids and I had a blast. We went to the Magic Kingdom, Hollywood Studios, Animal Kingdom, Epcot, Typhoon Lagoon and Blizzard Beach. As was our norm, we would get up at 6:00 am, have an early breakfast and get a jump start on the day. It was Jonathan's first time at Animal Kingdom; he absolutely loved it. At Disney's Hollywood Studios, Nori, Jonathan and I rode Rock 'N Roller Coaster three times; it immediately became our favorite ride.

Before we left Orlando, we made our traditional must stop at Uncle Julio's. The kids and I love Uncle Julio's. It is a national chain serving Tex-Mex cuisine, located right next to the Orlando Eye. Nori had her usual beef enchiladas; Jonathan ordered his chicken soft tacos, and I had the skirt steak fajitas. We always have to have our sure-fire chips and salsa with a few quarts of salsa to go, no kidding. For dessert, we had none other than their world-famous dessert piñata. The piñata is a chocolate covered shell, if you will, which you crack open with a wooden stick. Once cracked, strawberries, pineapple, churros and donut holes come gushing out. It comes served with melted chocolate sauce, caramel and whipped cream. It is ridiculously good…yummO.

As the kids and I returned from Orlando, it was nearing the end of July and I was going to be traveling quite a bit. I dropped the kids off at Yari's house, and on July 25, 2019, I was off to Atlanta, Georgia where Tony Robbins, Grant Cardone, Joseph McClendon, Shark Tank's Kevin O'Leary and Damon John, among many other speakers, would be present. It was a powerhouse of entrepreneurs and industry leaders. I had a front row seat to this two-day event, front and center to be precise. Wow, wow, wow. What an experience. Tony Robbins stood right in front of me. I remember dancing on the stage and the MC of the two-day event, author and Stay True CEO Loren Lahav, gave me two free tickets to a future event for bringing much needed energy to the room and the stage throughout the evening. She actually invited me and two other men, along with her business partner Kristy Kuhl, to a nice dinner at a steak house nearby.

Tony Robbins brought the house down. He is a man on a mission and his mission is to inspire and to give everything he has in this life to everyone around him. He said several things that have stayed with me. He mentioned that we all have a tendency to stay stuck in our lives. We tell ourselves and others that now is not the right time. Maybe it will be next month, next year, perhaps when the children grow up or when I lose twenty pounds, or, maybe after the holidays. This holds true for relationships, for career paths, for saying I'm sorry, for going back to school. It is all fear, it is all procrastination. If you continue to use procrastination, you will live your time here on this earth without full gratification.

Stop! He yelled. Stop being afraid, he exclaimed. Stop being afraid of what could go wrong and start being excited about what could go right. What if, instead of looking at things and saying, oh, my God, what if it doesn't work, you tell yourself what if it works out better than I could have ever imagined?

Remember, you don't have to be great to get started, but you have to get started to be great. What if you lived life like your prayers had already been answered? What would you do? Who would you be?

As he spoke, I was motivated. I was inspired. I was driven. I realized the words he spoke were penetrating my entire being. In using the power of decision, I have the capacity to get past any excuse that is holding me back and to change any and every single part of my life instantaneously.

This man was powerful, and he knew it, but he was as humble as they come. At the end of the evening, I had an opportunity to meet him, shake his hand, take a picture and speak to him for a little bit. This man, the one you see on television, on stages and in interviews is real. He is his true, authentic self. He doesn't do anything for accolades or photo ops. I know, without question, what his two primary human needs are, love and contribution to all people.

It was early August. My flight from Miami arrives in San Juan, Puerto Rico. I am ready to see my friend, Manny the Magician. As he pulled around the curb of Luis Marin Airport, I ran up to his car and gave him a huge hug and a kiss on the cheek. I don't typically give my male friends kisses on the cheek, but occasionally, when I'm really loving on you, be prepared cause it's coming. As we arrived at his home, he showed me the guest room decorated with puppets, magic paraphernalia and newspaper and magazine clippings of his accomplishments everywhere. He told me to make myself at home. I said hello to Nery, Richie and Eddie and we all changed and jumped in his beautiful pool. Manny is a little bit of a child star in Puerto Rico. If you think of what Mr. Rogers was in the United States years ago, that is similar to who he represents on this island. We shared many laughs and memories.

As we began talking, his wife Nery shared with me that she was a neuro coach, having studied with none other than the creator of NLP, Richard Bandler. She showed me a photo they had taken together. As we continued in conversation, she shared with me some of her dreams and desires. She wanted to open and create emotional intelligence classes in schools throughout Puerto Rico. For a quick moment, I thought someone had spiked my diet coke. What, I thought, really? How is this possible? We share the same dream. As we continued talking, it almost seemed that all the pieces of the puzzle were coming together.

Then in a conversation with Manny, I told him, "Hey, Manny. I have an idea I would like your help with." He said, "Sure Frank, what is it?" I asked him if he would be able to film some videos for me and edit them. Manny had been in television production for over twenty years. He has his own television show, his own channel, and his own magic sitcom. He told me to talk to his son Richie, who helped with the editing.

By the time I left Puerto Rico, Frankie M. Powers and Facebook Motivational Mondays, had begun. Every Monday, around 8:00 am, I would post a video to share about my life, the good and the bad, to help people know that they are not alone in their struggles and that their past does not dictate their future. I let others know that they get to choose to be joyous and happy, and that their life is not contingent upon their circumstances. It is contingent on what they do with the plate that they are served. You cannot control the cards you are dealt, but you can play the hell out of the hand that is given to you.

It went well. It went extremely well. There have been moments where I would get frustrated by the lack of comments or likes and then, all of a sudden, someone will come up to me somewhere, randomly, and say, "Thank you man. You have no idea how much I look forward to your Motivational Monday videos. You have made a significant impact in my life, as well as my family's". Whoa…my eyes swell up in the moments where I have heard that, and I humbly say, it has happened more times than I can count. On three occasions, I have had individuals come to me to tell me that they were on the brink of going to the other side and that it was I that gave them hope. That it was I that…that because of me, their families have them. I mean, if there was ever a doubt if I was on the right path, these instances confirmed it.

I arrived back in Miami. And, in early August, I went to see my accountant, Caesar, and I registered Frankie M. Powers, Life Coaching, LLC. I went to Wells Fargo to open my business account, and Frankie M. Powers was born. "Let's go!" I exclaimed!

For all those people reading this who are unfamiliar or skeptical about coaching, the word "coach" originated from the word stagecoach, which was a means of taking people from where they are to the place they wished to go to. It was a method of getting a person from one destination to another. A coach, a life coach, helps you break through the deep-seated inner blocks that are nestled inside of you in order to have the life that you ultimately desire. So where are you stuck? Do you have the relationships that you have always dreamed of? With your children? With your friends? With your partner? Are you stuck in your career, your job, your passions? Where are you in your health? Your spirituality, your hobbies?

Find a coach, invest in yourself. I am amazed at how many times people will tell me I can't afford it, or I don't have time. My response is, we make time for those things we truly value. Is your life worth so little? Your life is worth more than you are giving it. You were not meant to have an ordinary life. You were made by God, in the image of God. You were not meant to be ordinary; you were meant to be extraordinary. Give yourself the gift of life that you deserve. Find a coach, get a coach, hire someone who you can trust and watch your life soar like fireworks in a clear evening sky on the 4th of July.

I was soon headed to Philadelphia to see motivational speaker ET (Eric Thomas) for an event on August 9th and 10th. As I arrived in Philly, in the early morning hours of Thursday, August 8th, and got off the plane, I rented a car and checked into a Marriott Hotel in downtown Philly.

That night, being in Philly, meant having to have none other than a nice cheesy, grilled Philly cheesesteak from Cleaver's. It was simply phenomenal. The following morning before heading to the ET event I ran up the steps of the Philadelphia Museum of Art, otherwise known as "The Rocky Steps" and realized that much like Rocky, I was an overcomer. I then was off to see ET. ET is otherwise known as the hip-hop motivational preacher. What a powerful two days it was. The overall theme was, "Drive," about finding your why and not giving up. Why do you want to do this?! Who is your why? Why is your why?

My why was because I knew that this was the direction that God was leading me to. Because I refuse to one day stand before or kneel on the steps of the pearly gates of heaven and have God look at me and say, "Son, you knew what I wanted you to do. You...knew. There are millions of others that never saw the light, not because it wasn't there, but because they never found the switch. I wrote in the instructional manual for living (the Bible), that you, that every single man, woman and child alive, has My light inside of them. Many people never find the switch. You, my son, found the switch and did nothing." That is my why, my inner voice saying, I got it ET. Wait, there's more...Nori and Jonathan, my children. I want to...no, I need to...show my kids that anything is possible, that you can go from being broken down to have your heart broken open. That is my why ET!

As I sat in the airport waiting to board the plane, I received a text from Yari letting me know she was getting married in November. My reaction was, oh, wow, how do the kids feel about this? I didn't even know she was seeing anyone. Who she sees or not is really none of my business, and I would not have cared at all, except...well, there are two really big excepts, Nori and Jonathan. I texted her back congratulations and wished her well. I remember calling the kids later that evening, to see how they were doing. I did not ask them anything specific or out of the ordinary. It was my typical daily evening phone call between 8:00 and 9:00 pm.

I want to share a quick insight for all the single parents who are reading this. It is our responsibility to call our children. There was a time that I used to tell them they needed to be sure to call me. It was not until I learned that children have a lot of things going on in their heads, and they think differently than we do. As adults, and as their parents, that is one responsibility we should take off our children and put on ourselves.

11
CLIMBING THE LOWER SLOPES

"Use your heart as your compass to guide you to the light of God's kingdom within. There it will lead you to the true treasures of Love, Forgiveness and Service which will satisfy all that you need to live." -Frankie M Powers-

As I landed in Miami, I remember thinking to myself, I wonder how the kids are feeling about Yari getting married. Do they like him? How does he treat them? Are they uncomfortable? Does he have kids? The following morning, on August 13, 2019, I contacted Cynthia to set up an appointment. When I told Cynthia about Yari getting married, she told me that she had known for quite a while. She informed me that the kids would be having two-stepbrothers, but because of confidentiality, she was not able to say anything. I completely understood her position. All that mattered to me was that Nori and Jonathan were emotionally okay.

It was now August 25th, and what a day I have in store. My day starts at Christ Fellowship Church, where, on my 44th birthday, I chose to be baptized in my Christian faith. It was just my kids and I, and my Devil Dog brother, Edzo, who was with me in Hanley. It was also my one-year anniversary of being sober. What a year, I remember thinking. To think how in one year, my whole life changed. It was amazing, miraculous really. After service, I put on a Christ Fellowship t-shirt, walked into the pool, and a pastor dunked my head in the water and baptized me as a follower of Jesus Christ.

My baptism

After my baptism, I took Edzo to have a Cuban sandwich, that he had been craving for a while. Edzo was accompanied by his girlfriend, now fiancée, Bobbi, and his son Logan. I was grateful for Edzo; his friendship has been a true blessing for me.

When lunch was over, the kids and I drove home to rest for a few hours and get ready for Sabal Palms Alcoholics Anonymous' Birthday night celebration. It was my month and I was prepared that evening to say a few words about my experience, strength and hope, receive my one-year sobriety medallion and eat some cake.

I saw several of my Sabal Palm friends at the event. My children were there alongside me, as well as others family members. I was introduced to an old friend of mine, Eileen's sister, Diana. It was a chance encounter, really, but that encounter led me to a book that changed my perception on love, how I perceived love, how and why others show love, but most importantly, that simple book made me realize why words were always so important to me and it made me appreciate my father's way of loving me more so than I ever had before. It was that book, that easy to read in one day book, that made me see love in a whole new light. The book is called, "The Five Love Languages," by Gary Chapman. It explains that most of us show love in one particular form, and most of us feel love, only when it is expressed in a certain way. Mr. Chapman really changed the ball game with this one.

My beliefs, and what I am writing, is not from the five love languages, but is derived from my belief in them and my own conclusions that I firmly believe is the way that we feel love, is the one method that we felt the most unloved by during our childhood. Let me explain. The five love languages are:

1) Words of Affirmation
2) Acts of Service
3) Receiving Gifts
4) Quality Time
5) Physical Touch.

For me, my mom covered all five love languages. However, the one that I felt I lacked the most, and I never felt from my father, was words of affirmation. Words of affirmation mean everything to me, literally, figuratively, and even physically, if that makes sense. Telling me what you feel about me, or writing to me what I mean to you, is the greatest treasure that anyone can ever give me.

I remember being at boot camp, at Parris Island, and reminiscing about the letter my dad wrote me. Here I was, reading that letter in front of a group of thirty of the manliest men, future Marines, and that letter broke me.

When it comes to using all five love languages, I think I use them all. I didn't realize it at the time, but I think my grandfather's death made me try everything I could to get love any and every way imaginable. I know for certain there may be others walking this earth who love as much as me, but it is not possible for anyone to love more than me. At this moment, the song "I Would Do Anything for Love" by Meatloaf is playing in my head. At the end of the chorus he says, "I would do anything for love, but I won't do that," I never could quite figure out what that meant, but I can guarantee you I would do that and more.

It was now the week of August 26, 2019. Jonathan was starting fifth grade at

St. Kevin's Catholic School, and Nori was an incoming freshman at St. Brendan High School. I decided to coach one last season of Tamiami Basketball. I told Jonathan that if I can manage to get his school friends on the same team, that I would coach. Jessie, Pipa's mom, and Erika, Jay's mom, actually had their boys play up one year so they could play together. So did Camila, Max' mom. We had four childhood best friends playing on the same team and I was their basketball coach.

Life was a blur. I was wearing too many hats. I was starting a business, coaching basketball, my parents and I were at odds, and I am a single father with two kids in two different schools. I can't help but think of the Kelly Clarkson song at this moment, "What Doesn't Kill You Makes You Stronger".

It was now getting close to Labor Day weekend, and on Thursday, August 29, 2019, the kids and I took a flight to visit Manny in San Juan, Puerto Rico. I remember being hesitant to leave, because it appeared there was a major storm and possible hurricane heading our way, but I left anyway. Fortunately, the storm was a miss. The kids and I had a wonderful time in Puerto Rico. We went to El Yunque, a national rainforest and bathed in the freezing river. We spent the weekend traveling the island's beaches, bathing in Manny's pool, and building foundational memories. I have to say, my close friends truly are like family. All my life my family was small. My mother did not have any siblings and my dad's only sibling, my aunt, had no children. So, my friends are like the family I never had. It was a weekend filled with great fun and relaxation.

We arrived home from Puerto Rico on Monday, September 2nd, and Yari was throwing Nori a "15's" birthday party that following weekend, a party I was not invited to attend. That hurt deeply. Did I come to terms that I would not be invited? Yes. My daughter hadn't. She wanted her dad there and wasn't given that. I have no problem taking all the heat for the things I did or failed to do in my relationship with my ex-wife. What I did have a problem with is our kids suffering because of them. Despite this not being Nori's wishes, she decided to throw a party for Nori that would not give Nori the opportunity to share a dance with her father. For those of you who are unaware, the climax of the "15's" party is the father daughter dance.

So, on October 11th, with a great deal of help from Jessie and her family, I, as well, threw her a "15's" birthday party. I made sure to invite Yari. She never responded and did not make it. In spite of all this, Nori had a wonderful time. Before dancing with my daughter, the father/daughter dance, I made it a point to grab the microphone and say a few words to Nori. As I looked in her eyes, I told her, "If I could have painted a picture, made a list, or had spoken to God himself and asked Him what I wanted in a daughter, and if He would have granted me every single wish, it still would have paled in comparison to the precious gift He gave me in you."

In the meantime, my friendship with Jessie and the Barreras continued to become unbreakable. What Jessie and her family did, and continue to do for me, is unheard of. The kids and I have become part of the family. It is almost like she adopted all of us. God, I love those people. I hope and pray that God helps me to one day find a way to return the favor. During those difficult moments, and the ones that followed, they have been a bedrock by my side.

Jessie and The Barreras

Jonathan's birthday was coming soon. We celebrated with some close friends at the Venetian Pool. Jonathan is a really simple boy. He just wanted to be in the water. Well…the water with his closest friends. Thinking it over, Nori has always been simple too. In life, we often lose sight of the big picture. We get so caught up in our fast-paced lifestyle that we forget to stop and be present and notice that the things we often value as important are usually not the things that matter. It is the people, the love, the connections that matter so much more than the cars, the homes, and the pretentions. Western civilization has changed the world for the better part in thousands of ways, but in one very important way, we are so far behind. We are taught to seek happiness outside of ourselves instead of finding our happiness within us.

It was now November 1, 2019. I attended a Deepak Chopra event hosted by Unity on the Bay. The theme of the evening was, "I am Infinite Potential."

Deepak spoke about mindfulness and how it improves the quality of our lives while increasing one's performance, as well as how it extends our time and helps us cope with loss. He was soft spoken and gentle. He brought a peaceful energy into the room. The talk of mindfulness piqued my interest. I have always been a go, go, go kind of person. He brought to my attention the importance of stopping, pausing and taking a look as an observer and then proceeding.

On November 7th, Tony Robbins and his signature event, Unleash the Power Within (UPW), came to Miami. I cannot believe that in only one year, I went from discovering who this man was and what he stands for, to now being fully immersed in a new way of living, discovering the man God intended me to be. It was exactly one year ago the same weekend, that I discovered Tony Robbins in New Jersey. One can never underestimate what you can accomplish in a year. It is so much more than one could ever imagine. Last year this very weekend I flew to see Tony. Exactly one year later Tony Robbins holds an event in my very own city. Coincidence? Godincidence.

As the four-day event began, I was taken aback at how much retention of the information I had from the year prior. Several of my friends from Landmark and Dale Carnegie were also at the event. My dear friend Norma, Lisa T., Adam and Beth were crewing for the event. My friend Wilbert, from Landmark, was also partaking in the event with me. Some of the most valuable jewels that I came away with from this weekend was to change "I should do this" to "I must!" The way that you talk to yourself matters. If you tell yourself, I should, you will always find a reason to talk yourself out of it. Once you tell yourself I must, you will develop a "no matter what attitude".

In life, the difference between the doers and the dreamers is not intelligence and it is not their educational background. It is those people who are persistent and resilient in what they desire and develop a never give up attitude. One of Tony Robbins' favorite quotes of mine is, "Life is a dance between what you fear the most, and what you desire the most."

One other thing that Tony talked about that hit home with me was when he said, find what drives you, what motivates you, what you are passionate about and let that be the driving force that drives you through the rest of your life. Once you find it, take massive action and it will be impossible to fail. When you do that, you will look up one day and see that all your dreams have become your reality.

It was now nearing November 15th, the day Yari got married. Nori, Jonathan and I went to Michael's the day before. I remember asking if the kids had wanted to get something for their mom and Robert, her soon to be husband, for their wedding. They said, "Yes, Papi." I remember walking up to the Michael's employee and telling him we were looking for a collage picture frame for my ex-wife's wedding day. He looked at me as if I was crazy. I remember the kids and I laughing about it. I was happy for Yari and the kids. They really seemed to like Robert. Robert treated them well and I was appreciative that there would be a male presence in their lives on a daily basis. I was genuinely happy for them.

Thanksgiving was right around the corner and Jessie and Noel invited us to spend the day with them and their family at Noel's mom, Sonia's, home in West Palm Beach. I had no other plans, so the kids and I said yes. We were going to be having Thanksgiving dinner there and spend black Friday with them and their family as well. On Saturday, Nori, Jonathan and I woke up and headed out to the Holy Land Experience and Disney World for a few days, but not before the adventurer in me came out.

Jonathan's favorite basketball player is Russell Westbrook. Russell Westbrook played for the Houston Rockets at the time, and our favorite basketball team is, and forever shall be, the Miami Heat. A buddy of mine, from Houston, had a connection with the Houston Rocket's organization and he had a few tickets available for the game. The only thing was that the game was on November 27, 2019, the evening before Thanksgiving and…it was in Houston. I thought about it, checked the flights, I had a bunch of frequent flyer miles and I said what the heck, let's do it. I remember thinking YOLO (You Only Live Once).

I picked up the kids at school and at 5:00 pm we were flying into Houston. The kids had no idea. They were beyond excited. This was crazy. I mean, this was really crazy. The night before, the Miami Heat's aqua blue vice shirts had just been released. I was at the American Airline's Arena at approximately two in the morning, purchasing one for each of us to wear at the event.

We arrived at George Bush International Airport in Houston, quickly picked up our rental car, and went straight to our hotel near the airport. We checked in, dropped off our suitcase and went straight to the Toyota Center, home of the NBA's Houston Rockets basketball team. As we walked into the arena, Nori and Jonathan stopped, looked at me and gave me a huge hug and said, "Thanks, Papi, you really are the best." I will never forget the looks on their faces as they said those words to me. That is one of those moments that I will keep in my treasure chest of memories. We made it to the arena just in time, as the game had just started. Wow, that arena was awesome! I have to say the fans and people in Houston were incredible. Everyone was so kind and polite. We were not really used to that in Miami. The game was a blowout and the Heat's best player, Jimmy Butler, was out with an undisclosed injury. The Miami Heat didn't stand a chance. Nevertheless, it was an unforgettable experience, and Jonathan, being the big personality that he is and using his friendly attitude, even had a chance to pat Russell Westbrook on his shoulder as he was on his way to the locker room.

As we left the arena, we stopped for ice cream, then drove to the hotel. On the way to the hotel, I remember showing the kids where dad was just a few short months ago at NLP training.

As we arrived at the hotel, we took a quick shower and went straight to bed. We got roughly four hours of sleep that night. At 4:30 am the alarm went off, we brushed our teeth, said our morning prayers and off to the airport we went. I remember walking into the airport, and everyone was wishing one another a Happy Thanksgiving. We boarded the plane, sat in our seats and at 7:05 we were heading to Miami. In just a few short hours, we would be arriving home, changing clothes and driving off to Thanksgiving dinner, with our luggage to Orlando in tow, with Jessie and the Barreras.

It was now December, and we were in the midst of the holiday season. Jonathan's basketball season was over. My coaching business was doing better than I could have anticipated. Everything seemed to be going very well in my life. Everything except that my relationship with my parents was heavily severed.

It was now Christmas afternoon, and the kids came to spend the evening with me. They opened their gifts. I cooked a beef tenderloin with a mushroom gravy sauce and some smoked asiago scalloped potatoes. It melted in their mouths. It had been about seven years since I made that dish with them. They absolutely loved it.

Soon we were to be heading out on winter break vacation and Pigeon Forge, Tennessee was the destination. It was the Barreras and the Lopezs and we were off on a road trip. On December 28th we drove off and our first stop was Savannah, Georgia. We checked into our hotel and took our own personal tour of the Savannah river banks. What a beautiful city, I thought.

As the kids and I walked near the river and took pictures, Noel and I saw a Wet Willies. I used to love Wet Willies. Wet Willies is a frozen daquiri bar. It used to be one of my favorite stops on South Beach in my younger years, where I would spend countless days and nights there as I got hammered. For the first time in almost twenty years, I had a Wet Willies drink. However, for the first time ever, I had a Weak Willy (no alcohol). I guess I tried to relive some of those youthful memories.

After finishing the drink, we all stopped for an Italian dinner before it was time to head to the hotel to get some sleep, to recharge before our next stop, Pigeon Forge, Tennessee. We had two rooms, one was the boy's room, which consisted of Jonathan, Pipa, Noel, and me. The other was the girl's room which was Jessie, Nori, Gabi and Dani. It was now Sunday morning, December 29th. We woke up, had an early breakfast, and were off to the cabin we had rented in Pigeon Forge. Till this day, I will never figure out how Noel managed to tightly snuggle all our luggage in the rented SUV.

Around 6:00 pm, we finally arrived; our cabin was breathtaking. It had two floors, a small game room, a fireplace and a jacuzzi. It was…perfect. We headed out to Walmart and picked up an enormous quantity of groceries, then settled in for the evening. As we drove around the city, I was beyond surprised how many attractions and people came to Pigeon Forge to spend the holidays. There were so many attractions to experience, so many shows to watch.

The next day we got up and decided to go to the Titanic exhibit attraction. It was an interesting and historical experience. There were so many artifacts present before us that had been recovered from the famous sunken ship. Many of the discoveries were on display. Many of them were, in fact, recovered by the Titanic Museum's owner. In 1987, co-owner John Joslyn, co-led a six-million- dollar expedition to the site of where the Titanic sank. It was an adventure that was chronicled in a special television event called, "Return to the Titanic". The 2-hour program was the second highest rated documentary of all time and here we were, experiencing its discoveries.

The next day was New Year's Eve; we had no major plans. Another of Nori's very best friends, Sophia, and her family had also rented nearby. We were going to be spending the 31st and most of our trip together. Enrique, Sophia's dad, had made reservations for tickets at the world-famous Dollywood theme park for Thursday, January 2, 2020.

Life was changing and I was changing. In fact, I was never a tattoo guy, but I had just recently gotten myself one. I used to tell myself, how is that going to look on me when I am an old man? Would people look at me and say, look at that old guy with tattoos? (Yes, exactly, I was worried what others would say and think.)

The tattoo that I inked on myself was on my left wrist and it was a small cross. It was a symbol for surrender, for leaving my life and my future in His hands.

On January 2nd we awakened, and Jessie made everyone breakfast, cooked to order, as she did every morning. That was my second day of my exercise regimen. I had actually started the day prior, on January 1, 2020, at 5:00 am. Everyone thought I was crazy. They wondered why I did not just wait until I got back from vacation. I remember telling them that I had to be the change that I want to see in the world, and I had to practice what I preached. I was, in my estimation, forty-five pounds overweight and it was time for me to get to work. I remember stepping outside those early mornings and it was cold…damn cold. I did it though. Arnold Schwarzenegger once said, "You can have excuses, or you can have results. But you can't have both."

After having breakfast in the cabin, our next stop was Dollywood. Dollywood was a much bigger theme park than I anticipated. I could not have imagined the mere size of this place. It was filled with attractions, rides and roller coasters. There is a chapel in Dollywood called the Robert F. Thomas chapel, named after the doctor who delivered Dolly Rebecca Parton. There is also the Calico Falls school house, a one-room schoolhouse, that is a replica of how Tennessee schools appeared in the 1890's. We closed the park down that night.

There was so much to see and do. It is definitely a place that I would love to revisit someday. Dollywood is a theme park named after actress and world-renowned country singer, Dolly Parton. Dolly is a fun-loving, always smiling, bigger than life personality. She has a wonderful rags to riches story and southern girl charm. She dreamed of opening up a place where people could spend the day enjoying one another's smiles, laughter, and faith with friends and family. Well, Dolly…your mission was definitely accomplished.

The next morning, we arose and headed out to Gatlinburg. We were going snow tubing. We were all really excited. This was to be the highlight of our winter trip. I'm not quite sure what I enjoyed more, Dollywood or snow tubing. I really loved both. Snow tubing was exhilarating. I had never done it before. There was not a frown on anyone's face going down those hills. Every single person wore a smile. It was clean, good natured, outdoorsy fun. We enjoyed the air…the trees…the views and the mountains. It was beautiful.

The next day we were heading back home. We were not quite sure if we would make it, or if we would end up stopping somewhere to spend the night. So, we were off. Here is a special warning to whoever reads this and wants to take a car trip with me. I need stops. I mean…I really need stops.

Bathroom stops, stops to pee. Noel looked like Herman the Hermit from Yogi Bear's First Christmas. I laugh as I write this, hoping he does not get too upset. He would get so mad. I mean…he would yell, telling me to stop drinking fluids, but I couldn't. I always needed something available to drink. I was always thirsty. I never realized this till now.

After tiring out and making an overnight rest stop in Orlando, we awakened the following morning and drove home to Miami. The kids and I hugged Jessie and the Barreras and thanked them for an amazing trip. I let Jessie know that the following morning I would be dropping the kids off early, because I needed to be at the airport at 6:30 am.

12
THE SUMMIT IS IN SIGHT

"To sit in silence is to learn more about oneself than one could ever learn from others." -Frankie M Powers-

I woke up early in the morning of January 6th and dropped the kids off at Jessie's house, I went home and called an Uber. Next stop, Miami International Airport for a flight to Raleigh, North Carolina, to visit and wish my mother a happy 70th birthday. This trip for me was nerve-racking. I was filled with anxiety. I hadn't spoken to either one of my parents in over seven months. I was desperate for peace. I was heartbroken over the turmoil and distance between my family and me. I needed a resting place to land, to land my heart, to have my heart rest in my mother's love.

The flight was smooth. A few hours later, I landed in Raleigh. I walked over to the Hertz car rental booth and grabbed my vehicle. I put on google maps and proceeded to drive two and a half hours to their cabin home in Piney Creek, North Carolina.

My parents had no idea that I would soon be visiting them. The truth is, I had no idea if they were even going to be home. All I knew is that I had to be back in Raleigh by 5:00 am the following day, January 7th, for my flight back home to Miami.

As I drove up the mountain, I was remembering just how beautiful the landscape was. I saw several deer drinking water and crossing the riverbanks. I began thinking of my grandmother, Abuela Tata, and having lost her at the age of 70. I thought of my grandfather, Abuelo Tata, who never made it to age 60. I knew that I had to try to re-establish a relationship with my mom. I was willing and determined to take full responsibility for the deterioration of our connection.

When I pulled into the driveway, I saw that no one was home. So, I waited…and waited. After two hours, I contacted one of her close friends, Maria. She informed me that my parents had gone out for dinner and would be back in about an hour. My parents still did not know that I was there waiting for them, so the surprise was still on.

An hour later, my dad pulled into the driveway in his gray Toyota Tacoma pick-up truck. As they exited the car, they saw me waiting with flowers and a gift in hand. I wished my mom a happy birthday, gave her a big hug, and told her how much she meant to me. I was quite surprised at how unsurprised they seemed to be. Truthfully, I was a little hurt at how emotionless they were about me being there. I said hello to my dad, and then they asked me what I was doing there. I replied, "Well, mom, grandma and grandpa never made it to 71. You are my mom; I love you and I want to make peace with you. I want you in my life."

They invited me inside the cabin and offered me something to drink. After having some meaningless small talk, my mother and father gave me a verbal lashing. They were not screaming or being disrespectful, they just let me have it. They told me how much I had hurt them over the course of the years. How they felt disrespected and unappreciated by me. I quietly listened and then tried to take full responsibility for my actions and explained that I was sick. I wasn't making excuses; I was merely trying to explain to them that the man who I was is no longer the man that was standing before them. I felt rejected. I felt unwanted. I felt unloved.

After several hours of trying to make my case for their forgiveness of me, their son, and my sharing my desire to be part of their lives, I realized that I was being treated unfairly. My father responded, "It takes time. I can't just forgive you like that." I stood up and said, "Okay. Look, I took a flight from Miami to come over here to see you. I rented a car and drove two and a half hours to get here because you are my mom, and it's your birthday. I love you both so much. I have to be back at Raleigh Airport at 5:00 am and it is now 10:00 pm. I still have to drive two and a half hours to my hotel. If you don't want to forgive me and choose to not have me be a part of your life, then I have to respect that. Although it hurts me deeply, but I will have some personal dignity and love myself enough to not be around anyone who does not want me there."

When I stood up and went to say goodbye, in that moment, it seemed something clicked in my mom. She told me, "Frankie, I love you. I am sorry too." We both shed a few tears and shared a warm embrace. My father just kind of stayed steadfast.

It looked like he felt stuck in his emotions. They began to offer their home for me to sleep when they looked at the weather forecast and saw it called for heavy snow in the next few hours, and I had quite a trek to the airport. I said goodbye and drove away. As I left their cabin, I remember feeling like this was the beginning of re-establishing my relationship with my parents. I was overjoyed…for the moment.

I arrived at the hotel, took a quick shower and went straight to sleep. Four hours later, I awoke, had a quick breakfast at a Waffle House, and off to the airport to take my flight back home to Miami. Over the course of the last ten days, I had been in Savannah, Georgia, Pigeon Forge, Tennessee, Orlando, slept one night in my bed in Miami, and then to Raleigh, North Carolina to drive to Piney Creek, sleep in Raleigh, and now, finally I was headed back home. As soon as I sat on the plane, I took a nice nap until we landed at Miami International Airport.

Once I arrived home and finished working, by 7:00 pm, I was done. I went to bed and slept for fourteen hours straight. I had not slept that much in one day in over a year.

Over the course of the last several months, I had talked with many of my new friends and expressed an interest in telling my story, in writing a book. I was finally led to a renowned and respected editor and author of, "How Speaking Your Truth Could Save Your Life and How It Saved Mine", Lynn Everard. I scheduled to meet Lynn at my famous meeting place, Shuck & Dive. He explained to me the tools of the trade. He also advised me to be compassionate and patient with myself as I went over my tell all book, because he let me know that unhealed wounds and emotions were bound to be stirred up. Boy…he sure as hell was not lying. I like Lynn, he was real, he was honest, he was…a humble, gentle man. We agreed to start working together to get this book done. I told him the title, "From Rock Bottom to Mountaintops: My Journey through Faith, Hope and Love." He loved it.

It was mid-January 2020, and Jonathan, Pipa, Jay and Max had all opted out of Tamiami basketball to try a more competitive travel basketball league. It was a step up in competition, and Jonathan was ready for the challenge.

It was now March 4, 2020. I was on my way to Puerto Rico to visit my dear friend Manny the Magician. I had been running low on my Monday Motivational videos, and it had been a few months since I saw him last. The goal was to shoot twenty videos this time around. We came quite close, hitting eighteen. Manny, Nery, Richie and Eddie always treated me like family. Heck...Manny and I are family.

I arrived in Miami from Puerto Rico on March 9th with this new unknown pandemic invading the United States and the world. I was a little anxious. I began double dipping on the workout front. I was walking and lifting weights in the morning and doing so in the evening as well.

On the late afternoon of March 10th, as I was walking in the park near my parent's home, my dad saw me. He pulled over to the side of the street and we spoke for a little while. He was still upset with me, still angry over the incident that happened on July 2, 2019. Although the truth is it had nothing to do with that incident, but in his estimation, it did. By mine, he had been upset with me all of his life. As I write this, I realize it is not me. I know that these are childhood hurts, but needless to say, he is my father, I love him, and I just don't want to argue, so I walked away.

He drove around again and called me over. Again, I kindly told him to leave me alone. After the fourth time, he tells me to come near the car. As I approach his car, I notice his eyes were watery. As you can see by now, I am an emotional man. I am joyous, I am passionate and when I need to cry, I turn the faucets on and let it all out. Now my father...no, that's not him. That is not in his nature, or let me correct myself, he does not allow himself to fully express his emotions because he has been taught and instilled to believe, that doing so is a sign of weakness.

In this moment, seeing my father teary-eyed, I knew that he was not in his head, but he was in his heart. My dad looked me in the eye, which he seldomly did, and said, "Do you know what day it is today?" Immediately, I knew. Immediately, I remembered. I remember every year, but somehow it eluded me that year until that moment.

My father struggles with life, not financially, but with living. He walks around with body armor, guarded. He is in defense mode, from the moment he wakes up in the morning to the moment wherever he drifts off to sleep (be it the recliner, sofa, or sometimes, even, the bed). He is restless.

Now...there is one day out of the year that I have an opportunity to see my dad, to meet my dad, my real...dad. This is the man who he truly is behind the hurts, behind the pain, behind the scars of unmet expectations, or before life's battles cut him to the bone. Today, March 10th is that day. As some of you may remember, March 10th was the day I lost my beloved, favorite grandparent, my Abuelo Papo. He had told me that he had been emotional throughout the day and he had been seeking his dad, my Abuelo Papo, for guidance.

I lovingly put my hand on my father's left shoulder and said, "Dad, if he were to speak to you, would you be open to listening?" He looked at me puzzled. I said, "Look at me, Pops." Every once in a while, I would use that name as a term of endearment. I told him to stop living in anger, to stop living in the past. "It robs you, Dad. It cuts you. It disables you. He replied, "I can't…I can't. This is who I am!" I said, "No, dad, this is who you have chosen to be. There is a better way, Papi. I promise you. If you allow me to, I can guide you."

For one of the few times in my life, we began getting into a deep hearted conversation and immediately, when he started getting into his emotions, he said, "I can't. I can't anymore. This is draining me." It was. It's supposed to. The truth is people, that every single one of us starts packing on weight. We take on the weight of heartache, the weight of let downs and the weight of frustrations, burdens and disloyalty. If we don't unclog all that build up and drain our bodies, our minds, our hearts and our souls, we will forever be building walls and barriers of resistance towards those things that we most desire in our lives.

All of us must drain the swamp, our own swamp, from time to time in order to heal, in order to grow, in order to come back to the person, we were born to be. I respected my dad and his wishes and gave him the space he asked for. Space…giving people space is one of the most undervalued traits that any human being can have. The importance of letting people find their path in their own timing and giving assistance when asked, guidance only when sought, and only push when given permission, is one of the most important traits that anyone can have.

It saddens me to see my dad, who I love so dearly, carrying so many unhealed old wounds around with him. He prides himself with the euphemism that when things get tough, he puts on the backpack and powers through. However, the truth is that he has been piling tens of thousands of dead weights on that backpack, that the weight does not allow him to move forward. So, inevitably, as many people in Western civilization do, he stays stuck.

Me with my Parents

During this time, it was hard to meet with my clients at work. All interactions were done through phone conversations or facetime. They were my saving grace. Being able to be fully present with others was a huge gift that I had within me and that I had yet to realize its real significance and importance. My God-given abilities to remember things from people, friends, family and or clients, the smallest of details, has always made those around me feel deeply cared for and loved. The truth is, they feel it because it is real. I do care for them. I do love them. I was just born with a deep love affair with all people, whoever and wherever they are. It is genuine, it is true, it is…real.

Every time I have been around someone when they have a breakthrough in their life, I was having it with them. I am not just saying it. I was. During our time in life, when we invest in anything, a person, a job, our relationships, when we gain an accomplishment, it is rewarding, satisfying and it is also one of the three components to a life rooted in abundance. It is… fulfilling. So, I celebrate. I celebrate their accomplishments, my accomplishments, your accomplishments, and other's accomplishments. We need to learn to celebrate ourselves, as well as one another, more often. We tend to criticize ourselves, time and time again, for those things we do wrong, yet, when we finally achieve something, that we have been yearning and working for so long, we celebrate so very little. My call to action to every single one of you reading this is to learn to celebrate. Celebrate you, celebrate me, celebrate us, celebrate…often!

It was now April 13th, and due to Covid, we were all forced to celebrate Easter with church services online for the first time in my life. Hats off to the Pastors throughout the world for doing their best to make the adjustment as seamless as possible. However, there is no substitute for the experience of the human connection, with the gift of commuting together and worshipping with one another. According to a Gallup poll taken near the end of 2020, ratings of mental health during the time of Covid, and the turbulence going on in our country, mental health declined in every demographic Gallup measured – age, race, gender, income, marital status and political affiliation. Of all these demographics, mental health declined in every single area except one…weekly church attendees. "Feed your faith and watch your fears starve to death."

Our new norm of social distancing, wearing masks, having curfews, gyms being closed, restaurants available for takeout only, talk about a re-set, what the heck? People all around were irritable, driving erratically, not smiling and carrying pent up anger. Life had become a hot mess, but maybe, just maybe…there was an opportunity for people in the world to unite for the purpose of something greater than oneself, or, maybe not… yet.

Past the halfway point of May, I was feeling down, losing focus, I was desolate, hurt and sad. The human connection was dissipating. I still had my children 50% of the time. Their sports activities were cancelled, school classes were on Zoom, no outings and more and more of social media running rampant. I felt for them. I felt for all the children throughout the country, better yet, throughout the world.

I reached out to Cynthia and began to share with her my feelings, thoughts and emotions. She asked me permission to state an observation she had made. I told her sure, most definitely. She then reminded me of all the tools I had in place and all the things I had accomplished over the course of the last year and a half. What she hit me with next was beyond unexpected. It was as if she sucker-punched me in the gut. It was a jab that I so desperately needed to hear about one other thing I had been doing and projecting onto others. She told me, "Frankie, you are a manipulator." That, in fact, I had spent my life manipulating others, unknowingly and with good intentions. As I write this, I remember the quote that resonates with me, "The road to hell is paved with good intentions."

Before I tell you my reaction and response, I want to start by saying the irony is that I can so easily see this trait in others. I can see the tools I have. I can see the clearing and the pathway for personal freedom for other people. I can see their relationships and the hits and misses in their ability or inability to connect with others. I can see the bridge that needs to be built in order to connect with their children. Children, being quite simple, really, since life has not yet begun to hit them with upper cuts and body blows. I could even see how to speak to myself. Yet, sometimes, we are so blinded and so caught up in others that even with all the knowledge, expertise and experience we have cultivated and obtained, we find it hard to look in the mirror and really see ourselves. There is not a human being alive who is immune to this. Just like every single person has, or should have, a primary care physician, every single man, woman and child alive should have a therapist, counselor and/or coach.

In all honesty, I believe with absolute certainty that people need one even more so than their primary doctor. Because, although most of us only go to see our doctor when we are feeling ill or sick, our minds, our thoughts and our emotions are omnipresent. The quality of our lives, and the greater part of our health, is driven by our emotions, whether they are high or running low.

One negative event in your day can have a domino effect in your life and in the lives of those whose lives are intertwined with yours. Yet we don't make it of utmost importance to seek help when needed, which is constantly. There is a taboo, a stigma, with psychology and mental health that needs to be extinguished. If a human being has certain cancers and/or diabetes, most people would generally feel compassion and have empathy for them, even though, in many instances, these diseases were often self-inflicted, such as not exercising, one's diet, smoking, or poor health habits.

However, if the same person is now an alcoholic, drug addict, compulsive gambler, suffers from depression, anxiety, why are they deemed irresponsible, negligent or crazy? Why? Why! We judge them because somehow, we believe that they can do better, that somehow, we, ourselves, would do better or handle things differently. For example, "Well, I don't have that drinking problem. Why should they?" Who the hell do we think we are to compare our way to another's way? Why do we get so much satisfaction from making ourselves right at the expense of making another wrong? We all have different tastes, different likes, we all have a different…vice. Is it sleep medicine? Food? Another partner? What is your vice or coping method when life hits you hard?

Studies show that one in five people admit they suffer from mental health related problems. I firmly believe that study is skewed far too low. How many countless others will never even admit or make the concentrated efforts, or seek a different way, because they are too reluctant to accept that they have to surrender to a new belief, one in which they recognize that they are not the director of this show called life and are merely actors? "If there is no enemy within, the enemy outside can do no harm".

"Manipulator? Wow! How? What? What do you mean?" I asked, frantically. Cynthia began to tell me that she had seen this in me for a while throughout her conversations with Nori, and then, as I explained to her in depth, my conversations with others in my life. I sat and listened and before the session had ended, I thanked her. I told her thank you, I know how much of a risk you were taking being so bold and honest to tell me what you did, but it was exactly what I needed to hear from you. She reminded me that she had asked me permission before she delivered the much-needed body shot.

Nevertheless, I recognize that indeed it was a risk. Most people probably would not have taken it so kindly. It was perhaps the best beat down I had ever received. This reminds me of a wonderful quote by the legendary, and my favorite motivational speaker of all time, Les Brown. "When you get knocked down, make sure you land on your back, because if you can look up, you can get up." Yeah, I did. I landed on my back, but I could see clearly now. My vision had been blurred throughout much of my life, and I am not simply talking about alcohol, although that played a definitive role too.

Over the course of the next several weeks, I began observing myself. I began looking at everything through the eyes of, "Am I being manipulative in this moment? How have others perceived my actions? Oh, my God, was I acting on selfish means?" I prided myself in being selfless. I began to have empathy for myself. This reminded me that on December 30, 2018, while at a Christ Fellowship event with world-renowned author and Pastor, John Maxwell, when he said, "Every single one of you is selfish." The audience looked begrudgingly at him, and then he added, "You don't believe me? Okay. Every time you take a group picture, the first person you look for is yourself. If your eyes were closed in the picture, it was a horrible picture, but if you came out great, it was a wonderful picture."

I continued to play the tape of all the relationships with people that I had encountered throughout my life. I realized what a huge manipulator that I had been with my parents, my ex-wife, and even with my daughter Nori, which reminded me of a particular memory that occurred in June 2019.

I was at a T-Mobile store in west Miami awaiting my turn when I approached Nori and told her, "Look, Honey, I know that you must be tired of constantly being put in the middle with the situation between your mom and dad. I know that this is unfair to you and your brother, but, due to the fact that you are the older sister, you are the one who continues to be put in the middle of all this conflict. How 'bout you tell mom that you are tired of your parents not talking to each other and that you are tired of being put in the middle. Mom and Dad, if you guys can't figure out a way to get along for the sake of myself and my brother, then I am going to go live with my dad."

I remember thinking that this was a great idea and that it was for their best interest. I mean, the only reason that I deeply desired a civil relationship with Yari was because of Nori and Jonathan. That was it. I figured that if Yari was put in this situation, this may force her to find a way for us to engage and be amicable with each other. Well, Nori's response showed me maturity well beyond her fourteen years of age at the time. Her response was, "No, Dad, that would be manipulating, and I am not going to do that." Wow, what presence, what assertiveness, what grace my young daughter displayed.

I needed to hear and feel this manipulation knock-out punch that Cynthia landed. I needed to recognize this continuous pattern of behavior in order to rectify it. This realization also helped me share this experience with my friends, peers and clients. Every single experience that I learn and grow from I give to others so that they can receive it and grow from it as well. Contrary to the belief that we have been domesticated with for much of our lives, the purpose for us in this lifetime is not to accumulate as many things as we can. For when we are gone, we take nothing with us. It is, however, in giving away as much as we know, that withstands the test of time as our legacy.

During this time, I realized that throughout my journey and throughout my personal development, there was a certain component that I had shied away from. I had learned all about taking control of one's life, about taking full responsibility, about finding your purpose and your passion. I learned about living God's Will for you, about surrendering to what life is and what it brings you. I learned to seek fulfillment in life and to have faith, as if everything you have wished for has already come true. Yet, I had evaded for the most part, the part of slowing down, meditation, self-awareness and mindfulness.

I remember my dear friend, Norma, had spoken to me several times about the likes of Master Stephen Co, Jay Shetty and Anthony Profeta.

13
THE VIEW FROM
THE MOUNTAIN TOP

"God doesn't put a Goliath in front of you, unless He Knows that there is a David inside of you". -Frankie M Powers-

It was now the end of May 2020. I was heading to Cocoa Beach for a two-week stay for summer vacation. Somehow, a weekend workshop on the first weekend that I would be there, popped up in my Facebook feed during the few days that my kids were not going to be present with me. It was called, "Unleash the Healer Within." The workshop was hosted by world-renowned meditator, and the man I love to call, "The Prophetic Meditator," Anthony Profeta. It was the weekend of May 30th and 31st, and it unlocked the link that was missing in my life. During the weekend, I remember something Norma told me that stayed with me. Prayer is one talking to God, meditation is God speaking to you. That was powerful. That was downloaded in my memory bank and was so ever present and true for me.

By the end of the weekend, Anthony and I had become friends. He taught me that weekend what I believe to be one of the foundational building blocks rooted for an abundant life. It was the gift of being fully present, the gift of just being. This was a gift because it was already inside of me, however, just like any other gift, one must water the seeds so the tree can fully blossom. That is why therapists, counselors and coaches are so vital. They give people their full presence in that moment. They allow people to be fully seen.

This may seem like a simple formula, but how often are any of us fully present? We are most often thinking in the past or anxious about the future. We spend our days thinking of how this person hurt me or how my life could have been different if it wasn't for some situation or some individual. Stop, stop it. It is over. My friends, things happen, and you can't change them. We all do the best we can with what we know in the moment. If you knew then what you know now, you would have done things differently. Since you know better, next time you will do better. If you learn something from the situation, then celebrate, because you learned a lesson. If there is nothing you can do about the situation, let go of it because you cannot change it.

Many of us suffer from anxiety, fearful of what the future may bring or what is going to happen. What if I lose my job, then lose my home and am then out living in my car? What if I leave my relationship and I am all alone, and I never find love or am accepted? Do you see what is happening? Are any of these questions real? The answer is no. All of these things may happen, but are they realistically going to happen? You see, our minds have approximately 6,000 thoughts per day and 80% of those thoughts are negative and 95% of those thoughts are repetitive, so you continue to play the same things you are depressed about from your past, or anxious about your future, over and over again.

How 'bout if we reframe the situation? Say you do lose your job, but that gives you the opportunity to seek your dream job which is out there waiting for you. What if it ends up being the blessing that now gives you the time and the opportunity to open a business you've always dreamed of? What if, when you left the relationship that you had outgrown, you find someone who is everything that you could have ever wanted? What if…the situation that you see so direly, becomes the greatest blessing you could have ever imagined? This brings me to one of my favorite quotes of all time by, none other than, Dr. Wayne Dyer, "When you change the way you see the world, the world around you changes."

Most of us have heard the term multitasking. If you are doing multiple tasks at a given moment, you are probably doing many things poorly. It is scientifically proven that the mind cannot focus its attention on more than one thing at any given time. If you deviate to one thing, then get back to another, it generally takes eight to ten minutes to get completely re-focused on the original task at hand. The truth is, if we had the self-awareness to be fully present in the now, in the moment, we would by default gain more time. The hours on the clock may not change, but what we are capable of accomplishing does. We become more efficient at work, we build stronger relationships with those around us, and we discover the most undervalued desire that lays deep within all of us, we experience peace.

Needless to say, the act of being present, those two words, spoke volumes to me. Anthony Profeta, you nailed it my brother, I get it. I immediately signed up for his six-month, 100-hour, Mindfulness Meditation Teacher Training starting July 11, 2020.

After the weekend and the insights, I drove home to Miami to pick up my kids and headed back out to Cocoa Beach for some fun in the sun and…some family meditation. Yes, I decided to involve the children in my new discovery, and they thoroughly enjoyed it. Jonathan, to my surprise, really took a liking to it. He actually convinced me to drive an hour from where we were staying, on a Monday night, to Vero Beach, in order to do some sound bowl healing meditation. It was extremely gratifying as their father, to be able to plant the seeds for a more rewarding and fulfilling life for my children.

After enjoying the rays of the sun and some ocean front BBQ, an idea dawned on me. I was already doing Motivational Monday videos, and due to the pandemic and the feelings of disconnection that were occurring throughout the world, I decided to do Facebook videos as a family with the kids. The kids were like, oh, come on, dad, I don't want to do videos. I looked at them sheepishly and said, "You guys do Tik Tok videos all day, hours on end. Come on now guys." They looked at me and obliged.

They really didn't need much convincing. They asked me why I wanted to do this. I replied, "Well, you see, families used to talk a lot more and connect a lot more. People, as a whole, don't do that as often as they used to." In explaining to them these words, they quickly saw the value we could give to other families. I told them, "This is an easy way to serve other people just by being ourselves." They understood the true meaning of service and how important it was. I came up with a title, "Ties that Bind, Family Table Talk Thursdays". We loved it. The concept would be that every week one of us would pick a topic or question, unbeknownst to the rest of us, and then each of us would give our thoughts on the matter. We would encourage the audience to do their own family table talks at the dinner table. It went great. We felt good about it and others really seemed to enjoy it.

It was also during this time that I had registered for three online courses. "Moralities of Everyday Life," with a Professor from Yale; "Emotions: A Philosophical Introduction," from the University of Barcelona and "Science of Happiness," with a Professor from India. These courses gave me so much more enlightenment than I ever could have anticipated. It dispelled the notion that opposites attract. People who are polarly opposite cannot be attracted to one another, outside of a few nights of heated passion, because their fires burn differently.

I discovered that people are inherently good, and they do not want to purposefully, or intentionally, be the cause of someone's hurt or pain unless, of course, they happen to be a narcissist or psychopath, which, in fact, means they lack certain empathetic emotions. I learned about the science of happiness; that just small gestures and good deeds can give the same level of happiness to the giver as well as to the receiver and doing so, causes a ripple effect in the receiver to want to do good as well. I continued to receive lightning bolts of awarenesses and insights everywhere around me.

It was now the final weekend in June, and I enrolled in a few courses that piqued my interest. One was Chakras Energetic workshop; the other was Introduction to Ayurvedic Medicine. For many of you, these words may be foreign. Truth is, I had never heard of Chakras until the year, 2020. As I continued my thirst for wisdom and growth, Chakras intrigued me. The Chakras system originated in India between 1500 and 500 BC from the time of the Vedas. Chakras are spiritual energy centers within the human body that are lined up along the spine, neck, and crown of your head. There are seven Chakras, where each one corresponds to specific organs, as well as physical, emotional, psychological, and spiritual states of being that may influence your life. It is believed that through different stages of one's life, particular Chakras have a stored emotional memory that contributes to your belief or disbelief in relation to fears, promiscuity, communication styles, and the like. This fascinated me. I, literally, entered this workshop with a beginner's mind. I was a sponge. I learned what foundational concepts of healing meant, and began to understand who a chiropractor was, as well as, learned about acupuncture and Ayurvedic medicine.

Throughout the weekend, I learned about foods and nature and the importance of being outdoors, feeling the suns energy and its effect on the quality of our lives, as well as the quality of our relationships. I also realized that in the Western world we focus on the outer to fulfill the inner, as opposed to Asian culture where regardless of their circumstances, where they live, what they have to eat, their job status, most of them are whole and at peace regardless of what material possessions they have accumulated. This is because in Asian culture, from an early age, they are taught the path to enlightenment lies internally and not externally.

By Monday morning, June 29th, my path became quite clear. Throughout my journey in the human experience, people have always fascinated me. Not a day goes by that I do not want to be of help to someone in need. I remember growing up, my dad always telling me, "Why are you always trying to help everyone?" He couldn't understand it. Now, I want you to keep in mind this is not my real dad. My real dad is the one that shows up once a year, on March 10th, the anniversary of my Abuelo Papo's death. The one who doesn't understand me, that is the man that life beat him down to be.

In my search for helping others and feeling unloved, I got lost; alcohol gave me a cushion, a support system. Upon resurrection of my soul's purpose for me, and seeing God's calling for me clearly, I have set out on a path to help inspire and empower others to live their true, inherent destiny. As I continue this path with those who entrust me to seek it, there are millions which will never know, and have never known, of its inherent existence. I envision showering our youth, our children, our children's children, the future leaders of this roundabout place we call earth with the knowledge that I have obtained through my challenges, so that others never have to succumb to the desperate cries for help or despair that almost resulted in my very own death.

For quite some time, I foolishly believed that I had to run for office in order to achieve the goals of changing our educational system, not realizing, through sheer ignorance, that in doing so, I would become a puppet of all those who would contribute to my campaign and in thus doing so, I would not be able to enact those very things that propelled me to run in the first place. I would then have to deviate from my principles, values and beliefs, and thus become a sheep in wolf's clothing. I would never sell my soul to the devil. I lived that life once; I had to bury Frank in order to resurface Frankie. Thomas Jefferson so eloquently put it, "When it comes to style, swim with the current. When it comes to principles, stand like a rock." In changing the course of my purpose, I changed the trajectory, not the destination. It was this very week that I recognized, I did not need to be a legislator to change our educational system. I needed to be a testament to how it could actually happen.

I believe it is finally time that we change the way we educate our children in the classroom. It is time we start planting seeds of universal values and morals inside of them. It is time we teach them that feelings matter, that emotions and beliefs matter. If you believe the world is against you, it very well will be. If you believe the world is an ugly place, it will be ugly. If you believe, you can one day be the next innovator, inventor or fashion designer, you will be that too. When you ask children who they want to be when they grow up, what they desire to have, where they want to live, do you think anyone's answer is, I want to be a drug addict. I want to be an alcoholic. I want to be homeless. Is there any child amongst us that would answer, I want to live in a poor neighborhood, or live in a homeless shelter? The answer is an unequivocal NO! Then why is it that some people make it in life and others don't? The answer is quite simple, because what they believe becomes their reality. The quote that resonates with me in this moment is, "If you believe you can, or you believe you can't, you will."

In wake of the events that began in 2020 between Covid and the killing of people such as George Floyd, why is it that you think there is so much division amongst us? It is because of people's personal beliefs and feelings about it. I believe you should wear a mask; I believe you shouldn't. George Floyd. George Floyd…these riots had very little to do with George Floyd or Brianna Taylor and others. These riots were because black people and minorities have felt they have been oppressed (now, my friends, please stay with me here, please do not tune me out). The truth is, in many instances they have. I recently remember watching the embarrassment of the first Presidential debate with my children. I, as well as my children, had us all write our opinions on the horrendous political theatre we had witnessed. I had recorded Fox News and CNN. While they both agreed, the candidates did not conduct themselves appropriately, their opinions were completely skewed to the desired choice of each political commentator.

Most of us are not open to having a dialogue in conversation. We cannot fix the problem until we realize that we are the problem. You cannot put a band aid on a gunshot wound. What really mattered in this election, or in any election that comes our way, is us. It is you and I learning to speak softly and listen intently to realize that who we are, oftentimes, are not the people we want to be.

It is not until we realize that most of us have not been living our own lives but the lives someone else told us we had to live in order to have made it, in order to live the American dream. What we fail to realize is that my dream and your dream can be vastly different. None of our dreams are wrong, they are all right. Can you see it? Can you? Is it the white picket fence with a nicely kept yard? Can you feel it? Frankie, what do you mean, can you feel it? That's right. Oftentimes, what we visualize as the dream, and what we actually feel when we obtain it, don't match. You cannot keep searching for something to fill the hole, the void inside of you. You have to clean out the wound in order to heal and grow. If you do not heal old wounds, you pass on those beliefs, the anguish, the disappointments, the hurts through your lineage throughout your family's history.

Someone has to make the cut. Someone has to say the suffering ends with me. With me! A significant problem is that most people don't even know that they are wounded, they believe that this is their life. My friends and family, all of us have wounds and all of us need healing. It is time we stop hurting and time we start healing and loving. Let me share with you an adage from Terry Real. "Family dysfunction rolls down from generation to generation, like a fire burning everything in its path, until one person in one generation has the courage to turn and face the flames. That person brings peace to their ancestors and spares the children that follow."

It was now July 11, 2020. I am on my way to Indialantic, Florida to begin my six-month Mindfulness Meditation Teacher Training with Anthony Profeta. For some reason, meditation, prayer and mindfulness have become almost taboo words, words that have become unacceptable to even be spoken about in schools, public forums and in government. Why, I ask? Is it fear of how it can be construed, fear of the unknown? Are a certain set of values and/or principles undesirable in today's society? Why is quiet time or time to slow your thoughts, or observe your thoughts in silence, somehow unacceptable in our Western culture?

A few years ago, Bradley Cooper starred in a movie, "Limitless". In the role he played, he would take a pill and he could see everything clearly. He was laser focused. He was omnipresent. What if this was obtainable? The answer to that question is, perhaps it is.

The Mindfulness Meditation Teacher Training was a mind opening, better yet, mind clearing program designed to teach us a centuries-old practice that allow us to get to the root of who we really are, what our thoughts really are, and how to be able to find inner peace. What can each of us do if we were more aware of our thoughts, if we were able to be more focused on our tasks at work, at home, and in our relationships with those around us? Would our lives not be enriched and enhanced by default? We would be able to attain more, to do more, to be more. Awareness, self-awareness, is a golden ticket to a life of serenity, to peace of what is and to peace of our thoughts. We are not our thoughts, we are not our emotions, nor are we our behaviors. Every single one of us are energetic beings in a physical body, we are our souls.

Scientific studies have shown that just twenty minutes of meditation a day, in as short of a span of eight weeks, reduces pain, anxiety and depression by upwards of 57%. To give you an example, morphine reduces pain by up to 25%, so why are we, in society, so reluctant to experiment with or enhance our awareness? Is it the pharmaceutical companies offering us a quick fix that only provides half of the results that we, ourselves, can reach on our own? Is it Western culture's desire for us, as people, wanting everything and wanting it now? Everything in life that is worthwhile and fulfilling takes time. The road to glory is not instantaneous.

You cannot produce a baby in one month by getting nine women pregnant. Time…takes time.

Anthony is a man with innate wisdom. He reads anywhere between two to three books a week and has been doing so for well over a decade. I have never been around a man who has so much wisdom and exhibits so much peace. I was drawn to Anthony; he was a magnet that I wanted to extract jewels from.

It was now September 2020. Nori was about to turn sixteen-years old. I continued to seek calmness amongst life's storms. To search for the peace that can only be found inside of me. Peace, happiness, fulfillment, the answer to all life's questions are always found inside every one of us, in our hearts, in the quietness of our conscious awareness.

In the meantime, I have never seen so much division in my surroundings in my lifetime. Debates on different points of views are not encouraged; in fact, people are admonished for doing so. "Why can we not have a difference of opinion without being judged, insulted, or ridiculed?" I thought to myself.

It was NFL opening weekend, the weekend of September 11th through 13th. An awareness came to me that completely shifted my perception on certain racial issues. It gave me a whole new insight into something I had held as a firm belief inside of me. I was always taught to honor the American flag and the National Anthem. I believed anyone that stood against it, was being disrespectful, insulting and belittling all those men and women who lost their lives for my freedom. From the moment I first heard of Colin Kaepernick kneeling for the National Anthem, I judged it as a despicable and disrespectful act against all Americans. I vehemently objected to that political stance. I even purchased a shirt that read, "I kneel for the cross and stand for the flag." This particular weekend, I stepped back to observe myself and see this situation from a different perspective, a perspective that I had never even allowed myself previously to entertain. Was it my idea or was it instilled in me according to the beliefs that I held as true as a fingerprint or a birthmark?

Was kneeling for the flag really a form of disrespect to our soldiers (myself included), our countrymen and our freedoms? As the rumblings in my mind continued, I began to question how true these beliefs that I held as Truths were. Was Colin Kaepernick, and everyone else who kneeled for the flag, saying, "The hell with you America?" I took a step back, paused and then asked myself, why did I give it that meaning? Was that what Black Lives Matter or NFL players and athletes throughout the country in the coming years meant? As I sat in silence, I asked myself, "In all of human history, has anyone ever kneeled for anything outside of seeking forgiveness or asking for help? The answer to that question was a resounding NO! When? When!" When has it meant anything but asking for forgiveness or desiring help?! Never, to my knowledge; it hasn't. No man or woman has ever knelt on the ground for any reason outside of expressing remorse or sorrow or asking please, can you help me?

Damn me! Damn those that convinced me of seeing these acts in the way that I did. What if people who felt throughout their entire lives that they didn't have a chance or that they were always being looked at differently, just chose to get on their knees, take the moment and say, "Please America, can we just be seen as equals?" Can we just be seen, as Thomas Jefferson once penned, "We hold these truths to be self-evident. That all men are created equal, that we are endowed by our Creator with certain unalienable rights, among these are life, liberty and the pursuit of happiness." What if? What if we eased the pains and the burdens and heartache that have been handed down and that has been felt from generation to generation? It is time each of us help heal the suffering that has been felt throughout people's historical lineage. This is not to be done through reparations or special privileges, but through empathy, understanding and compassion. Seek to understand and not judge, seek to listen and not speak, seek to love and not hate. What if we changed the story? If we change the story, we change our life.

Throughout my forty-five-years of life, I have shared openly for all of you to see some of my countless struggles, heartaches and pains that I suffered through. I tried to limit, to the best of my ability, blaming anyone for what I felt was done to me. Everyone I have encountered in my life has been my teacher and my student. That is the essence of what life is all about. Some people cross our path for a moment, for a period of time and then either they outgrow us, or we outgrow them. This is part of the human experience. There are no accidents, there are no coincidences. People do the best they can with what it is they know. Individuals are as generous as they believe they can be. There are some people who chose to give more because they recognize and know the value of giving. There are countless others that take more because they know no better. I firmly believe that for everyone, if they would have known better, they would have done better, and now you know better, so you do better.

My life has been a huge blessing. I now know that I cannot suffer loss without first experiencing love. I kept seeking love in people outside of me. I felt the need for love when love was within me all along. My search for love taught me the gift, that even my life-long deep-rooted faith somehow failed to seep within me, the gift, the most precious gift, which is that of unconditional love. I love people. You can choose to love me or not, but I put no preconditions on who I love and that is the very essence of who I am. A follower of Jesus Christ. Agape love – unconditional love. Before Jesus died, He looked up to the heavens and said, "Father, please forgive them. They know not what they do." If He can forgive those who crucified Him, who am I not to forgive anyone who has hurt me? To anyone who has ever hurt me, pained me, or spoke ill about me, I forgive you. I forgive all of you, no apologies needed. I am beyond blessed to have been given the life that I have, and it is now time for me to give all the love I have inside of me to everyone and anyone who is open to receiving it. I now know as I look back at my life that I had to hit rock bottom before I reached the mountain tops.

On the Mountaintop

"God doesn't put a Goliath in front of you unless He knows that there is a David inside of you." -Frankie M Powers

Sending agape love to all of you.

Before

After

As a special thank you for purchasing my book you are invited to access the special audio version read by me by taking a photo of the QR Code below. In this way you will be able to hear me take you on my journey from Rock Bottom to Mountaintops.

ABOUT THE AUTHOR

Frankie M Powers is an Empowerment coach, Motivational Speaker and Author. Frankie spent most of his life rooted in anger, resentment and as a victim of his circumstances. Until….he hit Rock Bottom and said no more, deciding to be the Victor of his Life. As he awakened to the true essence of who he was, he found his purpose and committed all of himself to becoming the man that he is today. There is a quote that speaks directly to who Frankie M Powers is; "Don't go where the path may lead, go where there is no path and leave a trail."

On his way to the Mountain Top, he gave up every attachment and belief that he held as true and became a crusader in seeking, "The Truth." He fully immersed himself in "Mastering Oneself," through the likes of Cognitive Behavioral Therapy, Emotional Intelligence and Neuro Linguistic Programming (NLP). He deeply explored the study of human behavior, emotions and philosophies. He became a Certified Mindfulness Meditation Instructor, Dale Carnegie Top Performance Speaker and Certified Yogi. The result is a powerful transformation in body, mind and spirit. He is living proof that not only is changing your life possible but shattering your old limiting beliefs is fully attainable. His dream, his vision, is spreading his message to school districts and people throughout the world through education. This has led him to develop a "21 Step Keys" to living a life filled with Purpose, Passion, Abundance, Peace, Freedom, Love and Hope.

Frankie M Powers is a single father of two beautiful children, daughter, Nori and son, Jonathan. Frankie M Powers, needed to be broken down in order to be completely broken open. He knows the way to achieving a life that most fear to even dream about. And he can show you the way to achieving all the dreams that you have always envisioned in your relationships, career and well-being. "Everything that you have ever desired in your life is right in front of you. Make the impossible/Possible. Live Life on Your terms. Frankie M Powers can guide you there.

Please visit www.FrankieMPowers.com to learn more about Frankie and how he can best help and serve you and your needs.